T0301570

Firms within Families

Firms within Families

Enterprising in Diverse Country Contexts

Edited by

Jennifer E. Jennings

University of Alberta, Canada

Kimberly A. Eddleston

Northeastern University, USA

P. Devereaux Jennings

University of Alberta, Canada

Ravi Sarathy

Northeastern University, USA

 Edward Elgar
PUBLISHING

Cheltenham, UK • Northampton, MA, USA

Published by
Edward Elgar Publishing Limited
The Lypiatts
15 Lansdown Road
Cheltenham
Glos GL50 2JA
UK

Edward Elgar Publishing, Inc.
William Pratt House
9 Dewey Court
Northampton
Massachusetts 01060
USA

A catalogue record for this book
is available from the British Library

Library of Congress Control Number: 2015933447

This book is available electronically in the **Elgar**online
Business subject collection
DOI 10.4337/9781782546528

ISBN   978 1 78254 651 1 (cased)
ISBN   978 1 78254 652 8 (eBook)

Typeset by Servis Filmsetting Ltd, Stockport, Cheshire
Printed and bound in Great Britain by T.J. International Ltd, Padstow

Contents

Contributors

Tales Andreassi, PhD, is Director of GVCenn – Center of Entrepreneurship and New Ventures at Escola de Administração de Empresas de São Paulo, Fundação Getulio Vargas (Brazil). He has researched, written and lectured on various aspects of entrepreneurship and innovation, such as innovation in small companies, effectuation theory, entrepreneurship and gender and entrepreneurship education. His work has appeared in more than 20 academic journals and he is the author of eight books.

Kimberly A. Eddleston, PhD, is a Professor of Entrepreneurship and Innovation within the D'Amore-McKim School of Business, Northeastern University (United States). She is also a Toft Visiting Professor at Jönköping International Business School, a Research Fellow at the University of St. Gallen, and a Field Editor for the *Journal of Business Venturing*. Much of her research focuses on how family and gender influences entrepreneurship. Her articles have appeared in leading academic journals such as the *Academy of Management Journal, Journal of Applied Psychology*, *Journal of International Business Studies*, and *Strategic Management Journal*.

Melanie Ganter is a PhD candidate at the Center for Family Business, University of St Gallen (Switzerland). Her research interests include entrepreneurship, innovation and corporate social responsibility. Her research has been published in *Entrepreneurship Theory & Practice, Journal of Product Innovation Management* and the *Academy of Management Best Paper Proceedings*.

Jie Huang, PhD, is an Associate Professor in Entrepreneurship at the College of Economics and Management in the Huazhong Agricultural University (China). Her research focuses on rural entrepreneurship. Her work has been published in academic journals such as *Chinese Rural Economy*.

Jennifer E. Jennings (formerly Jennifer E. Cliff), PhD, is the Winspear Professor of Entrepreneurship and Family Enterprise at the University of Alberta School of Business (Canada). Much of her research focuses upon the roles of family and gender in entrepreneurial and family firm contexts. A former Field Editor at the *Journal of Business Venturing* and a long-time member of the Diana International network, she is the co-editor of another volume recently published by Edward Elgar: *Global Women's Entrepreneurship Research: Diverse Settings, Questions and Approaches.*

P. Devereaux Jennings, PhD, is a Professor of Strategy and Organization and Director of the Canadian Centre for CSR at the University of Alberta School of Business (Canada). His research on organizational strategy, entrepreneurship and the natural environment has been published in a variety of outlets, including: *Administrative Science Quarterly*, the *Academy of Management Journal*, the *American Journal of Sociology*, *Entrepreneurship Theory and Practice*, the *Journal of Business Venturing*, and *Organization Studies*. Dev is currently an Associate Editor at *Administrative Science Quarterly*.

Youngbin Joo is a PhD student at the University of Alberta (Canada). His research focuses on the management of innovation and entrepreneurship, with a particular emphasis on corporate environmental strategies. His research has been presented at the *Academy of Management* meetings.

K. Kumar, PhD, is the Apeejay Surrendra Chair Professor of Family Business and Entrepreneurship at the Indian Institute of Management, Bangalore (India). He has been a Visiting Professor of Entrepreneurship in Athens and Sydney, was an entrepreneur, CEO of Trigent Software Ltd., and recently published research on effectuation in international entrepreneurship within *Entrepreneurship Theory and Practice.*

Ravi Sarathy, PhD, is Professor of International Business and Strategy at the D'Amore-McKim School of Business, Northeastern University (United States). His research interests include global strategy, family business and industrial policy. His work has been published in outlets such as the *Journal of International Business Studies* and *California Management Review*, with his research on family business recently appearing in the *Journal of Management Studies* and *Small Business Economics.*

Philipp Sieger, PhD, is an Assistant Professor of Family Business at the University of St. Gallen (Switzerland). His research focuses on the nexus of family business and entrepreneurship. His work has been published in academic journals such as the *Journal of Management Studies*, *Journal of Business Venturing*, and *Entrepreneurship Theory & Practice.*

Li Tian, PhD, is an Associate Professor in the Business School of Nankai University (China). Her research focuses on new venture creation and the initial growth of new firms. Her work has been published in academic journals such as *Management and Organization Review* and *Chinese Management Studies.*

Maria José Tonelli, PhD, is a Full Professor at Escola de Administração de Empresas de São Paulo, Fundação Getúlio Vargas (Brazil), where she is the Director of NEOP – Research Center on Organizations and People. Her main research interests include gender, work and organization. Over the last five years, together with Professor Tales Andreassi, she has been conducting the Goldman Sachs Foundation 10,000 Women Program at FGV-EAESP.

Thomas Zellweger, PhD, holds the Chair of Family Business at the University of St Gallen (Switzerland). His research interests include strategic entrepreneurship, succession in family firms, and entrepreneurial finance. His articles appear in leading academic journals such as *Academy of Management Journal, Organization Science, Strategic Management Journal*, and *Journal of Management Studies*.

Yanfeng Zheng is an Assistant Professor at the University of Hong Kong (China). He earned his PhD in management from the University of Wisconsin Madison. His research interests revolve around the nexus of strategic management and entrepreneurship. His work has been published in leading journals such as the *Academy of Management Journal, Strategic Management Journal, Journal of Business Venturing*, and *Journal of Management Studies*.

Acknowledgements

Given the numerous individuals who contributed to a project of this scope, it is hard to know where to start with our acknowledgments. As such, we will simply follow the age-old advice to 'begin at the beginning' and proceed from there.

Our first thank you therefore goes to Alan Sturmer at Edward Elgar, for being quick to embrace the book's concept at the very outset yet patient with its evolution thereafter. We are also indebted to the scholars whom we initially approached to conduct the country-specific studies featured in this multi-country collaboration: Philipp Sieger and Thomas Zellweger in Europe, Yanfeng Zheng in China, Tales Andreassi and Maria José Tonelli in Brazil, and K. Kumar in India. Thank you for your trust in the project's potential and our ability to manage the process, for forming partnerships with other talented scholars to get the job done (thanks for coming onboard Melanie Ganter, Jie Huang and Li Tian), for securing such strong participation in your respective countries, for producing such great work in the first place, and for responding so tolerantly to our subsequent requests for refinement.

We are also grateful to those who lent a helping hand throughout the process and as the manuscript submission deadline drew nearer. Thanks to all of the business owner-managers (more than 1370) who responded to the surveys, to Nitu Nathani and Paula Torres for the excellent research assistance provided in India and Brazil respectively, to Grace Oliveira for the diligent administrative assistance, and to Youngbin Joo for pitching in on the references. And thank you, Christopher Cliff, for your help with the page formatting and proposed design for the front cover.

Finally, we thank one another for the intellectual curiosity, unflagging enthusiasm and good humor from start to finish.

Jennifer, Kim, Dev and Ravi

1. Introduction: a framework for studying the 'double embeddedness' of business enterprising

Jennifer E. Jennings, Kimberly A. Eddleston, P. Devereaux Jennings and Ravi Sarathy

Over a decade ago, Aldrich and Cliff (2003) called for a 'family embeddedness' perspective on entrepreneurship research, urging scholars to consider how family-related factors impact—and are impacted by—venture creation processes and outcomes (see also Rogoff and Heck, 2003). As noted by Sharma, Melin, and Nordqvist (2014), the reciprocal influence of family and business has been of even longer-standing interest within the family enterprise literature, arguably constituting the field's distinctive focus. While research in both areas has progressed rapidly, knowledge of the myriad ways in which the families and firms of owner-managers affect one another is far from complete. In the entrepreneurship literature, empirical studies consistent with the family embeddedness perspective remain relatively rare (for examples see Eddleston and Powell, 2012; Gras and Nason, forthcoming; Powell and Eddleston, 2013; Zellweger, Sieger, and Halter, 2011). And even in recent reviews of the family business literature, the need for greater attention to family variables is a dominant refrain (Danes, 2014; James, Jennings, and Breitkreuz, 2012; McKenney, Payne, Zachary, and Short, 2014; Yu, Lumpkin, Sorenson, and Brigham, 2012).

Paralleling the call for increased consideration of family-related factors is that for an enhanced appreciation of the broader economic, institutional and cultural environments in which business enterprises are also embedded. Within the entrepreneurship literature, the latter appeal is a salient if not primary theme cutting across numerous essays (for example, Ucbasaran, Westhead, and Wright, 2001; Welter, 2011; Zahra and Wright, 2011; Zahra, Wright, and Abdelgawad, 2014) and special issues of academic journals (for example, Bruton, Ahlstrom, and Obloj, 2008; Jennings, Greenwood, Lounsbury, and Suddaby, 2013; Krueger, Liñán, and Nabi, 2013). It is also a key raison d'être of the Global Entrepreneurship Monitor (GEM) initiative. Within the family business literature, the need for greater attention to the effects of broader external environments is increasingly recognized as just as germane (see, for example, Gupta and Levenburg, 2010; Howorth, Rose, Hamilton, and Westhead, 2010; Sharma et al., 2014; Wright, Chrisman, Chua, and Steier, 2014). Indeed, upon observing that only 7 of the 124 empirical articles within their recent bibliographic analysis included firms from more than one country, De Massis, Sharma, Chua, and Chrisman commented that 'cross-country empirical studies . . . are necessary for a better understanding of the role that culture and institutions play in modifying the effects of family influence on firms' characteristics, behaviors, and performance' (De Massis et al., 2012: 51).

In combination, the above-noted calls point to the need for research on what we have termed the 'double embeddedness' of business enterprising; that is, the joint embedding of firms within the meso and macro contexts of both families and countries, respectively. We responded to this need by creating a collaborative initiative comprised of research teams responsible for collecting, analyzing and interpreting data from a relatively standardized survey within one of five distinct macro environments: the United States, Switzerland/Germany, China, Brazil and India. This book summarizes the preliminary results from this collaboration. Below we explicate our choice of focal country contexts and collaborators, the study's guiding conceptual frameworks, and our overarching expectations regarding the relative influence of family-related factors on owner-managers and their firms within and across different socio-economic environments.

CHOICE OF FOCAL COUNTRY CONTEXTS AND COLLABORATORS

For comparability with much extant research within the family business and entrepreneurship literatures, we selected the United States as the baseline country context for our investigation. As documented by De Massis and his colleagues (2012), studies focused exclusively upon US firms constituted the largest proportion—45 percent—of major empirical family business articles published within academic journals between 1996 and 2010. As noted by Davidsson (2004; 2006; also see Felzensztein, Gimmon, and Aqueveque, 2013), US-based studies have historically been the norm for academic journal articles on entrepreneurship as well. Two of the book's editors, Dev Jennings and Jennifer Jennings, handled the US data collection and analysis effort, with doctoral student Youngbin Joo joining as a co-author on one of the chapters.

Given that a considerable amount of research on family businesses and entrepreneurial firms has also been conducted within Europe, we approached two highly prolific researchers based in the region—Philipp Sieger and Thomas Zelwegger—about their willingness to head the European component of the study. Fortuitously, our request dovetailed with the pending launch of their data collection effort targeting family owned and managed firms within Germany, the EU's strongest economy, and Switzerland, a small but prosperous economy outside the EU but closely integrated with European and world economies. These countries thus formed the second focal macro-environmental context of our study. Doctoral candidate Melanie Ganter joined as a co-author on one of the Swiss/German chapters.

Heeding calls for family business and entrepreneurship research conducted outside of developed economies of North America and Europe— and within developing or transition economies in particular (for example, Basco et al., 2014; Felzensztein et al., 2013; Gupta and Levenburg, 2010)— we then reached out to potential collaborators within three of the largest countries widely considered to have emerging economies: China, Brazil and India (Khanna and Palepu, 2013). As summarized within Table 1.1, these countries differ in pronounced ways from the United States, Switzerland and Germany. As indicated, this is so not only with respect to key characteristics of their economies but also with respect to institutional and sociocultural characteristics of especial relevance to our investigation; specifically, the existence and nature of institutional frameworks conducive to business enterprising as well as the nature of and emphasis placed upon the institution of family.

The project team for each of the emerging-economy contexts included scholars based in the region, at least one of whom had a positive prior working relationship with one of the editors. Ascendant entrepreneurship scholar Yanfeng Zheng led the China initiative, forming partnerships with collaborators Jie Huang and Li Tian, each of whom had previously conducted research on entrepreneurs in the country. The Brazil and India teams were constituted by two of the book's editors (Ravi Sarathy and Kimberly Eddleston) and scholars of entrepreneurship and/or family enterprise in either country; specifically, Tales Andreassi and Maria José Tonelli in Brazil, and K. Kumar in India.

OVERARCHING CONCEPTUAL FRAMEWORKS

Each country-focused team produced two chapters for this book. The first chapter, which appears within Part I, focuses upon the organizational level of analysis, featuring findings pertaining to the effects of family upon the strategic orientations and business strategies of owner-managed

Table 1.1 Key economic, institutional and sociocultural characteristics of the study's focal country contexts

Countries	Key Economic Characteristics[1]	Key Institutional Characteristics	Key Sociocultural Characteristics
United States	GDP $15.7 trillion; high per capita income = $49,922; world's largest economy. Over half of all companies in the US are family businesses.[2]	Advanced industrial society, abundant availability of venture capital, rule of law and protection of property rights; US Small Business Administration (SBA) and government procurement support small and family entrepreneurs.	Individualistic, diverse society; high propensity for risk-taking, widespread consumerism; highly mobile society.
Switzerland and Germany	GDP $363 billion for Switzerland (CH), GDP $3.2 trillion for German (DE); high per capita income = $45,418 for CH, $39,028 for DE; considered wealthy nations. At least 60% of all European companies are family businesses.	Advanced industrial economies, strong welfare state and worker rights, significant family firms presence 'Mittelstadt' protected by favorable inheritance tax regulations; quality educational system featuring apprenticeships and universities, leading to competitive STEM outcomes; federal and state support for new and established small businesses, including consultancy, financial services and training.	High value placed on planning, order, punctuality, and separation of work and family; in the past Lutheran influence on work and saving; growing immigrant population and assimilation issues.
China	Second largest GDP, $12.4 trillion; per capita income = $9,162; population 1.35 billion; fastest growing emerging market over the 1980–2010 period, export-oriented. Approximately 85% of private enterprises are family owned.	Significant government involvement in economy through state-owned enterprises; major recipient of FDI inflows, ~$120 billion annually; GDP growth at 9.3% annually; high levels of corruption, uneven implementation of laws, uneven IP protection; government support through the state councils and ministries providing loan guarantees for bank loans, lower tax rates, training and market exploration.	Somewhat guided by Confucian values, stressing harmony, group over individual welfare, and moderation; *Guangxi*, importance of networks and connections; central role of family, clan, paternalism, high power distance, and high long-term orientation.

4

Brazil	GDP $2.4 trillion; per capita income = $11,875; over-reliance on commodities, declining rates of growth as commodity prices falling. Approximately, 85–90% of businesses are family businesses.	High levels of labor inflexibility, income inequality, corruption; significant government bureaucratic controls on business, high tax burden at 34.8% of GDP; small business support through SEBRAE, SENAC and SENAI, and start-up financing through FINEP.	Extended family central part of culture; significant differences between industrialized south and rural poorer north of Brazil; diverse immigrant populations; personal relationships important in business.
India	GDP $4.7 trillion; lowest per capita income = $3,830; population 1.2 billion. Family firms account for two-thirds of India's GDP.[3]	High levels of corruption, high levels of business regulation, 5-year GDP growth of 6.8% annually, but high income inequality; large rural economy, poor transportation and infrastructure; low tax burden at 7% of GDP; small business support through Small Industries Development Organization (SIDO) and National Small Industries Corporation Ltd (NSIC) as well as financing support through State Bank of India and other banks.	Business groups dominant; reliance on political networks; high income inequality, importance of hierarchy derived from caste systems; chaotic democracy, tension between capitalist and socialist approaches to growth.

Notes:
1. All GDP and per capita incomes are PPP adjusted, in US $, for 2013.
2. Family Firm Institute, Inc. http://www.ffi.org/?page=GlobalDataPoints%22.
3. KPMG (2013) http://www.kpmg.com/Global/en/IssuesAndInsights/ArticlesPublications/family-business/Pages/family-owned-businesses-backbone-indias-economy.aspx.

Sources: Heritage Foundation Index of Economic Freedom 2014; Family Firm Institute, Inc.; 2013 data unless otherwise indicated.

enterprises and the implications for firm performance. The second chapter, which appears within Part II, focuses upon the individual level of analysis, featuring findings pertaining to the effects of family upon the work–family interface strategies and experiences of business owner-managers and the implications for their psychological well-being. The overarching conceptual frameworks guiding each chapter are introduced and briefly elaborated below.

Guiding Model for the Part I Chapters

Figure 1.1 presents the guiding model for each of the chapters in Part I. This conceptual framework was inspired by one of the conclusions drawn from De Massis et al.'s annotated bibliography of family business studies in general:

> In sum, business strategy is an emerging area that deserves much more research in the future. Research is needed to explore further, both conceptually and empirically, the extent to which family involvement can result in distinctive behaviors concerning business strategy and the effect of these differences on family firms' performance. (De Massis et al., 2012: 22–23)

Salvato and Corbetta's more circumscribed and recent review of research on family business strategies, in particular, provided further inspiration—especially their decree that the focus of such enquiries 'should be on the family itself' (Salvato and Corbetta, 2014: 316).

Of all the potential family-related factors that could have been considered,

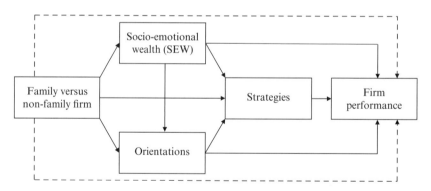

Note: Every conceptualized relationship is not explicitly examined within each Part I chapter; dotted lines signify that the family versus non-family distinction was considered primarily as a control variable in the performance models for most chapters.

Figure 1.1   Guiding conceptual framework for the chapters in Part I

the emphasis within the Part I chapters is upon the increasingly popular notion of 'socio-emotional wealth' (SEW). As elaborated by its originators and proponents, SEW refers to the motivation of family owners to preserve or enhance non-financial endowments and affective needs such as perpetuating the family's legacy and image, identifying with and exerting influence over the firm, and maintaining strong internal and external relationships (Berrone, Cruz, and Gómez-Mejía, 2012; Berrone, Cruz, and Gómez-Mejía, 2014; Gómez-Mejía, Haynes, Núñez-Nickel, Jacobson, and Moyano-Fuentes, 2007; Gómez-Mejía, Cruz, Berrone, and De Castro, 2011). To date, however, very few studies have explicitly measured the construct of SEW—let alone empirically investigated relationships with key variables of interest to business strategy scholars.

As implied by Figure 1.1, the chapters in Part I collectively examine the following fundamental questions related to SEW:

1. To what extent is SEW preservation and enhancement a motivation within owner-managed firms in general?
2. Is a concern for the preservation and enhancement of SEW higher within family than non-family firms in particular?
3. To what extent do SEW motivations influence standard variables of interest to strategy scholars, such as strategic orientations (in other words, towards growth, entrepreneurialism, and/or the long-term) and business strategies (in other words, exploration versus exploitation and causation versus effectuation)?
4. What is the impact of SEW motivations on firm performance relative to the effects of strategic orientations and business strategies?

Country-specific answers to the preceding questions can be found in the Part I chapters as follows: the United States (Jennings, Jennings, and Joo, Chapter 2); Switzerland/Germany (Sieger and Zellweger, Chapter 3); China (Zheng and Huang, Chapter 4); Brazil (Sarathy, Andreassi, Tonelli, and Eddleston, Chapter 5); and India (Sarathy, Kumar, and Eddleston, Chapter 6). Part I concludes with a comparative chapter assessing whether and how the answers to the above-noted questions vary across these diverse country contexts (Jennings, Sarathy, Eddleston, and Jennings, Chapter 7).

Guiding Model for the Part II Chapters

Figure 1.2 depicts the conceptual framework for each of the Part II chapters. Two emergent conversations within the entrepreneurship and family business literatures provided the overarching inspiration for this guiding model. One is the increased interest in the non-economic outcomes

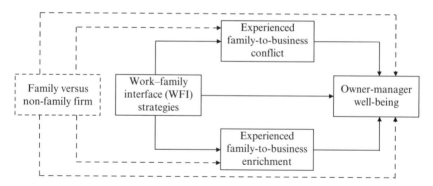

Note: Every conceptualized relationship is not explicitly examined within each Part II
chapter; dotted lines signify that the family versus non-family distinction was considered
primarily as a control variable in most chapters.

Figure 1.2   Guiding conceptual framework for the chapters in Part II

associated with business enterprising; specifically, the growing attention
paid to the personal well-being of owner-managers (see, for example,
the special section within the most recent GEM report by Amoró and
Bosma, 2014). The second is the increased awareness that comparatively
little attention has been paid to how work–family interface (WFI) factors
influence owner-managers and their firms (see, for example, Carr and
Hmieleski, 2014; McKee, Madden, Kellermans, and Eddleston, 2014;
Smyrnios et al., 2003; Werbel and Danes, 2010).

More specific inspiration came from two key distinctions raised by
entrepreneurship and family business scholars working within the WFI
paradigm. The first is the distinction between the *strategies* that owner-
managers use to manage the interface between work and family domains
and their *experiences* at this interface (Jennings and McDougald, 2007).
The second is the distinction between the *enrichment* versus *conflict* perspectives; that is, the notion that families and businesses can be 'allies'
as well as 'enemies,' capable of exerting both beneficial and detrimental
effects on one another (Eddleston and Powell, 2012; Powell and Eddleston,
2013). While advocates of either perspective have argued that WFI considerations possess implications for firm-level outcomes, the Part II chapters
follow most empirical work to-date in focusing upon outcomes at the
owner-manager level of analysis; specifically, on psychological indicators
of well-being.

As suggested by Figure 1.2, the chapters constituting the second part of
our study collectively address the following questions related to the WFI
of owner-managers:

1. What is the nature of the WFI strategies, experienced family-to-business conflict versus enrichment, and psychological well-being of business owner-managers in the focal country context?
2. To what extent do the WFI strategies enacted by business owner-managers influence their experienced family-to-business conflict and enrichment?
3. To what extent do the WFI strategies, experienced family-to-business conflict and experienced family-to-business enrichment of business owner-managers influence their psychological well-being?
4. Which of the WFI strategies and experiences are the most impactful for the psychological well-being of owner-managers?

Part II of the book is structured similarly to Part I, with the country-specific responses to the preceding guiding questions presented as follows: the United States (Jennings and Jennings, Chapter 8); Switzerland/Germany (Sieger, Ganter, and Zellweger, Chapter 9); China (Tian and Zheng, Chapter 10); Brazil (Sarathy, Andreassi, Tonelli, and Eddleston, Chapter 11); and India (Sarathy, Kumar, and Eddleston, Chapter 12). Part II also concludes with a cross-country comparison by the editors (Eddleston, Jennings, Jennings, and Sarathy, Chapter 13).

OVERARCHING EXPECTATIONS REGARDING THE RELATIVE INFLUENCE OF FAMILY-RELATED FACTORS

Heading into this study, we had two overarching expectations regarding the relative influence of family-related factors upon owner-managers and their firms. First, given the greater degree of family member involvement in the operation and/or governance that is likely within businesses deemed to be family enterprises by their owner-managers (Astrachan, Klein, and Smrynios, 2002), we were anticipating that our focal family-related constructs of SEW motivation and WFI experiences would be higher within and potentially exert stronger influences upon such organizations than those considered to be non-family firms. Second, in light of arguments and evidence that economic activity tends to be more intertwined with kinship ties and family households in regions beyond the developed Western world (see, for example, Gras and Nason, forthcoming; Gupta and Levenburg, 2010; Khavul, Bruton, and Wood, 2009; Peredo and McLean, 2013; Zellweger, Nason, and Nordqvist, 2012), we also expected that family-related considerations would exert stronger influences—either positive or negative—upon the outcomes of owner-managers and their firms within

China, Brazil and India than within the United States, Switzerland and Germany.

For details on the degree to which the empirical data supports these expectations at the organizational and individual levels of analysis, see the cross-country comparisons reported in Chapters 7 and 13, respectively. A broader discussion of the study's overall findings, limitations, contributions and implications appears in Chapter 14 (with key measurement scales and comparative methodological/sample details presented in Appendices A and B respectively). As will become apparent in the intervening country-specific chapters, however, the findings weren't exactly as we had anticipated.

REFERENCES

Aldrich, H.E. and J.E. Cliff (2003), 'The pervasive effects of family on entrepreneurship: Toward a family embeddedness perspective,' *Journal of Business Venturing*, **18** (5), 573–596.

Amoró, J.E. and N. Bosma (2014), 'Global entrepreneurship monitor 2013 global report.'

Astrachan, J.H., S.B. Klein, and K.X. Smyrnios (2002), 'The F-PEC scale of family influence: A proposal for solving the family business definition problem,' *Family Business Review*, **15** (1), 45–58.

Basco, R., A. Discua Cruz, G. Jimenez-Seminario, K. Ramachandran, L. Xin-chun, and F. Welter (2014), 'Call for papers: Family business in emerging, developing, and transition economies' http://euram-online.org/conference/2015/ (retrieved February 3, 2015).

Berrone, P., C. Cruz, and L.R. Gómez-Mejía (2012), 'Socioemotional wealth in family firms: Theoretical dimensions, assessment approaches, and agenda for future research,' *Family Business Review*, **25** (3), 258–279.

Berrone, P., C. Cruz, and L.R. Gómez-Mejía (2014), 'Family-controlled firms and stakeholder management: A socioemotional wealth preservation perspective,' in L. Melin, M. Nordqvist, and P. Sharma (eds), *The SAGE Handbook of Family Business*, London: Sage Publications, pp. 179–195.

Bruton, G.D., D. Ahlstrom, and K. Obloj (2008), 'Entrepreneurship in emerging economies: Where are we today and where should the research go in the future,' *Entrepreneurship Theory and Practice*, **32** (1), 1–14.

Carr, J.C. and K.M. Hmieleski (2014), 'Differences in the outcomes of work and family conflict between family- and non-family businesses: An examination of business founders.' *Working Paper*.

Danes, S.M. (2014), 'The future of family business research through the family scientist's lens,' in L. Melin, M. Nordqvist, and P. Sharma (eds), *The SAGE Handbook of Family Business*, London: Sage Publications, pp. 611–619.

Davidsson, P. (2004), *Researching Entrepreneurship*, Boston, MA: Springer.

Davidsson, P. (2006), 'Nascent entrepreneurship: Empirical studies and developments,' *Foundations and Trends in Entrepreneurship*, **2** (1), 1–76.

De Massis, A., P. Sharma, J.H. Chua, and J.J. Chrisman (2012), *Family Business*

Studies: An Annotated Bibliography, Cheltenham, UK and Northampton, MA USA: Edward Elgar Publishing.

Eddleston, K.A. and G.N. Powell (2012), 'Nurturing entrepreneurs' work–family balance: A gendered perspective,' *Entrepreneurship Theory and Practice*, **36** (3), 513–541.

Family Firm Institute (2013), 'Global data points,' www.ffi.org/?page=GlobalDataPoints (retrieved February 3, 2015).

Felzensztein, C., E. Gimmon, and C. Aqueveque (2013), 'Entrepreneurship at the periphery: Exploring framework conditions in core and peripheral locations,' *Entrepreneurship: Theory and Practice*, **37**, 815–835.

Gómez-Mejía, L.R., C. Cruz, P. Berrone, and J. De Castro (2011), 'The bind that ties: Socioemotional wealth preservation in family firms,' *The Academy of Management Annals*, **5** (1), 653–707.

Gómez-Mejía, L.R., K.T. Haynes, M. Núñez-Nickel, K.J. Jacobson, and J. Moyano-Fuentes (2007), 'Socioemotional wealth and business risks in family-controlled firms: Evidence from Spanish olive oil mills,' *Administrative Science Quarterly*, **52** (1), 106–137.

Gras, D. and R.S. Nason (forthcoming), 'Bric by bric: The role of the family household in sustaining a venture in impoverished Indian slums,' *Journal of Business Venturing*, http://dx.doi.org/10.1016/j.jbusvent.2014.10.002.

Gupta, V. and N. Levenburg (2010), 'A thematic analysis of cultural variations in family businesses: The CASE project,' *Family Business Review*, **23** (2), 155–169.

Heritage Foundation of Economic Freedom (2014), '2014 index of economic freedom,' http://www.heritage.org/index.

Howorth, C., M. Rose, E. Hamilton, and P. Westhead (2010), 'Family firm diversity and development: An introduction,' *International Small Business Journal*, **28** (5), 437–451.

James, A.E., J.E. Jennings, and R.S. Breitkreuz (2012), 'Worlds apart? Rebridging the distance between family science and family business research,' *Family Business Review*, **25** (1), 87–108.

Jennings, J.E. and M.S. McDougald (2007), 'Work–family interface experiences and coping strategies: Implications for entrepreneurship research and practice,' *Academy of Management Review*, **32** (3), 747–760.

Jennings, P.D., R. Greenwood, M.D. Lounsbury, and R. Suddaby (2013), 'Institutions, entrepreneurs, and communities: A special issue on entrepreneurship,' *Journal of Business Venturing*, **28** (1), 1–9.

Khanna, T. and K. Palepu (2013), *Winning in Emerging Markets: A Road Map for Strategy and Execution*, Boston, MA: Harvard Business Press.

Khavul, S., G.D. Bruton, and E. Wood (2009), 'Informal family business in Africa,' *Entrepreneurship Theory and Practice*, **33** (6), 1219–1238.

KPMG (2013), Website: http://www.kpmg.com/Global/en/IssuesAndInsights/ArticlesPublications/family-business/Pages/family-owned-businesses-backbone-indias-economy.aspx.

Krueger, N., F. Liñán, and G. Nabi (2013), 'Cultural values and entrepreneurship,' *Entrepreneurship and Regional Development*, **25** (9–10), 703–707.

McKee, D., T.M. Madden, F.W. Kellermans, and K.A. Eddleston (2014), 'Conflicts in family firms: The good and the bad,' in L. Melin, M. Nordqvist, and P. Sharma (eds), *The SAGE Handbook of Family Business*, London: Sage Publications, pp. 514–528.

McKenney, A.F., G.T. Payne, M.A. Zachary, and J.C. Short (2014), 'Multilevel analysis in family business studies,' in L. Melin, M. Nordqvist, and P. Sharma (eds), *The SAGE Handbook of Family Business*, London: Sage Publications, pp. 594–608.

Peredo, A.M. and M. McLean (2013), 'Indigenous development and the cultural captivity of entrepreneurship,' *Business and Society*, **52** (4), 592–620.

Powell, G.N. and K.A. Eddleston (2013), 'Linking family-to-business enrichment and support to entrepreneurial success: do female and male entrepreneurs experience different outcomes?,' *Journal of Business Venturing*, **28** (2), 261–280.

Rogoff, E.G. and R.K.Z. Heck (2003), 'Evolving research in entrepreneurship and family business: Recognizing family as the oxygen that feeds the fire of entrepreneurship,' *Journal of Business Venturing*, **18** (5), 559–566.

Salvato, C. and G. Corbetta (2014), 'Strategic content and process in family business,' in L. Melin, M. Nordqvist, and P. Sharma (eds), *The SAGE Handbook of Family Business*, London: Sage Publications, pp. 295–320.

Sharma, P., L. Melin, and M. Nordqvist (2014), 'Introduction: Scope, evolution and future of family business studies,' in L. Melin, M. Nordqvist, and P. Sharma (eds), *The SAGE Handbook of Family Business*, London: Sage Publications, pp. 1–22.

Smyrnios, K.X., C.A. Romano, G.A. Tanewski, P.I. Karofsky, R. Millen, and M.R. Yilmaz (2003), 'Work–family conflict: A study of American and Australian family businesses,' *Family Business Review*, **16** (1), 35–51.

Ucbasaran, D., P. Westhead, and M. Wright (2001), 'The focus of entrepreneurial research: Contextual and process issues,' *Entrepreneurship Theory and Practice*, **25** (4), 57–80.

Welter, F. (2011), 'Contextualizing entrepreneurship – conceptual challenges and ways forward,' *Entrepreneurship Theory and Practice*, **35** (1), 165–184.

Werbel, J.D. and S.M. Danes (2010), 'Work family conflict in new business ventures: The moderating effects of spousal commitment to the new business venture,' *Journal of Small Business Management*, **48** (3), 421–440.

Wright, M., J.J. Chrisman, J.H. Chua, and L.P. Steier (2014), 'Family enterprise and context,' *Entrepreneurship Theory and Practice*, **38** (6), 1247–1260.

Yu, A., G.T. Lumpkin, R.L. Sorenson, and K.H. Brigham (2012), 'The landscape of family business outcomes a summary and numerical taxonomy of dependent variables,' *Family Business Review*, **25** (1), 33–57.

Zahra, S.A. and M. Wright (2011), 'Entrepreneurship's next act,' *The Academy of Management Perspectives*, **25** (4), 67–83.

Zahra, S.A., M. Wright, and S.G. Abdelgawad (2014), 'Contextualization and the advancement of entrepreneurship research,' *International Small Business Journal*, **32** (5), 479–500.

Zellweger, T.M., R.S. Nason, and M. Nordqvist (2012), 'From longevity of firms to transgenerational entrepreneurship of families: Introducing family entrepreneurial orientation,' *Family Business Review*, **25** (2) 136–155.

Zellweger, T., P. Sieger, and F. Halter (2011), 'Should I stay or should I go? Career choice intentions of students with family business background,' *Journal of Business Venturing*, **26** (5), 521–536.

PART I

Family influences upon owner-managed businesses in diverse country contexts

2. The orientations, strategies and performance of family and non-family firms in the United States: how important is SEW?

P. Devereaux Jennings, Jennifer E. Jennings and Youngbin Joo

INTRODUCTION

This chapter focuses upon the family embeddedness of business strategy and performance of small and medium-sized enterprises (SMEs) in the United States. As noted by Sharma and Carney, privately held firms, in general, 'overwhelmingly dominate the economic landscape of our world' (Sharma and Carney, 2012: 233). To illustrate this point, they cited figures reported by Stuart (2011) estimating the number of US-based private enterprises with employees at over 6 million—a figure more than 1200 times greater than the country's 5000 or so publicly traded companies. Of these privately held businesses, the majority are SMEs; that is, small-sized enterprises with fewer than 250 employees and less than $50M in annual revenue; or, medium-sized enterprises with fewer than 500 employees and typically less than $500M in annual revenue (US SBEC, 2013). If sole proprietorships without employees are included, SMEs are estimated to account for approximately two-thirds of all US businesses (Astrachan and Shanker, 2003). They also account for about half of the country's employment (Astrachan and Shanker, 2003) and for approximately 46.0 percent of the nation's private non-farm gross domestic product (Breitzman and Hicks, 2008). Depending on the definition adopted, the proportion of SMEs in the US that are considered to be family owned ranges from 28.0 percent (US SBEC, 2013) to 70.0 percent (Astrachan and Shanker, 2003).

Despite their prevalence, privately held family firms constitute an understudied and thus particularly 'enigmatic organizational form' (Sharma and Carney, 2012: 233). This is due, at least in part, to the methodological challenges associated with their investigation. As a result, the family business field possesses 'limited available evidence' (Sharma and Carney, 2012: 235) regarding the comparative performance of family and non-family firms that are privately rather than publicly owned. Similarly, we would argue, family business scholars have not yet established empirically whether the strategies of privately held family and non-family firms differ significantly—and whether they do so in ways consequential for performance. Finally, the field is in need of empirical investigations that directly test the claim that the differential outcomes experienced by family firms are attributable to their greater focus upon non-economic goals, such as the preservation or enhancement of the family's socio-emotional wealth (Berrone, Cruz, and Gómez-Mejía, 2012).

This study addresses the above-noted gaps using primary data collected in 2012 from a stratified sample of 309 SMEs across the US. As such, it offers a rare glimpse into the elusive 'inner workings' of privately held family and non-family firms in the country. We start by presenting descriptive data on the characteristics of the participating firms, including comparative information on performance. We then summarize the findings pertaining to business strategy, detailing whether and how the family versus non-family SMEs differ with respect to the strategic concepts of exploration versus exploitation (for example, Cohen and Levinthal, 1990; He and Wong, 2004; Zahra and George, 2002) as well as causation versus effectuation (Sarasvathy, 2001). Following this we examine potential antecedents, presenting comparative data not only on traditional orientations (in other words, towards growth, entrepreneurialism and managing for the long-term) but also on the newer concept of socio-emotional wealth (SEW). We then conduct a series of multivariate regression analyses, conducted on both the full sample and the separate subsamples of family and non-family firms, to assess the relationships between SEW, the business orientations and strategies, and firm performance. We conclude with a discussion of the study's contributions, limitations and implications for research on family business strategy and performance. For a visual of our guiding conceptual framework, see Figure 1.1 in this book's introductory chapter (Jennings, Eddleston, Jennings, and Sarathy, Chapter 1).

DATA COLLECTION

Given that fine-grained data on the SEW motives, strategic orientations, business strategies and performance of privately held firms in the US is not readily available from public sources, we collected primary data for this study. The data were collected via an online survey administered by

Qualtrics, which is one of the world's leading suppliers of such services. We contracted this organization to secure a random sample of SMEs across a variety of industries and geographic regions of the US, stratified according to the following size categories: micro (0–10 employees), small (11–250 employees), and medium (251–500 employees). Although an owner-manager from 309 distinct firms agreed to participate, missing data on firm performance (in other words, 8 cases for the 12-month measure and 17 cases for the 5-year measure) and/or a handful of other variables reduced our sample size in some models.

CHARACTERISTICS OF THE FAMILY AND NON-FAMILY FIRMS

Demographic Characteristics

Of the 309 owner-managers who participated in the US-based study, 213 (68.9 percent) considered their businesses to be family firms, whereas 93 (30.1 percent) did not, and three firms (1.0 percent) had missing values.[1] As indicated in Table 2.1, more that 45 percent in both groups had fewer than 10 full-time employees (FTEs). In comparison with other research (for example, Anderson and Reeb, 2003; Chua et al., 2004; Palmer and Barber, 2001), then, our sample was constituted by a higher-than-average percentage of family firms, yet a proportion within the range reported in other studies (for example, Schulze et al., 2001). In comparison with Astrachan and Shanker's (2003) study of SMEs, the stratified nature of our sample resulted in a slightly lower percentage of very small firms.

More of the self-identified family firms tended to be in manufacturing (21.6 percent) and other industries (33.8 percent) than the self-identified non-family firms, which were concentrated in the personal and professional services sectors (41.8 percent). The family firms exhibited less national dispersion than the non-family firms (operating across 6.0 versus 9.5 states respectively on average), but slightly more international dispersion (operating in 3.5 versus 2.7 countries respectively on average). They also tended to be older and to be run more often by men than women and by those with a somewhat lower education level. The more traditional demographics of the family SMEs in the US sample fits with much of the extant literature characterizing family firms (for example, Miller, Le Breton-Miller, and Scholnick, 2008; Palmer and Barber, 2001; Zeitlin, 1974). In the vast majority of cases for both the family and non-family firms (88.7 percent and 87.1 percent respectively), however, it was the founder who responded to the survey.

*Table 2.1   Family versus non-family firm and owner-manager
             characteristics (US sample)*

Variables	Family firms (N = 213)	Non-family firms (N = 93)
Number of full-time employees		
0 to 10	59.65%	46.2%*
11 to 250	35.2%	47.3%*
251 to 500	1.4%	2.2%
Greater than 500	2.3%	3.2%
Industry categories		
Manufacturing	21.6%	10.8%*
Personal services	41.8%	58.1%**
Professional services	7.0%	10.8%
Other	33.8%	20.1%*
Other attributes of the firms		
Number of states with operations	6.0	9.5†
Number of countries with operations	3.5	2.7
Company age (years)	16.1	13.4
Owner-manager characteristics		
Male	52.7%	47.3%
Married	70.0%	57.0%*
Education (at least some university)	53.0%	68.5%†
Founder	88.7%	87.1%
Outcomes		
12-month average perceived firm performance (7-point scales)	4.48	4.51
5-year average perceived firm performance (7-point scales)	4.51	4.50
Owner-manager's perceived effectiveness in the business sphere (max of 100)	76	76
Owner-manager's satisfaction with the business (max of 100)	71	76

Note: † $p \le .10$, * $p \le .05$, ** $p \le .01$, *** $p \le .001$ (two-tailed tests).

Outcome Variables

Although the family and non-family firms exhibited noticeable differences on certain demographic characteristics, they did not differ significantly on outcomes such as firm performance, perceived effectiveness and business satisfaction. As indicated at the bottom of Table 2.1, the 12-month average and 5-year average indices of perceived performance[2] were virtually identical and moderate; in other words, scores of approximately 4.5 out of 7.0, with 4.0 being 'the same relative to competitors.' Not surprisingly, the owner-managers in both types of firms expressed equivalent levels of perceived effectiveness in the business sphere, both reporting scores of 76 out of 100. They also appeared to be equally satisfied with their businesses, with means of 71 and 76, respectively, out of 100. The first notable finding, then, pertains to the similar levels of performance exhibited by the family and non-family firms in our sample of US-based SMEs, as measured by a variety of indicators. We turn now to examining whether their strategies, orientations and concern for SEW were also more similar than different.

STRATEGIES, ORIENTATIONS AND SEW WITHIN THE FAMILY VERSUS NON-FAMILY FIRMS

Business Strategies

We investigated two sets of business strategies. The first set pertains to the distinction between *exploration* and *exploitation*. An exploration strategy involves a commitment to developing new technologies, products and markets (Cohen and Levinthal, 1990; He and Wong, 2004; Zahra and George, 2002). In contrast, an exploitation strategy focuses upon product and technology refinements conducted in the name of efficiency. When firms pursue both strategies with almost equal intensity, and attempt to configure the firm accordingly, firms are said to rely on a strategy of ambidexterity (Benner and Tushman, 2003).

Within entrepreneurship, and consequently among SMEs, exploration and exploitation are also used as strategies (for example, see Zahra and George, 2002). However, these strategies may fit less well than others because firms that are new and smaller tend to be, by definition, in a new technology, product area or market. Thus, it becomes more important to examine how such firms pursue product and market development in order to achieve their objectives. One accepted distinction in this regard is that between *causation* and *effectuation* (Sarasvathy, 2001). Causation refers to planning and mapping out product/market development in more linear, causal and projective terms whereas effectuation refers to responding to effects as the firm evolves.

The top section of Table 2.2 shows the degree to which these two sets of strategies were pursued by the family and non-family firms in the US sample. Following He and Wong (2004), exploration was measured by the average of four items regarding the importance, over the previous three

Table 2.2   *Family versus non-family business strategies, orientations and SEW (US sample)*

Variables	Family firms (N = 213)			Non-family firms (N = 93)	
	α	Mean	S.D.	Mean	S.D.
Strategies					
Exploration	.88	3.65	1.00	3.51	1.06
Exploitation	.89	3.76	.99	3.53*	1.05
Ambidexterity	.92	14.53	6.07	13.28	6.52
Causation	.87	3.79	.84	3.74	.80
Effectuation	.61	3.75	.74	3.66	.63
Orientations					
Growth	.77	3.1	.68	3.0	.71
Entrepreneurial	.83	3.82	.69	3.80	.66
Long-term	.73	3.66	.68	3.44*	.78
Socio-emotional wealth					
Family control	.89	4.06	.65	3.56***	.81
Identification	.81	4.43	.61	3.99***	.83
Bonds	.83	4.04	.71	3.90	.70
Emotion	.88	4.22	.65	3.98**	.89
Renewal	.65	3.70	.66	3.48*	.78
Composite measure	.89	20.29	2.30	18.96***	3.01

Note: $\dagger p \leq .10$, $* p \leq .05$, $** p \leq .01$, $*** p \leq .001$ (two-tailed tests).

years, of such objectives as 'introducing new generation of products' or 'entering new technological fields' (α = .88). Exploitation was measured by four items assessing the importance of such objectives as 'improving existing product quality' or 'reducing production costs' (α = .89). Each item for both scales was rated on a 5-point Likert scale ranging from '1 = very unimportant' to '5 = very important.' Ambidexterity was measured by multiplying the means of the two indices together. As indicated in Table 2.2, the owner-managers of both the family and non-family firms reported above-average means on all three measures. Even more notably, although the two types of firms did not differ with respect to degree of exploration, the family firms tended to exhibit significantly higher levels of exploitation and, consequently, almost significantly different levels of ambidexterity.

Following Chandler et al. (2011), causation was measured by the mean of four items such as 'we designed and planned business strategies' and 'we did meaningful analysis to select target markets,' each rated on a 5-point

Likert scale ranging from '1 = strongly disagree' to '5 = strongly agree' ($\alpha = .87$). Effectuation was measured on the same scale but by the mean of four different items, including 'we experimented with different products and/or business models.' As indicated in Table 2.2, both variables had means above 3.0 but it is apparent that these were not statistically different across the family and non-family subsamples. Because the Cronbach's alpha for the 4-item effectuation scale was low ($\alpha = .61$), we investigated alternate specifications but were unable to find any that exhibited greater internal reliability. As such, the findings for effectuation reported in our multivariate analyses, below, need to be interpreted with this caveat in mind.

Orientations

In recent years, both the strategic management and entrepreneurship literatures have moved towards studying the *antecedents* of different strategies as much as their effects. This intellectual shift is in keeping with early work, such as that on configurations (for example, Miller and Friesen, 1984), which recognized that strategy has several closely related correlates, and that emphasizing the role of culture and resource-based capabilities in firms (for example, Barney, 1991; Grant, 1996). Strategy in these formulations represents an attempt to design and leverage the deeper sources of firm value. As part of that effort, strategy researchers have added the concept of 'strategic intentions' or 'orientations' as a way of linking cognitions about capabilities to strategic practices and performance as an outcome (Bird, 1988; Hamel and Prahalad, 1989; Mantere and Sillince, 2007).

Three orientations concern us here: growth, entrepreneurial, and long-term. There is increasing evidence that large public firms (Collins, 2001), family firms (Miller and Le Breton-Miller, 2005), and small firms (Cliff, 1998) may deliberately limit growth or pursue slower growth trajectories in order to build deeper value in their firms. This appears to be so even if non-family firms, particularly those that are publically held, are presumed to be disciplined by the demands of the market, and thus less likely to engage in such alternatives. We measured a firm's growth orientation using eight items, inspired by Cliff (1998), that capture the extent to which the owner-manager intends to expand the business and is always seeking new ways to do so, or, conversely, sees expansion as a hazard and actually has some maximum size threshold in mind. Each item was rated on a 5-point Likert scale with higher values reflecting a greater orientation towards growth ($\alpha = .77$). As can be seen in Table 2.2, the owner-managers of the family and non-family firms in the US sample reported similar growth orientations. Notably, their means were also very close to the scale's mid-point of 3.0, reflecting a neutral orientation, on average, towards business growth.

Entrepreneurial orientation refers to the 'the processes, practices and decision making activities that lead to new [market] entry' (Lumpkin and Dess, 1996: 136). This construct is typically conceptualized and operationalized as being constituted by four dimensions: innovativeness, autonomy, aggressiveness, and risk-taking. Although each dimension can be measured and analyzed separately, we constructed a composite measure. Using the scale developed by Covin and Slevin (1989), entrepreneurial orientation was operationalized by the mean of eight items ($\alpha = .83$), with each item measured on a 5-point Likert scale. An illustrative item is 'we were flexible and took advantage of opportunities as they arose.' As indicated in Table 2.2, we did not find any evidence that the family and non-family SMEs in the US sample differed with respect to their degree of entrepreneurial orientation.

Finally, consistent with broader work on temporal rhythms and time horizons in organizations (Slawinski and Bansal, 2012; Lawrence, Winn, and Jennings, 2001) and with family business research on long versus short-term perspectives (Eddleston, Kellermanns and Zellweger, 2012; Zahra et al., 2004), we considered a firm's *long-term orientation*. Following Eddleston et al. (2012), we measured this variable by the average of four items, each rated on a 5-point Likert scale ($\alpha = .73$). Illustrative items include 'the firm is in business for the long run,' and 'the incentive for our (middle) management is tied to the long run performance of the firm.' As indicated in Table 2.2, and as might be expected from prior research (for example, Miller and Le Breton-Miller, 2005), the owner-managers of the family firms exhibited a significantly higher long-term orientation than those of the non-family firms.

Socio-emotional Wealth (SEW)

SEW refers to 'non-financial aspects of the firm that meet the family's affective needs, such as identity, the ability to exercise family influence, and the perpetuation of the family dynasty' (Gómez-Mejía et al., 2007: 106). More recently, Berrone et al. (2012) theorized five dimensions as constituting the core of this construct: family control, identification, bonds, emotion, and renewal (in other words, FIBER). These scholars recommended that each dimension be measured by multiple items, as we did here. An illustrative item for each dimension, in order, is as follows: 'I will never consider selling shares of the business outside my family,' 'If I lost the firm, I would feel like I had lost a little bit of myself,' 'In the business, we emphasize trust in relationships,' 'I am emotionally attached to the firm,' and, 'The firm is in the business for the long run.' Each item was measured on a 5-point Likert scale ranging from 'strongly disagree' to 'strongly agree.' We also created a composite SEW measure by summing the five averaged dimensions. As noted at the bottom of Table 2.2, the Cronbach's alphas for each FIBER dimension, as well as composite measure of SEW, were above .80 for the most part.[3] Moreover, almost every dimension (except for 'bonds') statistically discriminated between family and non-family firms. This was also so for the composite measure. As expected, in each case the family firms scored higher than the non-family firms.

THE RELATIONSHIPS BETWEEN STRATEGY, ORIENTATION, SEW AND PERFORMANCE

Results for the Full Sample

We are now in a position to explore the relationships between strategy and its potential antecedents on the performance of privately held SMEs in the US. Table 2.3 displays the regression results for the effects of strategy, orientation, and SEW on the 12-month performance index for the full sample of family and non-family firms combined. The convergence and divergence between these results and those for the 5-year performance index are discussed as we step through the table.

Model 1 is the baseline model containing controls at the industry, organization and individual levels. With the exception of industry dynamism, there does not appear to be a noticeable impact of industry type on performance. Among the organizational controls, logged firm size exerted consistently strong positive effects. It is also notable that the family firm dummy variable exerted a negative and marginally significant effect as additional variables were stepped into the models. Among the individual-level controls, being married was the only covariate that consistently made a (positive) difference to firm-level performance, although it should be noted, consistent with prior research (Miller et al., 2007), that the 'founder effect' was positive and statistically significant in some of the models.

Model 2 reports the findings for exploration and exploitation. Although exploration has a positive association with above-average performance, exploitation does not. Moreover, when exploration and exploitation were multiplied together in a supplemental analysis (available upon request), this 'ambidexterity' variable was positive and significant whereas exploration and exploitation became negative and significant. This implies that firms which simultaneously pursue both strategies perform substantially

Table 2.3   Net associations with prior 12-month performance index (US sample)

Variables	Model 1	Model 2	Model 3	Model 4	Model 5	Model 6
Controls						
Manufacturing	−.028	−.048	−.033	−.035	−.036	−.021
Personal services	.005	.208	.044	.064	.075	.036
Professional services	−.029	−.025	.024	.019	.036	.035
Industry dynamism	.128*	.035	.009	.043	.017	.014
Family firm	.018	.020	.001	−.127†	−.080†	−.080†
Number of states with operations	−.004	−.029	−.007	.018	.021	.004
Logged company size	.433***	.407***	.281***	.132**	.181**	.181**
Company age	.002	.021	.035	.043	.024	.058
Founder	.083†	.076†	.071	.057	.069	.068
Owner-manager male	−.018	−.005	−.019	−.016	−.028	−.028
Owner-manager married	.074†	.098*	.083†	.052	.083†	.078†
Owner-manager education	.003	−.009	−.029	−.038	−.028	−.023
Business strategies						
Exploration		.146*	.027	−.040	−.023	.001
Exploitation		.041	−.049	−.032	−.006	−.012
Causation			.349***	.233**	.246**	.139**
Effectuation			.130*	.070	.101†	.115†

Orientations						
Growth orientation				.126***		.139**
Entrepreneurial orientation				.133***		.044
Long-term orientation				.270***		
Socio-emotional wealth						
Family control					.025	
Identification					.103†	
Bonds					.055	
Emotion					-.083	
Renewal					.241***	
SEW composite measure						.181**
Overall model F	6.057***	5.726***	8.279***	9.192***	7.25***	7.83***
R square	.21	.24	.35	.39	.40	.40
Observations	289	274	263	261	249	243

Notes:
Values in the table are standardized OLS regression coefficients (beta values).
† $p \leq .10$, * $p \leq .05$, ** $p \leq .01$, *** $p \leq .001$ (in one-tailed, directional tests, two-tailed otherwise).

better than those pursuing just one. It should be noted, however, that when the process strategy variables of causation versus effectuation are entered in Models 3–6, exploration and exploitation are no longer significant (as is the case in secondary analyses of 5-year performance, both with and without ambidexterity).

As indicated in Model 3, the effects of causation and effectuation are significant and positive (and remain so, for the most part, in Models 4–6). The impact of causation is particularly robust, exerting an even larger standardized effect on performance than logged size. Effectuation has a more attenuated impact, and its influence is weaker in models of the 5-year performance index. This weaker effect may not be surprising given the previously noted problems with this scale's internal reliability.

Model 4 shows the effects for the three types of orientations. As a group, these variables improve the model's fit and R^2, though less dramatically than did the inclusion of the strategy variables themselves. Each of the orientation variables is positive and highly significant, with long-term orientation exhibiting the highest standardized coefficient of the three. The same pattern occurs when the 5-year performance index is used. It would seem, then, that a focus on growth, on being entrepreneurial, and on taking a long-run perspective are all positively associated with above-average performance for SMEs in the US. It is also noticeable that the strategy variable of effectuation is no longer significant and causation's impact drops considerably.

SEW has been touted as an alternative to—or potentially even the main theoretical determinant of—the above-noted orientation variables. In Model 5, the five FIBER dimensions are entered in place of the orientation variables; in other words, first, as an alternative. Combined, these dimensions result in a slightly higher R^2 than the orientation variables and the overall model F is comparable with that reported for Model 4 after accounting for the loss of degrees of freedom. The renewal dimension, in particular, has a very strong effect.

Model 6 shows the effects of the composite SEW measure net of the orientation variables. Due to multicollinearity between long-term orientation and the renewal dimension of SEW, we could not enter all five dimensions of SEW along with all three orientations in the same model. So we dropped long-term orientation and started with an examination of the SEW composite variable. Although this composite measure is positive and statistically significant, the overall model F and R^2 for Model 6 are not improvements over those for Model 5. Notably, however, a comparison of the statistically significant coefficients indicates that the composite measure of SEW exerts a comparable influence on firm performance as logged size—and a greater influence than either causation or growth orientation.

Results for Family versus Non-family Firms

Are these relationships between business strategy, orientations, SEW and firm performance the same for family and non-family firms? Based on our review of theory early in the chapter, one would certainly expect SEW to be more influential for the former group of firms than the latter. Also, our description of the mean and variance subsample differences in Table 2.2 would also lead us to believe that there should be variation in SEW's impact between family and non-family firms. Practically speaking, however, such differences may not be that easy to distinguish because the number of firms is not equivalent within each subsample, the degrees of freedom are reduced due to missing values, and the number of covariates to observations is rather large. Table 2.4, nevertheless, displays the results of our subsample comparison.

After controlling for industry, organizational and individual-level factors, we see that causation and effectuation (but not exploration and exploitation), for the most part, are significantly and positively associated with greater perceived firm performance. Causation appears to have a stronger effect among non-family firms, whereas effectuation does so among family firms. The results may not be that surprising, particularly in light of the agency theory/stewardship debate. Agency theorists argue that non-family firms are more likely to engage in strategic planning, something consistent with the professional training of non-family firm managers and with non-family firm market orientation (Salvato and Corbetta, 2014). But stewardship theorists would argue that family firms do strategize, just in a more organic way that is based on many family inputs and tailoring the firm's operation to the particular expression of the family's goals (Miller and Le Breton-Miller, 2005).

Turning to the three orientations, the findings reported in Table 2.4 indicated that the growth and long-term orientations exert effects similar to those reported for the full sample, but entrepreneurial orientation does not. The stronger positive effect of growth orientation in Models 1 and 5 for the family sample, compared with no effect in Models 2 and 6 for the non-family sample, might also have been expected. After all, family firms, given their focus on control and continuity might not wish to grow as aggressively (Chua et al., 1999; Miller and Le Breton-Miller, 2005); thus, those that do grow might be more distinctive from those that do not in terms of performance relative to competitors. Conversely, growth expectations are supposed to be automatically built into non-family firms, so variation in espoused versions of it may not really make as much of a difference for performance (Anderson and Reeb, 2003; Fama and Jensen, 1983). Using the same logic, the lower significant positive effect of long-term

Table 2.4 *Net associations with prior 12-month performance index—subsample comparison (US family and non-family firms)*

Variables	Family Model 1	Non-family Model 2	Family Model 3	Non-family Model 4	Family Model 5	Non-family Model 6
Controls	Included	Included	Included	Included	Included	Included
Business strategies						
Exploration	.038	-.128	.039	-.023	.056	.043
Exploitation	-.058	.007	.006	-.006	-.054	.007
Causation	.083	.398**	.163†	.246**	.122	.253*
Effectuation	.164*	.063	.187†	.101†	.180*	.117
Orientations						
Growth orientation	.170**	-.018			.186**	-.037
Entrepreneurial orientation	.106	.135			.066	-.080
Long-term orientation	.255***	.380**				
Socio-emotional wealth						
Family control			.061	-.115		
Identification			.091	-.015		
Bonds			-.068	.394**		
Emotion			-.133	.046		
Renewal			.245***	.326**		
SEW composite measure					.085	.370**
Overall model F	5.439***	3.662***	5.554***	3.555***	5.60***	3.285***
R square	.44	.53	.42	.56	.40	.51
Observations	172	77	172	76	167	75

Notes:
Values in the table are standardized OLS regression coefficients (beta values).
† $p \le .10$, * $p \le .05$, ** $p \le .01$, *** $p \le .001$ (in one-tailed, directional tests, two-tailed otherwise).

orientation in Models 1 and 5 for the family sample versus Models 2 and 6 for the non-family firms might also be anticipated. Long-term orientations are expected by agency and stewardship theory to be higher in family than non-family firms, and empirically the means are higher and the variances lower in the family subsample (as previously reported in Table 2.2).

The results for SEW are even more surprising. As indicated in Models 3 and 4, more of the FIBER dimensions were statistically significant within the *non*-family than within the family subsample (in other words, bonds and renewal in the former versus only renewal in the latter). Moreover, the effects of renewal were stronger amongst the non-family firms. Similarly, as indicated in Models 5 and 6, the composite measure of SEW exerted a positive and statistically significant impact upon performance only within the subsample of *non*-family firms. On the face of it, then, it would seem that the FIBER dimensions and the SEW composite measure are more important to the performance of firms that are marginally family owned and operated than amongst those that are considered by their owner-managers to be family firms.

Exploring SEW's Impact on Selected Orientations and Strategies

Given the significant direct effects for the SEW composite variable and many of its subdimensions on firm performance noted above, as a final set of analyses we explored the associations between the SEW measures and selected orientations (in other words, growth and entrepreneurial) and strategies (in other words, causation and effectuation).[4] The results are displayed in Table 2.5. As indicated, perhaps the most striking result is the statistically significant effect of the composite SEW measure within every single one of the models. Moreover, the consistently positive coefficient for this measure indicates that stronger SEW motivations tend to be associated with higher growth and entrepreneurial orientations as well as with higher levels of both causation and effectuation process strategies. Notably, this appears to be the case for the family and non-family firms alike.

Also notably, the results for the separate FIBER dimensions of SEW are not quite as consistent across the orientations and strategies—especially when the distinction between family and non-family firms is taken into account. For instance, a comparison of Models 2 and 3 reveals that growth orientation is influenced by the dimensions of family control, identification and bonds within family firms—but by the dimensions of emotion and renewal within non-family firms. In contrast, a comparison of Models 5 and 6 indicates that entrepreneurial orientation is positively influenced by the dimensions of family control and bonds within family and non-family firms alike. A comparison of Models 8 and 9, however,

Table 2.5 *The impact of SEW and the FIBER dimensions on orientations and strategy (US sample)*

	Growth Orientation			Entrepreneurial Orientation		
	Full Sample Model 1	Family Model 2	Non-family Model 3	Full Sample Model 4	Family Model 5	Non-family Model 6
Controls and Covariates	Included	Included	Included	Included	Included	Included
SEW Composite	.182***	.165***	.155†	.458***	.354**	.607***
Family Control	-.122†	.161**	-.1156	.161**	.155**	.158*
Identification	.143*	.106†	-.007	.106†	.117†	.065
Bonds	-.012	.407***	-.185	.407***	.421***	.405***
Emotion	.048	.016	.269†	.016	-.046	.138
Renewal	.199**	.002	.329**	.002	-.043	.162

	Causation			Effectuation		
	Full Sample Model 7	Family Model 8	Non-family Model 9	Full Sample Model 10	Family Model 11	Non-family Model 12
Controls and Covariates	Included	Included	Included	Included	Included	Included
SEW Composite	.404***	.348***	.517***	.221***	.229***	.217**
Family Control	.037	.117*	-.022	-.010	-.002	.155**
Identification	.081	.033	.224**	.101†	.158*	.117†
Bonds	.281***	.355***	.006	.137**	.203*	.421***
Emotion	.076	-.043	.285**	.038	-.010	-.046
Renewal	.171**	.148**	.156†	.055	.027	.143

Note: SEW composite measure entered in separate models from the FIBER dimensions.

shows that a causation strategy tends to be influenced by the dimensions of family control, bonds and renewal within family firms but primarily by the dimensions of identification and emotion within non-family firms. Finally, a comparison of Models 11 and 12 suggests that an effectuation strategy tends to be influenced by the dimensions of identification and bonds for both types of firms—and by the dimension of family control in the case of the *non*-family firms. These distinctions are quite complex, warranting further study in their own right.

In sum, when considered together, the pattern of findings reported in Table 2.4 and Table 2.5 lends support for the overall expectations regarding the effects of SEW as conveyed in Figure 1.1 of this book's introductory chapter (Jennings et al., Chapter 1). More specifically, they suggest that such motives are not only directly associated with firm performance but also indirectly associated through their influence upon strategic orientations and business strategies.

DISCUSSION

Summary and Implications

If we were asked to sketch a quick portrait of privately held SMEs in the US based upon our survey findings—particularly with respect to the similarities and differences between family and non-family firms—what features would we choose to emphasize? One would certainly be the lack of any statistically significant differences between the two groups of firms on a variety of performance indicators. We would also call attention, however, to the statistically significant differences that we did observe in terms of their business strategies, orientations, and emphasis placed upon SEW motives. In comparison with their non-family counterparts, our survey findings suggest that privately held family firms in the US are more likely to be pursuing a strategy of exploitation and to possess a long-term orientation. Perhaps not surprisingly, the owner-managers of the family firms also tended to be more concerned about SEW considerations.

These findings offer several noteworthy contributions to and implications for the family business literature. Most fundamentally, they help shed light on the methodologically elusive and thus 'much under-studied' (Sharma and Carney, 2012: 238) privately owned family firm (at least within the US). In particular, they suggest that these firms neither under-perform nor over-perform relative to their non-family SME counterparts. As such, theoretical and empirical work dedicated to predicting and demonstrating such differences may not hold much promise. Instead, our findings suggest that continued work on the different strategies and orientations of family and non-family firms—and the differential impacts of these strategies and orientations across the two types of privately held firms—is likely to prove more fruitful.

Even more specifically, our study makes contributions to emergent work adopting an SEW lens on the family firm. Methodologically, we offer much-needed, multi-item measures of the FIBER dimensions theorized by Berrone et al. (2012). Empirically, we demonstrated that the composite measure as well as several of the subdimensions exerted significant effects on perceived firm performance and certain strategic orientations and business strategies. These findings help establish the predictive validity of the SEW construct and its constituent dimensions, which we hope will stimulate further theoretical and empirical work from this overarching perspective.

Limitations

It is important to consider our study's findings, contributions and implications in light of its limitations. For one, the small size and stratified nature of our sample means that it is only partly representative of privately held family and non-family SMEs in the US. As such, we cannot say for certain that our results are generalizable to the entire population of such firms in this country. Related to the sample, it is important to keep in mind that a large number of the small-sized firms were sole proprietorships. Such organizations might benefit from separate analysis in the future.

A second limitation pertains to our reliance upon a third-party contractor for the administration of the survey, which meant that we did not have access to the sampling frame and thus no way of potentially obtaining objective performance data to corroborate the subjective measures provided by the anonymous owner-managers. Consequently, we also have no means of collecting subsequent over-time data from the participants. Both of these outcome-related issues are problematic within strategy research in general. We hope that our analysis of outcomes within the family sphere that appears within Part II of this book provides partial compensation.

A third limitation pertains to the lack of consistently provided data on family shareholdings. Indeed, only half of the owner-managers provided such information about their firms. As a result, it is difficult to compare our results with those for other studies, in which family versus non-family firms are distinguished primarily (if not solely) by family ownership level.

As noted by De Massis et al. (2012), however, self-identification has been used as an operational criterion within approximately 15.0 percent of extant family business studies.

Conclusion

In light of the above-noted limitations, we respond as follows to the overarching question articulated within our chapter's title. Although family and non-family SMEs in the US do not appear to differ on various aspects of perceived performance, they do exhibit notable differences with respect to their strategies, orientations, and concern for preserving or enhancing SEW. The latter concern is an important predictor of perceived performance—particularly, and rather surprisingly, within SMEs that were *not* considered to be family firms by their owners. In our view, then, the most immediate next step for future research is to assess the causality of this intriguing observed relationship.

ACKNOWLEDGEMENTS

The data collection for this chapter was supported by SSHRC grant number 410-2009-0321. The authors would like to thank Stephanie Cornforth for her excellent research assistance.

NOTES

1. While there were too many missing data on family shareholding and participation in management to establish more clearly the variations in family ownership and control among these firms, we remind readers that all of the sampled firms were owner-managed and that many of those not considered as a 'family firm' by the survey respondents appeared to have owner-managers with some shareholdings. Thus, by some definitions, the non-family subsample might also be thought of as marginally family owned and controlled.
2. Twelve-month and 5-year performance were each measured by the mean of a 7-item scale ranging from 1 = 'worse relative to competitors' to 7 = 'better relative to competitors,' with the midpoint 4 = 'the same relative to competitors.' The items included growth in sales, growth in market share, growth in profitability, return on equity, return on total assets, profit margin on sales, and ability to fund growth from profits. See Appendix B of this book for the full scales used to measure the core constructs in this study.
3. The high reliability (alphas) of the SEW dimensions might also be evidence of common method bias. But when the 30 items were factor analyzed, only seven dimensions had eigenvalues over one, and four of them, after varimax rotation, explained most of variance. These four factors were associated with the items for emotion and identification (jointly), bonds, control and renewal, respectively. Thus, in the US sample, we feel that the FIBER measures empirically capture the dimensions of SEW as theorized by Berrone et al. (2012).
4. Given exploration and exploitation did not have significant main effects on performance

and that Table 2.5 is focused on showing the indirect effects on performance for SEW through mediator variables, like orientations and strategies, we did not report the results for exploration and exploitation in Table 2.5. Long-term orientation, as alluded to in the chapter, overlaps with, conceptually and empirically, the renewal dimension of SEW; thus, long-term orientation was not included as a mediator variable, nor in Table 2.4 when SEW's impact on performance was modelled.

REFERENCES

Anderson, R.C. and D.M. Reeb (2003), 'Founding family ownership and firm performance: Evidence from the S&P 500,' *Journal of Finance*, **58** (3), 1301–1327.

Astrachan, J.H. and M.C. Shanker (2003), 'Family businesses' contribution to the US economy: A closer look,' *Family Business Review*, **16** (3), 211–219.

Barney, J. (1991), 'Firm resources and sustained competitive advantage,' *Journal of Management*, **17** (1), 99–120.

Benner, M.J. and M.L. Tushman (2003), 'Exploitation, exploration, and process management: The productivity dilemma revisited,' *Academy of Management Review*, **28** (2), 238–256.

Berrone, P., C. Cruz, and L.R. Gómez-Mejía (2012), 'Socio-emotional wealth in family firms: Theoretical dimensions, assessment approaches, and agenda for future research,' *Family Business Review*, **25**, 258–279.

Bird, B. (1988), 'Implementing entrepreneurial ideas: The case for intention,' *Academy of Management Review*, **13** (3), 442–453.

Breitzman, A. and D. Hicks (2008), *An Analysis of Small Business Patents by Industry and Firm Size*. SBA Office of Advocacy.

Chandler, G.N., D.R. DeTienne, A. McKelvie, and T.V. Mumford (2011), 'Causation and effectuation processes: A validation study,' *Journal of Business Venturing*, **26** (3), 375–390.

Chua, J.H., J.J. Chrisman, and E.P. Chang (2004), 'Are family firms born or made? An exploratory investigation,' *Family Business Review*, **17** (1), 37–54.

Chua, J.H., J.J. Chrisman, and P. Sharma (1999), 'Defining the family business by behavior,' *Entrepreneurship Theory and Practice*, **23** (4), 19–40.

Cliff, J.E. (1998), 'Does one size fit all? Exploring the relationship between attitudes towards growth, gender, and business size,' *Journal of Business Venturing*, **13** (6), 523–542.

Cohen, W.M. and D.A. Levinthal (1990), 'Absorptive capacity: A new perspective on learning and innovation,' *Administrative Science Quarterly*, **35** (1), 128–152.

Collins, J.C. (2001), *Good to Great*, New York: HarperCollins Publishers.

Covin, J.G. and D.P. Slevin (1989), 'Strategic management of small firms in hostile and benign environments,' *Strategic Management Journal*, **10** (1), 75–87.

De Massis, A., P. Sharma, J.H. Chua, and J.J. Chrisman (2012), *Family Business Studies: An Annotated Bibliography*, Cheltenham, UK and Northampton, MA, USA: Edward Elgar Publishing.

Eddleston, K.A., F.W. Kellermanns, and T.M. Zellweger (2012), 'Exploring the entrepreneurial behavior of family firms: Does the stewardship perspective explain differences?,' *Entrepreneurship Theory and Practice*, **36** (2), 347–367.

Fama, E.F. and M.C. Jensen (1983), 'Separation of ownership and control,' *Journal of Law and Economics*, **26** (2), 301–325.

Gómez-Mejía, L.R., K.T. Haynes, M. Núñez-Nickel, K.J. Jacobson, and J. Moyano-Fuentes (2007), 'Socioemotional wealth and business risks in family-controlled firms: Evidence from Spanish olive oil mills,' *Administrative Science Quarterly*, **52** (1), 106–137.

Grant, R.M. (1996), 'Toward a knowledge-based theory of the firm,' *Strategic Management Journal*, **17** (S2), 109–122.

Hamel, G. and C.K. Prahalad (1989), 'To revitalize corporate performance, we need a whole new model of strategy,' *Harvard Business Review*, **67** (3), 63–76.

He, Z.L. and P.K. Wong (2004), 'Exploration vs. exploitation: An empirical test of the ambidexterity hypothesis,' *Organization Science*, **15** (4), 481–494.

Lawrence, T.B., M.I. Winn, and P.D. Jennings (2001), 'The temporal dynamics of institutionalization,' *Academy of Management Review*, **26** (4), 624–644.

Lumpkin, G.T. and G.G. Dess (1996), 'Clarifying the entrepreneurial orientation construct and linking it to performance,' *Academy of Management Review*, **21** (1), 135–172.

Mantere, S. and J.A. Sillince (2007), 'Strategic intent as a rhetorical device,' *Scandinavian Journal of Management*, **23** (4), 406–423.

Miller, D. and P.H. Friesen (1984), *Organizations: A Quantum View*, Englewood Cliffs, NJ: Prentice Hall.

Miller, D. and I. Le Breton-Miller (2005), *Managing for the Long Run: Lessons in Competitive Advantage from Great Family Businesses*, Boston, MA: Harvard Business Press.

Miller, D., I. Le Breton-Miller, and B. Scholnick (2008), 'Stewardship vs. stagnation: An empirical comparison of small family and non-family businesses,' *Journal of Management Studies*, **45** (1), 51–78.

Miller, D., I. Le Breton-Miller, R.H. Lester, and A.A. Cannella (2007), 'Are family firms really superior performers?,' *Journal of Corporate Finance*, **13** (5), 829–858.

Palmer, D. and B.M. Barber (2001), 'Challengers, elites, and owning families: A social class theory of corporate acquisitions in the 1960s,' *Administrative Science Quarterly*, **46** (1), 87–120.

Salvato, C. and G. Corbetta (2014), 'Strategic content and process in family business,' in L. Melin, M. Nordqvist and P. Sharma (eds), *The SAGE Handbook of Family Business*, London: Sage Publications, pp. 295–320.

Sarasvathy, S.D. (2001), 'Causation and effectuation: Toward a theoretical shift from economic inevitability to entrepreneurial contingency,' *Academy of Management Review*, **26** (2), 243–263.

Schulze, W.S., M.H. Lubatkin, R.N. Dino, and A.K. Buchholtz (2001), 'Agency relationships in family firms: Theory and evidence,' *Organization science*, **12** (2), 99–116.

Sharma, P. and M. Carney (2012), 'Value creation and performance in private family firms: Measurement and methodological issues,' *Family Business Review*, **25** (3), 233–242.

Slawinski, N. and P. Bansal (2012), 'A matter of time: The temporal perspectives of organizational responses to climate change,' *Organization Studies*, **33** (11), 1537–1563.

Stuart, A. (2011), 'Missing public companies: Why is the number of public traded companies in the U.S. declining?,' retrieved from http://ww2.cfo.com/growth-companies/2011/03/missing-public-companies/ (accessed February 4, 2015).

US SBEC (2013), 'United States Small Business Entrepreneurship Council Web

Page,' retrieved from http://www.sbecouncil.org/about-us/facts-and-data/ (accessed February 4, 2015).

Zahra, S.A. and G. George (2002), 'Absorptive capacity: A review, reconceptualization, and extension,' *Academy of Management Review*, **27** (2), 185–203.

Zahra, S.A., J.C. Hayton, and C. Salvato (2004), 'Entrepreneurship in family vs. non-family firms: A resource-based analysis of the effect of organizational culture,' *Entrepreneurship Theory and Practice*, **28** (4), 363–381.

Zeitlin, M. (1974), 'Corporate ownership and control: The large corporation and the capitalist class,' *American Journal of Sociology*, **79** (5), 1073–1119.

3. The performance of Swiss and German family firms: investigating strategies, orientations and SEW as determinants

Philipp Sieger and Thomas Zellweger

INTRODUCTION

In this chapter we center our attention on the performance drivers of family firms in Switzerland and Germany and compare the corresponding results with the findings generated in the US. Investigating family firms is justified as this organizational form not only constitutes the majority of all firms globally (Sharma and Carney, 2012), but in particular in Switzerland and Germany. In fact, more than 88 percent of all firms in Switzerland are defined as family firms (Frey, Halter, Klein, and Zellweger, 2004), and numbers for Germany are similar (Klein, 2000). While more than 99 percent of all companies in Switzerland are small and medium-sized (Frey et al., 2004), the share of family firms varies with firm size; more specifically, the share of family firms decreases with increasing firm size, which is in line with findings from Germany (Klein, 2000). The social and economic impact of family firms is remarkable. In Germany for instance, family controlled firms provide 60 percent of all jobs and account for 51 percent of the total sales of the German economy (cf. www.familienunternehmen.de).

Even though the interest of both academics and practitioners in family firms has been rising significantly in recent years, the existing body of knowledge in the field is still rather fragmented (Sharma, 2004; Sharma and Carney, 2012). Hence, further investigations are necessary, in particular concerning one of the main goals of all family firms: success across generations (Chua, Chrisman, and Sharma, 1999; Habbershon, Nordqvist, and Zellweger, 2010). What is driving long-term success of family firms is still a matter of debate, whereby the underlying main determinants are still not sufficiently known.

Addressing this critical knowledge gap, we investigate a sample of 322 long-living family firms from Switzerland and Germany and test to what extent different business strategies (exploration, exploitation, causation, effectuation), business orientations (growth and entrepreneurial orientation), and socio-emotional wealth (SEW) considerations (in terms of family control, identification, bonds, emotion, and renewal) are related to each other and ultimately affect family firm performance in a joint way. More specifically, we investigate four different types of relationships:

1. How are SEW considerations related to business orientations?
2. How are SEW considerations related to business strategies?
3. How are business orientations related to business strategies?
4. How are SEW considerations, business orientations and business strategies jointly related to family business performance?

Before proceeding with our analyses, we describe our methodology and the characteristics of the family firms that are included in our sample. The chapter concludes with a discussion of the study's contributions and implications for research on family business performance.

METHODOLOGY

We used the 'Amadeus/Bureau van Dijk' database that offers financial information for public and private companies across Europe to identify large and long-living family firms from Switzerland and Germany. To be included in our study, at least 25 percent of the equity had to be held by a single family, and the company had to have at least EUR 80 million in revenues. Our specially developed questionnaire was entered into a survey software program; then, an email invitation was sent to a total of 6781 family firm owners in the spring of 2012. Using two reminder emails, we received 322 completed questionnaires that form the basis for this chapter. Although this corresponds to a response rate of only 4.7 percent, given the unique nature of the target group we feel this rate is satisfactory.

CHARACTERISTICS OF FAMILY FIRMS IN OUR SAMPLE

We start by noting that our sample differs considerably from the sample that has been generated in the US in two main aspects. First, our sample does not include non-family firms, as our online survey was only sent to individuals who were identified as being owners of a family-controlled

Table 3.1   Family firm and owner characteristics for the Swiss/German
            sample

Variables	Values
Number of full-time employees	
1 to 10	1.2% of all firms
11 to 250	29.5% of all firms
251 to 500	18.5% of all firms
Greater than 500	50.8% of all firms
Industry categories	
Manufacturing	41.6%
Professional/personal services	18.3%
Other	40.1%
Other attributes of the firms	
Number of countries with operations	14.9
Company age (years)	86.9
Owner-manager characteristics	
Male	85.4%
Married	70.0%
Education (at least some university)	68.0%
Founder	9.9%
Outcomes	
Average perceived firm performance (1 = much worse, 7 = much better)	5.2
Owner-manager's perceived effectiveness in the business sphere (max of 100)	80
Owner-manager's satisfaction with the business (max of 100)	82.7

Note: Firm performance was measured with four items that refer to its relative
performance compared with competitors over the last three years.

firm. In fact, the average percentage of equity owned by the family in our
sample is 86.2 percent, whereas the share of firms where the family owns
less than 50 percent of the equity is only 11.7 percent. Hence, we will not
compare family firms to non-family firms in our chapter, but will focus
instead on within-family firm comparisons. Second, as shown in Table 3.1,
while the US sample is highly skewed towards small firms with fewer than
10 full-time employees (FTEs), our sample is skewed towards large firms
with more than 500 FTEs. We regard this as a unique chance to compare
family-firm-related findings across different size firms.

Regarding industry sector, we see that 41.6 percent of our firms are active in manufacturing, which is almost twice as high as in the US sample; 18.3 percent are offering professional or personal services, and the remaining 40.1 percent are allocated to other industry sectors such as construction, trade, and others. Our family firms are very international, as the average number of countries with operations is higher than 14; moreover, the family firms are almost 90 years old on average, which indicates that they are likely to be in the hands of the third or fourth generation. The owner-managers that answered our survey are mostly male, married, and well-educated, whereby the shares of males and the level of education are clearly higher than for instance in the US sample. Given the high firm age, it is not surprising to see that less than 10 percent of all respondents are the actual founders of the firm. However, 76.9 percent of the respondents are active in the management of their firm.

The average firm performance in our sample according to our measure that is described in detail in the next section is medium to high (5.2 on a 1 to 7 scale), and the owners seem to be pretty happy with their firm: both the owners' perceived effectiveness in the business sphere and the actual satisfaction with the business are equal or higher than 80 (on a 0 to 100 scale). These scores are clearly greater than in the US sample.

To conclude, we note that this chapter is based on a very unique sample that differs considerably from other samples used in this book: our family firms are much larger, older, more international, and more concentrated in the manufacturing industry. Regarding the owners surveyed, the share of males is much higher, as is the level of education. Firm performance and the owners' satisfaction are also both higher. This promises interesting insights from the analyses presented below.

AN OVERVIEW ABOUT STRATEGIES, ORIENTATIONS, SEW AND FIRM PERFORMANCE

Prior to presenting the results, we first provide a theoretical overview about the constructs that we are examining (and their measures). First, in order to discuss the strategies employed in family firms that may be influenced by both SEW and orientations—and that are likely to have a direct effect on performance—we rely on the distinctions between exploration versus exploitation (Cohen and Levinthal, 1990; He and Wong, 2004; Zahra and George, 2002) as well as causation versus effectuation (Sarasvathy, 2001). The first pair refers to *what* family firms are mainly doing. An exploration strategy comprises product or market diversification and thus a commitment to developing new technologies, products, and markets. An exploitation strategy, in contrast, is represented by product and technology refinements that aim for efficiency and scoping down markets. When firms pursue both strategies simultaneously, one speaks of ambidexterity (Benner and Tushman, 2003). To measure exploration and exploitation we rely on an 8-item measure used by He and Wong (2004) that asks business owners to indicate how important different objectives are to the firm. An objective indicating exploration is 'Open up new markets,' whereas one indicating exploitation is 'Reduce production cost.' The ambidexterity variable was calculated by multiplying the standardized exploration and exploitation measures. *How* firms pursue their selected strategy is also interesting. One accepted distinction in this regard is between causation and effectuation (Sarasvathy, 2001). Causation refers to planning and mapping out a firm's strategy in more linear, causal, and projective terms; effectuation refers to responding to effects as the firm evolves. Put differently, firms following a causation logic have a given goal and search for means to achieve that goal; firms following an effectuation logic, instead, start with given means at hand without a pre-defined goal (Sarasvathy, 2001). Both strategies are measured using the scale developed by Chandler, DeTienne, McKelvie, and Mumford (2011). One of the five items that we use for causation is 'We designed and planned business strategies'; one of the 11 items related to effectuation is 'We tried a number of different approaches until we found a business model that worked.' If not mentioned otherwise, the responses to all our items were anchored at 1 (strongly disagree) and 7 (strongly agree).

Second, we investigate different orientations that may affect the choice of strategies and ultimately firm performance and may themselves be affected by SEW considerations outlined later in this chapter. Scholars agree that orientations may be crucial antecedents of strategy (Bird, 1988; Mantere and Sillince, 2007; Miller and Friesen, 1983). In our chapter we focus on two particularly important orientations: growth orientation and entrepreneurial orientation. The first one is chosen because it is not naturally given that all firms strive for the highest possible growth. Rather, many firms, particularly those that are founder or family managed (Cliff, 1998; Miller, Le Breton-Miller, and Scholnick, 2008), may choose a slower growth path or even limit growth as they may want to create other values in their firm. We measured growth orientation by a 6-item scale inspired by Cliff (1998). A sample item is 'I am always searching for new ways to grow my business.' An entrepreneurial orientation refers to the 'the processes, practices and decision making activities that lead to new [market] entry' (Lumpkin and Dess, 1996: 136). It normally consists of five dimensions: namely, autonomy, innovativeness, risk taking, proactiveness, and competitive aggressiveness. In our chapter, to avoid unnecessary complexity, we rely on an aggregate 6-item measure based on Covin and Slevin (1989) and do not investigate all the dimensions separately.

Third, the notion of 'socio-emotional wealth' (SEW) is one of the most influential concepts that has been developed and applied in family business research in recent years (Berrone, Cruz, and Gómez-Mejía, 2012; Gómez-Mejía, Haynes, Núñez-Nickel, Jacobson, and Moyano-Fuentes, 2007; Zellweger, Kellermanns, Chrisman, and Chua, 2012). SEW refers to 'non-financial aspects of the firm that meet the family's affective needs, such as identity, the ability to exercise family influence, and the perpetuation of the family dynasty' (Gómez-Mejía et al., 2007: 106). Put differently, it describes the non-financial benefits for the family that are associated with firm ownership. As proposed by Berrone et al. (2012), SEW is conceptualized as consisting of five key dimensions: family control, identification, social bonds, emotion, and renewal (taken together: FIBER). In our survey, all five dimensions were measured with multiple items, using measurement instruments proposed and/or validated in previous research. For family control we used items such as 'I will never consider selling shares of the business outside my family' and 'I wish that the future president of the business will be a family member' (Berrone et al., 2012). For identification we used items such as 'I am highly concerned about how the firm is viewed in public' and 'I will not engage in strategic actions that may damage the image of the business.' To capture the bond aspect of SEW we used items based on Uzzi (1996) such as 'In the business, we prefer dealing with people we know' and 'In the business, our networks provide us with many useful referrals.' For the emotional dimension we draw on items originally developed by Richins (1994) that capture the owner's emotional attachment to the firm. An example is 'I am emotionally attached to the firm.' Finally, for the renewal dimension, we rely on items that capture the intention of the family to renew family bonds through dynastic succession, meaning the family's long-term orientation with the ultimate aim to hand the business down to future generations (Berrone et al., 2012; Eddleston, Kellermanns, and Zellweger, 2012). A sample item is 'The firm is in the business for the long run.' We investigate these separate dimensions of SEW, as well as an aggregate measure of the construct ($\alpha = .78$), as antecedents to orientations, strategy, and ultimately firm performance in our models.

To do so, we also need to measure actual firm performance in a reliable way. Because reliable performance data about privately held firms, which represent the majority of the firms in our sample (88.3 percent), are very difficult to obtain, it is customary to rely on self-reported performance data. We thus asked respondents to rate their company's performance compared with their competitors over the last three years in the dimensions:

Table 3.2   Strategies, orientations and SEW in the Swiss/German sample

Variables	α	Mean	S.D.	Min	Max
Strategies					
Exploration	0.73	5.3	1.2	1	7
Exploitation	0.77	5.6	1.1	1	7
Ambidexterity	0.76	30.3	10.1	1	49
Causation	0.74	3.8	0.7	1.8	5
Effectuation	0.55	3.3	0.7	2.73	4.45
Orientations					
Growth	0.68	4.3	0.8	2.5	6
Entrepreneurial	0.73	4.3	1.0	1	7
Socio-emotional wealth					
Family control	0.79	5.1	1.8	1	7
Identification	0.69	6.2	0.9	2.33	7
Bonds	0.78	5.0	1.2	1	7
Emotion	0.68	6.1	1.0	1.33	7
Renewal	0.50	5.9	1.0	2.67	7
Composite measure	0.78	5.6	0.9	1.33	7

growth of sales, growth of market share, growth of profitability, and return on equity ($\alpha = .84$) (adapted from Dess and Robinson, 1984; Eddleston, Kellermanns, and Sarathy, 2008). Each of the four performance indicators was measured on a 7-point Likert-type scale ranging from *much worse* (1) to *much better* (7).

Cronbach's alphas, means, standard deviations, and minima/maxima are shown in Table 3.2. With two exceptions, all alphas are above 0.60. For the composite SEW measure that includes all five FIBER dimensions, we conducted a factor analysis to assess the validity and overall quality of our measure. Five dimensions with eigenvalues higher than 1 emerged, explaining 68 percent of the total variance. All items included in that measure loaded on their expected components without cross-loadings.

EMPIRICAL ANALYSES ACCORDING TO OUR CONCEPTUAL MODEL

In the following sections we present the findings from the different multivariate regression models that examined our four guiding research questions. We first investigate the link between SEW and orientations;

second, we take a closer look at the SEW–strategies relationship; third, we test the connection between our orientations and strategies; and finally, we build a comprehensive model wherein we test the combined effects of strategies, orientations, and SEW on family firm performance.

The Relationship between SEW and Orientations

Our expectation is that the different dimensions of SEW as well as SEW as a whole will affect the growth orientation and entrepreneurial orientation of our family firms. The results of the corresponding regression analysis are presented in Table 3.3.

In Model 1 we see that none of the FIBER dimensions is significantly related to growth orientation; neither is the aggregated SEW measure in Model 2. We need to note that our measure for growth orientation was included in a follow-up survey that we conducted where only 55 responses could be collected. Hence, the non-findings in Model 1 and Model 2 could be partly attributed to the small sample size. Nevertheless, we can see differences between the FIBER elements. The strongest coefficients are shown for identification and renewal, whereby identification is positively related to growth orientation. Hence, when family firm owners identify strongly with their firm, this seems to be conducive to a positive attitude towards growth. A positive association between identification and growth orientation is also found in the US sample. A focus on renewal, in turn, seems to inhibit growth aspirations. As mentioned, these findings have to be interpreted with care as they are not significant from a statistical point of view.

Model 3 shows that both family control and bonds are significantly and negatively associated with entrepreneurial orientation. This stands in contrast to the US sample, wherein both elements are significantly and positively related to entrepreneurial orientation. The negative tendency in our sample, and hence the contrasting result compared with the US findings, is confirmed when we investigate the aggregate SEW measure: while it is very close to the ambitious significance level of 0.05 ($p = 0.06$), its coefficient is clearly negative. Hence, and very interestingly, SEW seems to inhibit entrepreneurial orientation amongst the family firms in our Swiss/German sample.

The Relationship between SEW and Strategies

In this section we discuss the relationships between SEW and its five FIBER sub-dimensions on the four strategies included in our model (in

Table 3.3 *The relationship between SEW (FIBER dimensions) and orientations in the Swiss/German sample*

Variables	Model 1 Growth orientation			Model 2 Growth orientation			Model 3 Entrepreneurial orientation			Model 4 Entrepreneurial orientation		
	B	S.E.	p	B	S.E.	p	B	S.E.	p	B	S.E.	p
Constant	*5.371*	*1.088*	***	*5.054*	*1.014*	***	*5.265*	*.441*	***	*5.452*	*.444*	***
Control variables												
Manufacturing	-.036	.122		-.055	.112		-.006	.072		-.003	.071	
Personal/professional services	-.153	.144		-.111	.124		-.163	.070	*	-.148	.070	*
Industry dynamism	.072	.119		.080	.110		.123	.070	†	.072	.069	
Self-perception as family firm	.390	.239		.346	.215		-.098	.075		-.064	.075	
Number of countries	-.017	.074		-.027	.065		.052	.072		.056	.072	
Logged company size	.382	.156	*	.374	.137	**	.172	.071	*	.189	.071	**
Company age	-.059	.101		-.081	.097		-.011	.061		-.014	.062	
Founder	-.505	.543		-.313	.510		-.496	.230	*	-.597	.231	*
Owner-manager male	-.166	.089	†	-.160	.081	†	.015	.065		-.018	.063	
Owner-manager married	-.363	.155	*	-.292	.136	*	-.007	.062		.017	.062	
Owner-manager education	.190	.136		.119	.122		.009	.070		.045	.068	

Table 3.3 (continued)

Variables	Model 1 Growth orientation			Model 2 Growth orientation			Model 3 Entrepreneurial orientation			Model 4 Entrepreneurial orientation		
	B	S.E.	p	B	S.E.	p	B	S.E.	p	B	S.E.	p
Socio-emotional wealth												
Family control	-.055	.135					-.218	.072	**			
Identification	.087	.101					-.060	.067				
Bonds	.068	.135					-.138	.067	*			
Emotion	-.011	.144					-.015	.072				
Renewal	-.083	.149					.100	.070				
SEW composite measure				.029	.152					-.146	.076	†
Overall model F	2.708*			2.257*			2.395**			2.081*		
R square	0.439			0.392			0.163			0.11		
Observations	54			55			214			216		

Note: † = p < 0.10, * = p < 0.05, ** = p < 0.01, *** = p < 0.001.

other words, exploration/exploitation and causation/effectuation). The results of our respective regression analyses are shown in Table 3.4.

Model 1 shows that out of the FIBER dimensions only 'renewal' is positively related to a causation strategy (marginally significant, $p = 0.08$). In Model 2, the aggregated SEW measure fails to reach statistical significance, which leads us to conclude that SEW and its sub-dimensions are not strongly affecting the causation strategy choice. For effectuation (Models 3 and 4) we see a similar picture: while family control is negatively and significantly related to an effectuation strategy, renewal is positively and significantly related. The first finding opposes the US findings, whereas the second one is in line with them. Different from the US chapter, the SEW composite measure is not significant. We note, however, that the sample sizes for Models 1–4 are small, which might partly explain the non-significance of some of our variables.

The findings related to an exploration strategy depicted in Models 5 and 6 tell us that SEW in general does not seem to affect exploration strategies, as neither the FIBER dimensions nor the aggregated measure reach statistical significance. An exception is that renewal is close to marginal significance ($p = 0.11$) and thus seems to have a slightly positive effect. In contrast, we find more initial evidence, in Models 7 and 8, that SEW seems to be positively related to an exploitation strategy. We find a very strong, positive and significant effect of identification on exploitation; similarly, the aggregated SEW measure is positively related to exploitation and almost reaches marginal significance ($p = 0.12$).

The Relationship between Orientations and Strategies

In addition to SEW, the basic orientations discussed above are assumed to affect the family firms' strategic choices. In order to be able to conduct regression analyses as meaningful as possible, we focus on orientations and strategies where we have enough responses in our dataset. Hence, we do not investigate growth orientation and causation/effectuation strategies. Corresponding results would need to be interpreted with great care, and we have explored the respective relationships with SEW already; hence, we chose not to delve deeper into those areas but to focus on the most promising concepts. Table 3.5 illustrates the relationships between entrepreneurial orientation and exploration/exploitation strategies.

Model 1 shows that, as expected, entrepreneurial orientation is positively and significantly related to an exploration strategy. This is not too surprising as an exploration strategy is a very 'entrepreneurial' strategy that contains many elements of entrepreneurship, such as the development of new products and new markets. However, it still shows that basic

Firms within families

Table 3.4   The relationship between SEW (FIBER dimensions) and strategies in the Swiss/German sample

Variables	Model 1 Causation			Model 2 Causation			Model 3 Effectuation		
	B	S.E.	p	B	S.E.	p	B	S.E.	p
Constant	*6.159*	*.964*	***	*6.646*	*.945*	***	*3.506*	*.568*	***
Control variables									
Manufacturing	.198	.107	†	.140	.103		.029	.063	
Personal/prof. services	.081	.120		.012	.106		.123	.070	†
Industry dynamism	−.135	.105		−.148	.101		.082	.062	
Perc'd as family firm	.198	.213		.388	.201	†	−.319	.126	*
Number of countries	.004	.063		−.013	.060		.063	.037	†
Logged company size	.290	.128	*	.301	.125	*	−.112	.075	
Company age	.056	.090		.086	.090		.006	.053	
Founder	−1.144	.480	*	−1.350	.472	**	.000	.283	
Owner-manager male	.026	.077		−.005	.075		.052	.045	
Married	.101	.137		.067	.128		.007	.081	
Educ. level	.065	.120		.087	.113		−.047	.070	
Socio-emotional wealth									
Family control	−.159	.115					−.206	.068	**
Identification	−.010	.090					.017	.053	
Bonds	.087	.117					−.005	.069	
Emotion	.000	.109					.076	.064	
Renewal	.239	.133	†				.281	.078	**
SEW composite				.038	.135				
Overall model F	1.691+			1.653			2.075*		
R square	0.403			0.306			0.454		
Observations	57			58			57		

Note: † = p<0.10, * = p<0.05, ** = p<0.01, ***=p<0.001.

orientations and chosen strategies are related, which supports the validity of our conceptual model. A significant relationship between entrepreneurial orientation and exploitation strategy could not be found ($p > 0.90$). One might even expect a negative relationship there; in fact, the coefficient of the entrepreneurial orientation measure is slightly negative (−0.004). However, also exploiting something by reducing costs, for instance, can still include entrepreneurial improvements such as implementing new corresponding ideas. But this link to entrepreneurship does not seem strong in our analysis.

Table 3.4   (continued)

	Model 4 Effectuation			Model 5 Exploration			Model 6 Exploration			Model 7 Exploitation			Model 8 Exploitation		
	B	S.E.	p	B	S.E.	p	B	S.E.	p	B	S.E.	p	B	S.E.	p
	4.066	.662	***	5.313	.528	***	5.316	.519	***	6.335	.504	***	6.262	.511	***
	−.044	.072		.089	.087		.070	.083		.118	.083		.112	.082	
	.033	.075		−.147	.083	†	−.155	.082	†	.012	.080		.001	.081	
	.042	.071		.417	.084	***	.413	.081	***	.139	.080	†	.162	.080	*
	−.103	.140		.073	.090		.072	.087		.067	.086		.121	.086	
	.051	.042		.069	.086		.088	.084		−.060	.082		−.103	.083	
	−.081	.087		.226	.085	**	.209	.083	*	.138	.081	†	.119	.082	
	.019	.063		−.031	.074		−.032	.072		.121	.070	†	.115	.071	
	−.208	.331		.015	.275		.012	.270		−.360	.263		−.327	.266	
	−.003	.052		.095	.078		.068	.074		.023	.075		.055	.072	
	−.026	.089		−.041	.074		−.018	.072		−.060	.070		−.073	.071	
	−.088	.079		−.134	.083		−.100	.079		−.176	.080	*	−.203	.078	*
				−.061	.087					−.112	.083				
				.046	.080					.278	.076	***			
				−.021	.080					.104	.077				
				−.070	.086					−.020	.082				
				.137	.084					−.051	.081				
	.075	.095					.001	.089					.138	.087	
	0.529			4.173***			5.321***			3.082***			2.733***		
	0.124			0.253			0.239			0.2			0.139		
	58			214			216			214			216		

The Overall Picture: Antecedents to Family Firm Performance

In this section we finally bring together the different pieces that we have been developing so far. We thus investigate critical performance antecedents in family firms together, namely exploration/exploitation strategies, entrepreneurial orientation, and SEW with its FIBER sub-dimensions. As in the preceding analysis, we only include constructs in our final regression models where we have enough valid cases in our dataset. Table 3.6 gives an overview of our results.

Model 1 includes our control variables only. We see that company size is strongly and positively related to firm performance as assessed by the respondents, which holds true also for all other models in Table 6. We deduce that in our context, size indeed matters. In Model 2, we have

Firms within families

Table 3.5   *The relationship between entrepreneurial orientation and*
              strategies in the Swiss/German sample

Variables	Model 1 Exploration			Model 2 Exploitation		
	B	S.E.	p	B	S.E.	p
Constant	*3.509*	*.650*	***	*6.329*	*.673*	***
Control variables						
Manufacturing	.065	*.079*		.098	*.082*	
Personal/professional services	−.106	*.079*		−.001	*.082*	
Industry dynamism	.401	*.075*	***	.197	*.077*	*
Self-perception as family firm	.086	*.083*		.099	*.086*	
Number of countries	.079	*.079*		−.077	*.081*	
Logged company size	.147	*.081*	†	.121	*.084*	
Company age	−.020	*.068*		.137	*.070*	†
Founder	.203	*.262*		−.354	*.271*	
Owner-manager male	.073	*.070*		.051	*.073*	
Owner-manager married	−.021	*.069*		−.066	*.071*	
Owner-manager education	−.119	*.075*		−.213	*.078*	**
Orientations						
Entrepreneurial orientation	.332	*.077*	***	−.004	*.080*	
Overall model *F*	7.344***			2.494**		
R square	0.303			0.128		
Observations	216			216		

Note: † = p < 0.10, *=p < 0.05, ** = p < 0.01, *** = p < 0.001.

added our exploration/exploitation strategies. Exploration is positively
and significantly related to firm performance; exploitation almost reaches
the marginal significance level of 10 percent ($p = 0.12$) and has a positive
coefficient. With adequate care we can thus conclude that exploitation is
also likely to contribute to firm performance. A combination of those two
strategies, labelled ambidexterity, hence should also bear positive implications for firm performance. This is in line with the findings in the US
chapter where exploration is positively and significantly related to firm
performance. When we add entrepreneurial orientation in Model 3, we see
that it is positively and marginally significantly related to firm performance
($p = 0.07$), which again supports the US findings. When other variables are
added in Models 4 and 5 we consistently see a positive coefficient of entrepreneurial orientation with encouraging p-values ($p = 0.06$) in Model 4
and $p = 0.03$ in Model 5. In Model 4, we add the FIBER dimensions. The
analysis shows that only renewal is marginally significantly related to firm

Table 3.6 Antecedents to family firm performance: strategies, orientations and SEW in the Swiss/German sample

Variables	Model 1			Model 2			Model 3			Model 4			Model 5		
	B	S.E.	p	B	S.E.	p	B	S.E.	p	B	S.E.	p	B	S.E.	p
Constant	5.388	.513	***	5.306	.506	***	5.137	.512	***	5.014	.511	***	5.051	.509	***
Control variables															
Manufacturing	-.109	.083		-.131	.081		-.130	.081		-.087	.083		-.124	.080	
Personal/professional services	.036	.082		.062	.081		.078	.081		.078	.080		.069	.080	
Industry dynamism	.093	.078		.004	.082		.013	.081		-.037	.085		-.049	.083	
Self-perception as family firm	-.114	.086		-.137	.084		-.129	.084		-.105	.086		-.095	.085	
Number of countries	.067	.082		.061	.081		.061	.080		.039	.082		.021	.081	
Logged company size	.254	.083	**	.206	.083	*	.186	.083	*	.196	.083	*	.191	.082	*
Company age	-.034	.070		-.043	.070		-.041	.069		-.080	.070		-.077	.070	
Founder	-.104	.267		-.066	.263		.021	.266		.088	.266		.074	.265	
Owner-manager male	-.075	.074		-.093	.073		-.088	.072		-.063	.074		-.058	.071	
Owner-manager married	-.062	.072		-.052	.071		-.053	.070		-.059	.070		-.056	.070	
Owner-manager education	-.026	.078		.014	.078		.004	.078		-.012	.080		.006	.077	

Table 3.6 (continued)

Variables	Model 1 B	Model 1 S.E.	Model 1 p	Model 2 B	Model 2 S.E.	Model 2 p	Model 3 B	Model 3 S.E.	Model 3 p	Model 4 B	Model 4 S.E.	Model 4 p	Model 5 B	Model 5 S.E.	Model 5 p
Strategies															
Exploration				.199	.086	*	.151	.089	†	.138	.089		.149	.089	†
Exploitation				.127	.081		.137	.081	†	.108	.083		.111	.080	
Orientation															
Entrepreneurial orientation							.147	.082	†	.162	.084	†	.177	.082	*
Socio-emotional wealth															
Family control										-.030	.084				
Identification										.092	.079				
Bonds										-.030	.077				
Emotion										.132	.082				
Renewal										.134	.081	†			
SEW composite measure													.206	.086	*
Overall model *F*	1.748†			2.319**			2.409**			2.375**			2.643**		
R square	0.087			0.131			0.145			0.189			0.165		
Observations	214			214			214			214			216		

Note: † = p < 0.10, * = p < 0.05, ** = p < 0.01, *** = p < 0.001.

performance ($p = 0.10$); emotion is very close to being marginally significant ($p = 0.11$). This is a first indication that SEW tends to be positively related to performance. The crucial and positive role of renewal is also visible in the US data. In Model 5, we add the aggregated SEW measure instead of the FIBER measures and find a significant and positive relationship with firm performance (again, as in the US chapter).

DISCUSSION AND IMPLICATIONS

In this chapter we set out to generate new insights into the performance of large, long-living family firms in Switzerland and Germany. Overall, our analyses generated numerous valuable findings. On a general level, we believe that our approach of investigating strategies, orientations, and SEW as determinants of family firm performance from their owner's perspective has proven to be very useful, as we have been able to identify connections between these three elements and separate connections with performance. As a whole, and as a key contribution of our chapter, this allows us to better explain the performance of family firms. More specifically, while we were not able to establish a link between SEW and growth orientation, our findings clearly point to a negative relationship between SEW and entrepreneurial orientation, which stands in contrast to findings from the US. This is a valuable insight because our data also shows that firm size is positively related to firm performance; hence, growth orientation should be ultimately related to performance as well (assuming that growth orientation is actually leading to growth). Our findings pertaining to the SEW–strategy link are rather mixed. A link between SEW and causation is hard to see; and evidence regarding the SEW–effectuation link is ambiguous because one FIBER dimension is positively related, one is negatively related, and the aggregate SEW measure is not related at all. Also, while the SEW–exploration link could not be established, our findings support a positive association between SEW and exploitation. While we confirm the entrepreneurial orientation–exploration link, our final analysis with regard to firm performance leads to additional important insights.

Taken together, we see that four factors seem to drive family firm performance in the Swiss/German sample: firm size, exploration, entrepreneurial orientation, and SEW as a whole (whereas support for the single FIBER dimensions is only moderate). If we were to identify the performance drivers of Swiss and German family firms, those four elements would be our answer in a nutshell. However, our findings regarding the connections between strategies, orientations, and SEW allow us to draw a more fine-grained picture. And in this picture, we believe a very central role is played by SEW. The reason is that the SEW–performance relationship seems to be multi-faceted and complex. While we see an overall positive effect of SEW on performance it also negatively affects entrepreneurial orientation; which, in turn, is positively related to performance and to exploration (which, as a main effect, is also positively related to performance). SEW, however, seems to support an exploitation rather than an exploration strategy, with the former having a tendency towards a positive relationship with performance. Furthermore, SEW does not support a growth orientation; firm size, however, is positively related to firm performance. In other words, SEW seems to have a positive direct effect on performance but both positive and negative indirect effects as well.

These intriguing findings contribute to different streams of literature and open up promising avenues for future research. On a general level, we add to the family business literature, as the performance of long-living family firms is one of the most important research subjects in the field (Habbershon et al., 2010; Sharma, 2004; Zahra and Sharma, 2004). Our findings pertaining to how strategies, orientations, and SEW affect each other and how they affect performance enriches literature on strategy in family firms (Astrachan, 2010), entrepreneurial orientation in family firms (Zellweger and Sieger, 2012), and SEW in general (Berrone et al., 2012; Gómez-Mejía et al., 2007; Zellweger et al., 2012). More specifically, we enhance the existing body of knowledge about how SEW considerations may affect orientations and strategic choices, how orientations may affect strategic choices, and how these elements are all related to firm performance.

Building on our findings, we call for additional research in this area. In particular, scholars are encouraged to explore the critical role of SEW in the context of family firm performance in more detail. We believe we have only scratched the surface so far. More needs to be known about the detailed relationships with strategic choices, which could be achieved by analyzing datasets where all four strategic choices can be examined adequately. In fact, the limited sample size for some of our variables is one of the major limitations of our approach that could be overcome by future research efforts. Also with regard to the SEW–orientations link we call for future research because we found a negative SEW–entrepreneurial orientation relationship (whereby scholars in other countries found a positive one). This deserves future research attention. Here, important contingency factors such as firm performance itself could be explored; it could be expected that when SEW is endangered, entrepreneurial orientation might rise. Also, while our sample is unique in terms of the size of the firms in our sample, an explicit comparison of small and large family firms (and maybe even with small and large non-family firms) bears a lot of potential. Last but not least, we call for explicit cross-country comparisons covering not only different countries but also different cultural and economic contexts.

Conclusion

What makes a family firm successful in the long run is maybe the most fascinating question in family business research. With our chapter we have tried to provide a novel view on family firm performance by testing the effects of strategies, orientations, and SEW on the performance of long-lived Swiss and German family firms. As a main result we show that SEW seems to play a very central but also multi-faceted and sometimes ambiguous role that deserves future research attention.

REFERENCES

Astrachan, J.H. (2010), 'Strategy in family business: Toward a multidimensional research agenda,' *Journal of Family Business Strategy*, **1** (1), 6–14.
Benner, M.J. and M.L. Tushman (2003), 'Exploitation, exploration, and process management: The productivity dilemma revisited,' *Academy of Management Review*, **28** (2), 238–256.
Berrone, P., C. Cruz, and L.R. Gómez-Mejía (2012), 'Socioemotional wealth in family firms: Theoretical dimensions, assessment approaches, and agenda for future research,' *Family Business Review*, **25** (3), 258–279.
Bird, B. (1988), 'Implementing entrepreneurial ideas: The case for intention,' *Academy of Management Review*, **13** (3), 442–453.
Chandler, G.N., D.R. DeTienne, A. McKelvie, and T.V. Mumford (2011), 'Causation and effectuation processes: A validation study,' *Journal of Business Venturing*, **26** (3), 375–390.
Chua, J.H., J.J. Chrisman, and P. Sharma (1999), 'Defining the family business by behavior,' *Entrepreneurship Theory and Practice*, **23** (4), 19–39.
Cliff, J.E. (1998), 'Does one size fit all? Exploring the relationship between attitudes towards growth, gender, and business size,' *Journal of Business Venturing*, **13** (6), 523–542.
Cohen, W.M. and D. Levinthal (1990), 'Absorptive capacity: A new perspective on learning and innovation,' *Administrative Science Quarterly*, **35** (1), 128–152.
Covin, J.G. and D.P. Slevin (1989), 'Strategic management of small firms in hostile and benign environments,' *Strategic Management Journal*, **10** (1), 75–87.
Dess, G.G. and R.B. Robinson (1984), 'Measuring organizational performance in the absence of objective measures: The case of the privately-held firm and conglomerate business unit,' *Strategic Management Journal*, **5** (3), 265–273.
Eddleston, K.A., F.W. Kellermanns, and R. Sarathy (2008), 'Resource configuration in family firms: Linking resources, strategic planning and technological opportunities to performance,' *Journal of Management Studies*, **45** (1), 26–50.
Eddleston, K.A., F.W. Kellermanns, and T.M. Zellweger (2012), 'Exploring the entrepreneurial behavior of family firms: Does the stewardship perspective explain differences?,' *Entrepreneurship Theory and Practice*, **36** (2), 347–367.

Frey, U., F. Halter, S. Klein, and T. Zellweger (2004), *Family Business in Switzerland: Significance and Structure*. Paper presented at the FBN 15th World Conference, Copenhagen, DEN.

Gómez-Mejía, L.R., K.T. Haynes, M. Núñez-Nickel, K.J.L. Jacobson, and J. Moyano-Fuentes (2007), 'Socioemotional wealth and business risks in family-controlled firms: Evidence from Spanish olive oil mills.' *Administrative Science Quarterly*, **52** (1), 106–137.

Habbershon, T., M. Nordqvist, and T. Zellweger (2010), 'Transgenerational entrepreneurship.' In M. Nordqvist and T. Zellweger (eds), *Transgenerational Entrepreneurship: Exploring Growth and Performance of Family Firms across Generations* (pp. 1–38). Cheltenham, UK and Northampton, MA, USA: Edward Elgar Publishing.

He, Z.L. and P.K. Wong (2004), 'Exploration vs. exploitation: An empirical test of the ambidexterity hypothesis,' *Organization Science*, **15** (4), 481–494.

Klein, S.B. (2000), 'Family businesses in Germany: Significance and structure,' *Family Business Review*, **13** (3), 157–181.

Lumpkin, G.T. and G.G. Dess (1996), 'Clarifying the entrepreneurial orientation construct and linking it to performance,' *Academy of Management Review*, **21** (1), 135–172.

Mantere, S. and J.A.A. Sillince (2007), 'Strategic intent as a rhetorical device,' *Scandinavian Journal of Management*, **23** (4), 406–423.

Miller, D. and P.H. Friesen (1983), 'Strategy-making and environment: The third link,' *Strategic Management Journal*, **4** (3), 221–235.

Miller, D., I. Le Breton-Miller, and B. Scholnick (2008), 'Stewardship vs. stagnation: An empirical comparison of small family and non-family businesses,' *Journal of Management Studies*, **45** (1), 51–78.

Richins, M.L. (1994), 'Valuing things: The public and private meaning of possessions,' *Journal of Consumer Research*, **21** (3), 504–521.

Sarasvathy, S. (2001), 'Causation and effectuation: Toward a theoretical shift from economic inevitability to entrepreneurial contingency,' *Academy of Management Review*, **26** (2), 243–263.

Sharma, P. (2004), 'An overview of the field of family business studies: Current status and directions for the future,' *Family Business Review*, **17** (1), 1–36.

Sharma, P. and M. Carney (2012), 'Value creation and performance in private family firms: Measurement and methodological issues,' *Family Business Review*, **25** (3), 233–242.

Uzzi, B. (1996), 'The sources and consequences of embeddedness for the economic performance of organizations: The network effect,' *American Sociological Review*, **61** (4), 674–698.

Zahra, S.A. and G. George (2002), 'Absorptive capacity: A review, reconceptualization, and extension,' *Academy of Management Review*, **27** (2), 185–203.

Zahra, S. and D.D. Sharma (2004), 'Family business research: A strategic reflection,' *Family Business Review*, **17** (4), 331–346.

Zellweger, T. and P. Sieger (2012), 'Entrepreneurial orientation in long-lived family firms,' *Small Business Economics*, **38** (1), 67–84.

Zellweger, T., F. Kellermanns, J. Chrisman, and J. Chua (2012), 'Family control and family firm valuation by family CEOs: The importance of intentions for transgenerational control.' *Organization Science*, **23** (3), 851–868.

4. The antecedents and outcomes of business strategies within privately-held family and non-family SMEs in China

Yanfeng Zheng and Jie Huang

INTRODUCTION

This chapter focuses upon the strategies of privately-owned, small and medium-sized enterprises (SMEs) in China. As is the case for many countries around the world, a large percentage of Chinese SMEs are family firms, constituting an indispensable component of the national economy and undergirding the country's economic growth. The recent Chinese Family Business Survey conducted by Forbes (2013), for instance, revealed that 711 of the 2470 companies (28.8 percent) listed in the 'A share' equity market of mainland China for that year were family owned. As noted by Kwan, Lau, and Au (2012), the proportion of *privately-held* businesses in this emerging-market context that are family firms is estimated to be even higher.

While Sharma and Carney (2012) have noted that privately-held family firms are under-studied, in general, this is especially so in the case of China. Moreover, although questions such as whether and how family and non-family SMEs differ in terms of their strategic choices have been proposed but not yet carefully examined (Berrone, Cruz, and Gómez-Mejía, 2012), this is particularly so for countries outside of Europe and North America. There is thus a need for family business researchers to bridge the gap in our understanding of the differences between family and non-family SMEs in such contexts—and to examine how any differences affect firm performance. We note that empirical examination of such questions from the socio-emotional wealth (SEW) perspective, in particular, is desired (Berrone et al., 2012).

This study aims to address the above-noted gaps by collecting and analyzing large-scale survey data from a stratified sample of 296 SMEs across China. The remainder of this chapter is organized as follows. The next section summarizes our data collection procedure. Following that, we provide descriptive statistics on the sampled firms, focusing on a comparison between the family and non-family SMEs with respect to their strategies, orientations and importance placed on SEW; in other words, 'non-financial aspects of the firm that meet the family's affective needs, such as identity, the ability to exercise family influence, and the perpetuation of the family dynasty' (Gómez-Mejía, Haynes, Núñez-Nickel, Jacobson, and Moyano-Fuentes, 2007: 106). We then analyze whether these variables differentially impact the performance of the family and non-family firms. We conclude with the theoretical and practical implications of our study.

METHODOLOGY AND SAMPLE

We collected large-scale survey data on SMEs in China primarily through local associations of such enterprises across all of the country's provinces except Tibet. We contacted these local business organizations for their assistance in disseminating the survey to their member SMEs, which are defined by the Chinese economic bureau as companies with fewer than 500 employees. To enhance the credibility of the survey, we collaborated with two major research universities in China in the name of examining the business landscape of SMEs across the country. To increase the value of the survey in the eyes of the local SME organizations and the participating firms, we promised the participating SMEs access to summary statistics and consultancy. We also offered assistance to the local business organizations, in the form of drafting annual reports.

Prior to launching the survey, we discussed the desired number of participants with the local contacts. In areas with a relatively higher concentration of SMEs, such as the province of Zhejiang, we asked the local organization to reach out for more participants. As such, our approach resembles that of stratified sampling. The local contacts were provided with an online and paper version of the survey, both of which were translated from the US version into Chinese. The survey launched in October 2012 and closed in January 2013.

In total, we collected 243 and 110 responses from the online and mail versions, respectively, with younger owner-managers generally preferring the former mode. After obtaining the surveys, we randomly chose 10 percent of the responses and contacted the respondents for validation, correcting any inaccurate responses. We excluded any surveys for which the responses were either incomplete or unable to be validated. We ended up with 296 firms with complete data for analyses.

Demographic Characteristics of the Family and Non-family Firms

Of the 296 complete responses from owner-managers who participated in the China-based study, 107 considered their businesses to be family firms (36.1 percent) while 189 (or 63.9 percent) did not. The percentage of family firms is comparable with—yet slightly higher than—the percentage of publicly traded companies that are family firms (as reported above). The higher percentage in our privately owned SME sample may be due to the desire to retain ownership control within the family.

As indicated in Table 4.1, approximately one-third of the family firms (33.6 percent) but almost half of the non-family firms (43.9 percent) had fewer than 10 full-time employees (FTEs). In contrast, 57.0 percent versus 52.9 percent of the family and non-family firms, respectively, had 10–250 FTEs. It thus appears that family SMEs in China generally hire more employees than non-family SMEs.

The majority of the SMEs tended to operate in the manufacturing or personal services sectors rather than the professional services sector, which is to be expected in an emerging economy. The distributions across the different sectors were fairly similar for the family and non-family firms.

In terms of national and international dispersion, the family SMEs in China tended to operate in a broader number of provinces and countries than the non-family SMEs. This was so even though the two groups were highly similar in age, averaging 7.6 and 7.4 years respectively.

Given the relatively young age of the firms, it is not surprising that the large majority were still headed by the founder (approximately 83 percent in both cases). Interestingly, a lower proportion of the family than non-family SMEs were headed by a male owner-manager (62.6 percent versus 69.8 percent respectively). The owner-managers of the family firms were also slightly more likely to possess a university education (58.9 percent versus 51.2 percent) and more likely to be married (86.0 percent versus 78.8 percent respectively).

Outcome Variables for the Family and Non-family Firms

As far as the outcome variables of perceived firm performance are concerned, the family and non-family firms did not differ much. Specifically, we measured current and past perceived performance on a 7-item Likert scale with each item rated from '1 = much worse' to '7 = much better.' An example item is: 'How would you rate your firm's performance relative to your competitors over the last twelve months on sales growth?' As indicated at the bottom of Table 4.1, the 12-month average and 5-year average indices of perceived performance relative to peers were virtually

Table 4.1   Family versus non-family firm and owner-manager
*   characteristics (China sample)*

Variables	Family (n=107; coded as 1)	Non-family (n=189; coded as 0)
Number of full-time employees		
1 to 10	33.6%	43.9%
11 to 250	57.0%	52.9%
251 to 500	6.5%	2.1%
Greater than 500	2.8%	1.1%
Industry categories		
Manufacturing	29.9%	28.5%
Personal services	29.0%	32.8%
Professional services	16.8%	15.3%
Other	24.3%	23.3%
Other attributes of the firms		
Number of provinces with operations	5.4	4.3
Number of countries with operations	2.2	1.2
Company age (years)	7.6	7.4
Owner-manager characteristics		
Male	62.6%	69.8%
Married	86.0%	78.8%
Education (at least some university)	58.9%	51.2%
Founder	83.2%	83.1%
Outcomes		
12-month average perceived firm performance (7-point scale)	4.8	4.9
5-year average perceived firm performance (7-point scale)	4.9	4.8
Owner-manager's perceived effectiveness in the business sphere (max of 100)	74.4	73.4
Owner-manager's satisfaction with the business (max of 100)	72.0	74.1

Note: Bivariate comparisons revealed that none of the above-noted values differed significantly between the family and non-family firms.

identical and above the scale's midpoint for both the family and non-family firms. Moreover, when asked how effective they perceived themselves as business owner-managers on a scale ranging from 0 to 100, the family and non-family owner-managers expressed equivalent levels of perceived effectiveness; in other words, scores of 74.4 versus 73.4 respectively. With respect to their *satisfaction* with business, however, the owner-managers of family SMEs appear to be slightly less satisfied but this difference is not statistically significant (72.0 versus 74.1 out of 100). This is a potentially interesting phenomenon that may invite further investigation on the well-being of family versus non-family firm owner-managers. We now turn to examining whether the strategies, orientations and concern for SEW tend to be similar or different within the two types of SMEs.

STRATEGIES, ORIENTATIONS AND SEW WITHIN THE FAMILY VERSUS NON-FAMILY FIRMS

Business Strategies

We investigated two sets of business strategies suggested by the literature. The first set refers to the distinction between *exploration* and *exploitation*. An exploration strategy involves a commitment to developing new technologies, products and markets; conversely, an exploitation strategy focuses on product and technology refinements in the hope of improving efficiency (March, 1991; He and Wong, 2004). When firms pursue both strategies with almost equal intensity, they are said to rely on a so-called strategy of *ambidexterity* (Benner and Tushman, 2003). The second set of strategy variables captures the distinction between *causation* and *effectuation* (Sarasvathy, 2001). Whereas most strategy studies assume that owner-managers ought to plan ahead and develop business strategies in a more linear and causal manner (in other words, causation), a sizeable amount of research conducted during the past decade has revealed that an effectuation strategy—in other words, responding to effects as firms evolve—is quite popular among entrepreneurial firms.

The top section of Table 4.2 shows the degree to which these two sets of strategies were pursued by the family and non-family firms in the China sample. Exploration was measured by a 4-item index on which the firm's owner-manager rated the importance, over the previous three years, of such objectives as 'introducing new generation of products' or 'entering new technological fields' on a 5-point Likert scale ranging from 1= 'very unimportant' to 5 = 'very important' (α = .85). Exploitation was measured along the same 5-point Likert scale, but by a 4-item index consisting of objectives such as 'improving existing product quality' or 'reducing production cost' (α = .84). Ambidexterity was measured by multiplying the means of the two indices together (α = .89). As indicated, the owner-managers of both the family and non-family firms reported above-average means on all three measures. Overall the two types of SMEs exhibited

Table 4.2 *Family versus non-family business strategies, orientations and SEW (China sample)*

Variables	α	Family		Non-family	
		Mean	S.D.	Mean	S.D.
Strategies					
Exploration	.85	3.87	.76	3.86	.90
Exploitation	.84	4.07	.64	4.11	.71
Ambidexterity	.89	16.08	5.02	15.97	5.60
Causation	.84	4.00	.59	3.96	.63
Effectuation	.86	3.89	.54	3.88	.62
Orientations					
Entrepreneurial	.81	3.94	.80	3.87	.74
Long-term	.75	3.82	.58	3.80	.53
Socio-emotional wealth					
Family control	.83	3.88	.50	3.48***	.61
Identification	.82	4.09	.67	4.00	.62
Bonds	.75	3.57	.69	3.62	.55
Emotion	.88	4.25	.65	4.03*	.61
Renewal	.78	3.72	.87	3.53*	.76
Composite measure	.87	3.90	.57	3.73**	.45

Note: † $p \leq .10$, * $p \leq .05$, ** $p \leq .01$, *** $p \leq .001$ (two-tailed tests).

virtually identical degrees of exploration and exploitation, and consequently comparable levels of ambidexterity.

Causation was measured by the mean of four items such as 'we designed and planned business strategies' and 'we did meaningful analysis to select target markets,' each rated on a 5-point Likert scale ranging from '1 = strongly disagree' to '5 = strongly agree' (α = .84). Effectuation was measured on the same scale but by the mean of four different items, including 'we experimented with different products and/or business models' (α = .86). As indicated in Table 4.2, the family and non-family SMEs in the China sample did not differ much with respect to these strategies either.

Orientations

Strategy researchers have added the concept of 'strategic intentions' or 'orientations' as a way of linking cognitions about capabilities to strategic practices and performance as an outcome (Bird, 1988; Hamel and Prahalad, 1989). Orientations include decision-making practices and processes, thus capturing the deeper behavioral precursors underlying strategies. Here we examine two types of orientations that seem suited to SMEs and family businesses: entrepreneurial orientation and long-term orientation.

Entrepreneurial orientation refers to the 'the processes, practices and decision making activities that lead to new [market] entry' (Lumpkin and Dess, 1996: 136). This construct has been extensively studied in the entre-preneurship literature. It is typically conceptualized and operationalized as being constituted by four dimensions: innovativeness, autonomy, aggres-siveness, and risk-taking. We followed the conventional approach by devel-oping a composite measure that sums up the scores on each dimension. Specifically, it was operationalized by the mean of an 8-item scale with each item measured on a 5-point Likert scale ranging from '1 = strongly disagree' to '5 = strongly agree' (α = .81). As shown in the middle of Table 4.2, we did not find any statistical difference in the entrepreneurial orientation of the family and non-family SMEs in the China sample.

Consistent with broader work on temporal rhythms and time horizons in organizations (Acona et al., 2001; Slawinski and Bansal, 2012), and with family business research on long versus short-term perspectives (Eddleston et al., 2012; Zahra et al., 2004), we also considered a firm's *long-term orientation*. Following Eddleston et al. (2012), we measured this variable by a 5-item scale (α = .75), which included such items as 'the operation of business is able to serve its long-term target,' and 'I do not evaluate the short-run achievement of new investment.' All items were rated on a 5-point Likert scale that ranged from '1 = strongly disagree' to '5 = strongly agree.' Counter to expectations from prior research (for example, Miller and Le Breton-Miller, 2005), we did not observe any sig-nificant differences between the long-term orientations of the family and non-family SMEs in the China sample.

Socio-emotional Wealth

As noted earlier, SEW refers to non-financial benefits for an entrepre-neur's family that derive from business ownership. More recently, Berrone et al. (2012) proposed five dimensions as constituting the core of this construct: family control, identification, bonding, emotion, and renewal (in other words, FIBER). We followed the suggestions raised by these researchers and measured each dimension by multiple items. An illustra-tive item for each, respectively, is as follows: 'In the business, most execu-tive positions are occupied by family members,' 'Customers often associate my name with products and/or services of this firm,' 'In the business, employees are treated as if they are part of one family,' 'If I lost the firm, I would feel like I had lost a little bit of myself,' and, 'I see the business as a legacy to be transferred to the next generation.' Each item was measured on a 5-point Likert scale ranging from 'strongly disagree' to 'strongly agree'; each dimension was measured by four to five items. We also created a composite SEW measure by summing the five averaged dimensions.

As noted at the bottom of Table 4.2, each FIBER dimension as well as the composite measure of SEW exhibited high levels of reliability (all $\alpha \geq 0.75$). Moreover, all five dimensions except identification and bonding statistically discriminated between the family and non-family firms. A significant difference between the two types of businesses was also observed for the composite measure. In all cases of significant differences, the family firms scored higher than the non-family firms.

THE RELATIONSHIPS BETWEEN STRATEGY, ORIENTATION, SEW AND PERFORMANCE

Results for the Full Sample of SMEs

After detailing the characteristics of the sampled SMEs in China, we now examine the potential impacts for firm performance. Table 4.3 displays the regression results for the effects of the strategy, orientation, and SEW measures on the 12-month performance index for the full sample of family and non-family firms combined.

Model 1 is the baseline model comprised of control variables at the industry, organization and individual levels. At the industry level, firms in the manufacturing industry appear to be lagging behind other industry groups in terms of performance, possibly due to the hyper-competition within this sector in China. Industry dynamism exerted a positive and significant effect on performance but this effect disappeared when we entered the business strategy, orientation and SEW variables. Of the organizational controls, logged firm size was the only one to exhibit a statistically significant (and in this case positive) effect. Notably, the family firm indicator variable was non-significant, as were all of the individual-level controls.

Model 2 reports the findings for exploration and exploitation. Overall, exploration demonstrated a consistent and positive impact on performance but exploitation did not. In fact, exploitation appeared to be negatively impacting SME performance. Moreover, when exploration and exploitation were multiplied together (in supplementary analyses available upon request), the ambidexterity variable was significant and positive, indicating that firms which simultaneously pursue both strategies perform substantially better than those pursuing just one approach. When the process strategy variables of causation versus effectuation were entered in

Table 4.3   Net associations with prior 12-month performance index (China sample)

Variables	Model 1	Model 2	Model 3	Model 4	Model 5	Model 6
Controls						
Manufacturing	−0.147*	0.143*	−0.117†	−0.119†	−0.120†	−0.134*
Personal services	−0.077	−0.094	−0.082	−0.045	−0.093	−0.057
Professional services	0.055	0.049	0.041	0.048	0.045	0.041
Industry dynamism	0.250***	0.141*	0.074	0.027	0.071	0.022
Family firm	−0.055	−0.043	−0.032	−0.053	−0.050	−0.068
Number of states with operations	0.037	0.036	0.052	0.033	0.078	0.061
Logged company size	0.262***	0.226***	0.193***	0.171***	0.201***	0.173***
Company age	0.024	0.015	0.019	0.004	0.014	0.001
Founder	0.038	0.030	0.047	0.033	0.044	0.032
Owner-manager male	0.086	0.052	0.044	0.068	0.052	0.071
Owner-manager married	0.064	0.067	0.053	0.053	0.056	0.062
Owner-manager education	0.029	−0.004	−0.011	−0.019	−0.004	−0.016
Business strategies						
Exploration		0.272***	0.214***	0.171**	0.213***	0.176*
Exploitation		−0.062	−0.157*	−0.126†	−0.169*	−0.121†
Causation			0.150†	0.034	0.151†	0.051
Effectuation			0.143†	0.022	0.109	0.015
Orientations						
Entrepreneurial orientation				0.166**		0.195**
Long-term orientation				0.298***		0.290***
Socio-emotional wealth						
Family control					−0.078	
Identification					0.034†	
Bonds					0.384***	
Emotion					.0192	
Renewal					0.043†	
SEW composite measure						.096*
Overall model F	5.25***	5.70***	6.04***	6.67***	6.67***	6.69***
R square	.18	.22[a]	.26[a]	.28[a]	.27[a]	.29[a]
Observations	296	296	296	296	296	296

Notes:
Values in the table are standardized OLS regression coefficients (beta values).
a R square significantly different from the baseline model of controls (Model 1).
† $p \leqslant .10$, * $p \leqslant .05$, ** $p \leqslant .01$, *** $p \leqslant .001$ (two-tailed tests).

Models 3–6, the impact of exploration and exploitation changed very little. In the China context, then, it appears that causation and effectuation exert effects independent of exploration and exploitation strategies.

As indicated in Model 3, the effects of causation and effectuation are marginally significant and positive but their effects became non-significant with the orientation and/or SEW variables entered in the models. The impact of causation is slightly stronger than effectuation but the effect sizes of both variables are comparable. This weaker effect may be attributable to the lower applicability of effectuation for SMEs in the China context.

Model 4 shows the effects for the two types of orientations. As a group, the two orientation variables improve the model's fit. A more rigorous F test on the change in R-squared showed a significant difference at the 0.01 level. Each of the orientation variables is positive and highly significant, with long-term orientation exhibiting the stronger standardized coefficient. The same pattern occurs when the 5-year performance index is used. It would seem, then, that being entrepreneurial yet also taking a long-run perspective are positively associated with above-average performance for SMEs in China.

SEW has been theorized by prior studies as an alternative to—or potentially even the main theoretical determinant of—the above-noted orientation variables. In Model 5, the five FIBER dimensions are entered in place of the orientation variables. Most had a statistically significant impact on performance, with the bonding dimension exerting the strongest effect. That being said, the five dimensions of SEW did not improve the fit of the model in comparison with the orientation variables, as indicated by the slightly lower R-squared value.

Model 6 shows the effects of the composite SEW measure net of the orientation variables. Although this composite measure is positive and statistically significant, the overall model fit for Model 6 is not better than the one of Models 4 or 5. Moreover, the effect size of the composite measure of SEW appears to be smaller than that for the orientation variables. Although informative, this smaller effect size might be due to the combination of both family and non-family SMEs in the sample. On that note, we next examine whether the effects of the strategy, orientation and SEW variables differ between the two subsamples.

Results for Family versus Non-family Firms

Are these relationships between business strategy, orientations, SEW and firm performance the same for family and non-family SMEs in China? Given our earlier literature review and the descriptive differences reported

Table 4.4   Estimation of prior 12-month performance: comparison between family and non-family SMEs in China

Variables	Family Model 1	Non-family Model 2	Family Model 3	Non-family Model 4	Family Model 5	Non-family Model 6
Controls	Included	Included	Included	Included	Included	Included
Business strategies						
Exploration	0.202	0.152	0.312*	0.173†	0.239†	0.164†
Exploitation	−0.083	−0.161†	−0.218†	−0.178†	−0.138	−0.155
Causation	0.010	0.061	0.077	0.171	−0.004	0.085
Effectuation	−0.036	0.073	−0.032	0.210†	−0.082	0.087
Orientations						
Entrepreneurial orientation	0.165	0.164*			0.170	0.170*
Long-term orientation	0.249†	0.274**			0.236†	0.285**
Socio-emotional wealth						
Family control			−0.379*	−0.184		
Identification			.013	.041†		
Bonds			.428***	.418**		
Emotion			.105†	.037		
Renewal			.500**	−.147		
SEW composite measure					.197*	.003
Overall model *F*	3.83***	4.96***	3.36***	3.55***	3.49***	4.45***
R square	.31	.33	.39	.26	.43[a]	.33
Observations	107	189	107	189	107	189

Notes:
Values in the table are standardized OLS regression coefficients (beta values).
a   *R* square significantly different from the baseline model of controls (Model 1).
† $p \le .10$, * $p \le .05$, ** $p \le. 01$, *** $p \le .001$ (two-tailed tests).

in Table 4.2, one might anticipate SEW to be more salient for the former group than the latter. Empirically, however, such differences may not be that easy to distinguish because the number of firms in each subsample is not equivalent. We nonetheless explored the potential heterogeneity between the two subsamples, the results of which are reported in Table 4.4.

Models 1 and 2 indicate that after controlling for industry, organizational and individual-level factors, the first set of strategy variables (exploration and exploitation) appear to exert only a marginal impact on the performance of either the family or non-family SMEs. The second set of strategy variables (causation and effectuation) exerted virtually no impact on the performance of either type of business. The non-significant effects for causation were particularly surprising given that the family business literature implies that such a strategy could be more impactful in such firms due to tendency for family businesses to be less professionalized.

As further indicated within Models 1 and 2, both of the orientation variables appear to exert stronger positive effects on the performance of the non-family than the family SMEs. Indeed, entrepreneurial orientation was found to be a significant predictor only for the non-family firms and long-term orientation exerted only a marginally significant positive impact on the performance of the family firms. Although the smaller size of the family firm subsample might be contributing to these apparent differences, it is interesting that the non-family firms appear to benefit more than the family firms from possessing a long-term orientation in particular.

As indicated within Models 3 and 4, the results for the separate dimensions of SEW reveal that each exerted a differential impact on the performance of the family and non-family firms. Family control, for example, was significantly (and negatively) associated with firm performance for the family but not the non-family firms. In contrast, identification was significantly (and positively) associated with the performance of the non-family but not the family firms. The bonding dimensions was significantly and positively related to the performance of both firms, but more strongly so for the family businesses. The emotion dimension was also more impactful for the family firms; indeed, this dimension showed no significant association with the performance of the non-family businesses. The renewal dimension exhibits the most striking difference, exerting a positive and highly significant impact on firm performance within the subsample of family firms but a non-significant impact in the non-family subsample.

Combined, the preceding set of results suggests that a concern for SEW is more strongly associated with the performance of family than non-family SMEs in China. The results presented in Models 5 and 6 for the composite measure of SEW reinforce this conjecture. As indicated, the estimate for this composite measure is positive and significant for the family subsample but non-significant in the non-family subsample. This difference is notable given the larger size of the latter subsample.

DISCUSSION

Summary

We are able to draw some preliminary conclusions regarding privately-held SMEs in China based upon our survey findings—particularly regarding similarities and differences between the family and non-family firms. Our first major finding is that there is a lack of any notable difference between the two groups on a variety of performance indicators. More specifically, our survey results reveal that the owner-managers of family and non-family SMEs in this country do not differ in terms of perceived firm performance relative to peers over a 12-month or 5-year period, perceptions of their own effectiveness as owner-managers, or their satisfaction within the business sphere. Moreover, the two subsamples do not appear to differ with respect to business strategies such as exploration versus exploitation or causation versus effectuation—or in terms of their entrepreneurial or long-term orientations. They did, however, exhibit notable differences regarding their emphasis on SEW motives, with the owner-managers of the family firms expressing greater emphasis overall and on several constituent dimensions, as expected from the literature.

In unreported analyses (available upon request), we also explored some strategic considerations particularly salient within the context of China. More specifically, we surveyed the informants with regard to how much focus they placed on maintaining relationship with governmental agencies, as the government is still a dominant player in this context (Luo, Xue, and Han, 2010) and it is possible that family and non-family SMEs take different approaches toward such organizations. Once again, however, we found little difference between the two subsamples (averages of 3.40 for the family SMEs and 3.36 for the non-family SMEs, respectively, out of 5.00). That being said, maintaining relationships with governmental agencies appears to play an important role in the performance of family and non-family firms alike, as this context-specific variable was found to be positively and significantly related with the prior 12-month performance index for both groups of firms.

The preceding results point to a rather homogeneous business population between family and non-family SMEs in China. In general, they seem to follow similar strategies and business practices and achieve similar performance. When we examined whether the impacts of the strategy variables on firm performance differed between the family and non-family subsamples, however, we obtained some interesting results that offer more nuanced understanding. Although an entrepreneurial orientation and a long-term orientation both exhibited larger positive effects in the non-family than the family subsample, the SEW variables showed the most striking differences between the two types of firms. As would be expected from the family business literature, all of the constituent dimensions except for identification were more strongly associated with firm performance in the case of the family firms. This was also the case for the composite SEW measure, which was not significantly associated with the performance of the non-family SMEs despite the larger size of this sub-sample. Notably, however, the effect of the family control dimension of SEW was *negatively* related to firm performance in the case of the family firms.

Contributions and Implications

Our findings make several significant contributions to and offer several implications for the family business literature. Most fundamentally, they help shed light on the methodologically elusive—and thus 'much under-studied' (Sharma and Carney, 2012: 238)—privately-owned family firm (especially in the China context). In particular, they suggest that these firms neither under-perform nor over-perform relative to their non-family SME counterparts. As such, theoretical and empirical work dedicated to predicting and demonstrating such differences may not hold much promise. Instead, our findings suggest that continued work on the different strategies and orientations of family and non-family firms—and the dif-ferential impacts of these strategies and orientations across the two types of privately-held firms—is likely to prove more fruitful.

Even more specifically, our study makes contributions to emergent work adopting a SEW lens on the family firm. Methodologically, we offer much-needed, multi-item measures of the FIBER dimensions theorized by Berrone et al. (2012), all of which exhibited a Cronbach's alpha at or above 0.75. Empirically, we demonstrated that these dimensions exerted separable effects on perceived firm performance—and that our compos-ite measure of SEW (which had a Cronbach's alpha of .87) explained a similar proportion of the variance in this outcome. These findings help establish the predictive validity of the SEW construct and its constituent dimensions, which we hope will stimulate further theoretical and empirical work from this overarching perspective.

Limitations

It is important to consider our study's findings, contributions and impli-cations in light of its limitations. For example, despite great effort put into the design of the survey, the small size and stratified nature of our sample means that it is only partly representative of privately-held SMEs in China. As such, we caution readers not to generalize our findings to the entire population of such firms in this country, which contains more than 20 million SMEs (Beijing SME Online, 2012). Future studies could take advantage of other large-scale survey opportunities, such as those sponsored and initiated by governmental agencies or semi-governmental agencies, to gain more comprehensive understanding of the inner workings of SMEs in China.

A second limitation pertains to our dependence upon a third-party contractor for the administration of the survey and contact with the local business organizations. Although we had extensive communication with the contractor regarding how to gather representative sample firms—and even participated in some meetings with the local SME organizations—we did not have complete control over the exact target firms. We tried to remedy this weakness by conducting follow-up interviews with more than twenty sampled firms to verify our survey results. Future studies with more direct access to SMEs can design a better sampling frame and even a longitudinal survey to validate and extend the analyses presented in this chapter.

Conclusion

In light of the above-noted limitations, we respond as follows to the overarching question implied within our chapter's title. Although family and non-family SMEs in the China do not appear to differ on various aspects of firm characteristics and perceived performance, they do exhibit notable differences with respect to the emphasis placed on SEW motives and the impact of this emphasis upon firm performance. Our findings seem to be compatible with the prediction that SEW plays a more important role in family firms than non-family firms, although the overall difference needs to be examined more carefully across each individual dimension.

ACKNOWLEDGEMENTS

We acknowledge the financial support from Seed Funding for Basic Research from the University of Hong Kong (project code: 201210159009) and General Research Fund of HK SAR (project code: HKU 793513B). We also thank Pok Yin Chow and Judy Zhu for their research assistance.

REFERENCES

Ancona, D. G., Perlow, L. A., and Okhuysen, G. A. (2001), 'Taking time to integrate temporal research,' *Academy of Management Review*, **26**, 512–529.
Ancona, D., P. Goodman, B. Lawrence, and M. Tushman (2001), 'Time: A new research lens,' *Academy of Management Review*, **26** (4), 645–663.
Beijing SME Online (2012), 'China SME report 2012,' retrieved from http://www.sme.gov.cn 2012-10-29 (accessed September 8, 2013).
Benner, M. and M. Tushman (2003), 'Exploitation, exploration, and process

management: The productivity dilemma revisited,' *Academy of Management Review*, **28** (2), 238–256.

Berrone, P., C. Cruz, and L. Gómez-Mejía (2012), 'Socioemotional wealth in family firms: Theoretical dimensions, assessment approaches, and agenda for future research family,' *Family Business Review*, **25** (3), 258–279.

Bird, B. (1988), 'Implementing entrepreneurial ideas: The case for intention,' *Academy of Management Review*, **13** (3), 442–453.

Eddleston, K., F. Kellermanns, and T. Zellweger (2012), 'Exploring the entrepreneurial behavior of family firms: Does the stewardship perspective explain differences?,' *Entrepreneurship Theory and Practice*, **36** (2), 347–367.

Forbes China (2013), 'Chinese Family Business Survey 2013,' retrieved from http://www.forbeschina.com/review/201309/0028419.shtml (accessed September 8, 2013).

Gómez-Mejía, L., K. Haynes, M. Núñez-Nickel, K. Jacobson, and H. Moyano-Fuentes (2007), 'Socioemotional wealth and business risk in family-controlled firms: Evidence from Spanish olive oil mills,' *Administrative Science Quarterly*, **52** (1), 106–137.

Hamel, G. and C. Prahalad (1989), 'Strategic intent,' *Harvard Business Review*, **May-June**, 63–76.

He, Z. and P. Wong (2004), 'Exploration vs. exploitation: An empirical test of the ambidexterity hypothesis,' *Organization Science*, **15** (4), 481–494.

Kwan, H., V. Lau, and K. Au (2012), 'Effects of family-to-work conflict on business owners: The role of family business,' *Family Business Review*, **25** (2), 178–190.

Lumpkin, T. and G. Dess (1996), 'Clarifying the entrepreneurial orientation construct and linking it to performance,' *Academy of Management Review*, **21** (1), 135–172.

Luo, Y., Q. Xue, and B. Han (2010), 'How emerging market governments promote outward FDI: Experience from China,' *Journal of World Business*, **45** (1), 68–79.

March, J. (1991), 'Exploration and exploitation in organizational learning,' *Organization Science*, **2** (1), 71–87.

Miller, D. and I. Le Breton-Miller (2005), *Managing for the Long Run: Lessons in Competitive Advantage from Great Family Businesses*. Boston, MA: Harvard Business School Press.

Sarasvathy, S. (2001), 'Causation and effectuation: Toward a theoretical shift from economic inevitability to entrepreneurial contingency,' *Academy of Management Review*, **26** (2), 243–264.

Sharma, P. and M. Carney (2012), 'Value creation and performance in private family firms: Measurement and methodological issues,' *Family Business Review*, **25** (3), 233–242.

Slawinski, N. and P. Bansal (2012), 'A matter of time: Temporal perspectives in organizational responses to climate change,' *Organization Studies*, **33** (11), 1537–1563.

Zahra, S., J. Hayton, and C. Salvato (2004), 'Entrepreneurship in family vs. non-family firms: A resource based analysis of the effect of organizational culture,' *Entrepreneurship Theory and Practice*, **28** (4), 363–381.

5. Strategies and motives of family and non-family firms in Brazil: socio-emotional wealth and firm performance in an emerging market

Ravi Sarathy, Tales Andreassi,
Maria José Tonelli and Kimberly A. Eddleston

INTRODUCTION

Family business research has been marked by inconsistent findings regarding the influence of the family on the business, which has led to confusion in the field (Rutherford, Kuratko, and Holt, 2008). While family firms might be expected to suffer from fewer governance problems due to the combination of family ownership and control (Fama and Jensen, 1983; Jensen and Meckling, 1976), family firms research in *developed* countries shows that family firms confront unique problems including nepotism, parental altruism, managerial entrenchment, and stagnation (Schulze, Lubatkin, Dino, and Buchholz, 2001). A family's ability to exploit minority shareholders in some emerging markets has even led some scholars to describe family firms as 'villains' (Morck and Yeung, 2003; Peng and Jiang, 2010).

However, some recent research on family firms in emerging markets suggests that due to institutional voids in emerging markets, the family can be a key resource that contributes to firm performance (Khanna and Palepu, 2000; Miller, Lee, Chang, and Le Breton-Miller, 2009). Family control may allow a firm to more efficiently navigate unreliable and fluctuating market rules and government regulations (Park, Li, and Tse, 2006). Family ties can foster trust and social capital, which are valuable in reducing transaction costs when formal market-supporting institutions are lacking (Luo and Chung, 2005). In the absence of rules of law, property rights and formal institutions, the family can provide the firm with a stable employment base that works to protect the family's wealth and assets (Gedajlovic, Carney, Chrisman, and Kellermanns, 2012). Therefore, the family can be 'virtuous' in an emerging market, contributing to the success of the family firm (Banalieva, Eddleston, and Zellweger, in press).

In this chapter we consider these two views of family involvement, comparing the strategies, motives and performance of family and non-family firms in Brazil to determine if family involvement offers businesses an advantage. This chapter thus offers unique insight into privately held family and non-family firms in Brazil—one of the world's key emerging markets.

FAMILY FIRMS IN BRAZIL

The family is the foundation of social structure in Brazil (Watson, Barreira, and Watson, 2000) and therefore it is not surprising that the vast majority of entrepreneurial businesses in the country are family run (Gomes, 2013). Approximately 85 percent of all small businesses in Brazil are family firms with more than 10 million families involved in entrepreneurship (GEM Brasil, 2012). More specifically, 1.5 million families are supporting nascent entrepreneurs, 3.9 million are involved in new firms, and 5.2 million families are associated with established firms. In comparison, the US, which has 60 percent more citizens between the ages of 18 and 64, has only 7.5 million families engaged in some level of entrepreneurship. Thus, a greater proportion of families in Brazil are involved in entrepreneurship than in the US. Additionally, 18 percent of the largest companies in Brazil are family run, and many of them, started between 1925 and 1975, are now led by a later generation.

Because many Brazilian families aim to pass a strong, sustainable business on to the next generation, family firms in the country tend to focus on long-term growth (Gomes, 2013). In Brazil, adult children tend to remain close to their parents, both geographically and socially, and families tend to maintain close ties with extended family members (in other words, aunts, uncles, cousins, godparents), encouraging both the children and extended family members to join the family business. Because Brazil has a high unemployment rate, particularly for young adults between the ages of 18 and 24 (Endeavor Brazil, 2012), a family business is often an important source of employment for family members.

Family businesses in Brazil contribute 50 percent to the nation's GDP (Family Firm Institute, n.d.). While there is little research comparing family and non-family firms in Brazil, preliminary results by the Brazilian Institute of Corporate Governance (IBGC) show that publicly held family-controlled firms tend to be more valuable, profitable, and solvent—and offer higher dividend payouts—than non-family listed firms. The same report indicates that public family firms in the country also tend to maintain better governance practices than the average firm in the Brazilian market.

STUDY METHODOLOGY

The data for our Brazilian study was gathered through the common survey instrument used in the multi-country investigation study featured within this book. The questions were translated from English to Portuguese and then back-translated to verify that content and meaning had not changed. The survey was administered in face-to-face settings to over 200 owner-managers between September 2012 and September 2013. The respondents were business owners who had interactions with entrepreneurship programs at the Fundacao Getulio Vargas in Sao Paulo, Brazil's largest city and the center of Brazilian economic activity.

CHARACTERISTICS OF THE FAMILY AND NON-FAMILY FIRMS

As indicated in Table 5.1, 56 percent of the participants (N = 118) identified themselves as owner-managers of 'family firms,' with 94 self-reported to be heading non-family firms and a few firms unable to be characterized due to missing data. The vast majority of the family firms (73 percent) and non-family firms (80 percent) were very small; that is, they reported only 1–10 full-time employees. Only three family firms and one non-family firm reported having more than 251 full-time employees. Thus, our data appears to be in line with previous reports that found that 98 percent of all companies in Brazil are SMEs (Endeavor Brazil, 2012). When considering the specific number of full-time employees, the family firms were approximately five times larger than the non-family firms, with an average of 56 versus 12 employees, respectively. The family firms were also significantly older than the non-family firms, with respective average ages of 11.08 versus 4.72 years.

The Brazilian firms that provided industry information were primarily in the service industry (71 percent of the sample). In comparison, 55 percent of the firms in the US sample reported being in the service industry. Although no non-family firms reported being in manufacturing, eight family firms were manufacturers.

Regarding the characteristics of the owner-managers in our sample, those heading family firms were more likely to be married and less likely to

Firms within families

Table 5.1   Family versus non-family firm and owner-manager characteristics (Brazil sample)

Variables	Family	Non-family
Number of full-time employees		
1 to 10	72.9%	79.8%
11 to 250	24.6%	19.1%
251 to 500	1.7%	1.1%
Greater than 500	0.8%	0%
Industry categories (%)		
Manufacturing	10.2%	0%**
Services	66.7%	77.4%
Other	23.1%	22.6%
Other attributes of the firms		
Company age (years)	11.08	4.72***
Average no. of employees	56.05	11.78
Owner-manager characteristics		
Male	28.5%	31.6%
Female	71.4%	68.4%
Married	69.7%	53.7%
Education (at least some university)	78.1%	88.4%**
Founder	73.1%	96.8%***
Outcomes		
12-month average perceived firm performance (7-point scale [converted to 5-point scale])	4.54 [3.24]	4.73 [3.38]
5-year average perceived firm performance (7-point scale [converted to 5-point scale])	4.60 [3.29]	4.55 [3.25]
Perceived effectiveness in the business sphere (max of 10)	7.15	7.21
Satisfaction with the business (max of 10)	6.29	5.99
N	118	94

Note: † $p \le .10$, * $p \le .05$, ** $p \le .01$, *** $p \le .001$ (two-tailed tests).

be highly educated or founders than those heading non-family firms. The participating owner-managers of both the family firms (71 percent) and non-family firms (68 percent) were more likely to be female than male. This high proportion of women entrepreneurs is in line with previous reports on entrepreneurship in Brazil (Kelley, Brush, Green, and Litovski, 2011).

Turning to business outcomes, while we see that the family firms reported slightly lower 12-month perceived firm performance than non-family firms (means of 4.54 versus 4.73 on a 7-point scale), the family firms also reported slightly higher 5-year perceived firm performance (means of 4.60 versus 4.55 on a 7-point scale).[1] Although these scores are similar to those reported by the US family and non-family firms, the Brazilian owner-managers appear to be much less satisfied with their businesses than those in the US sample. While the owner-managers of family firms and non-family firms in the US were somewhat satisfied with their businesses (71 percent versus 76 percent out of a maximum of 100 percent), the family firm owner-managers and non-family firm owners in Brazil reported scores of only 63 percent and 60 percent. However, in regards to perceived effectiveness, the owner-managers in Brazil and US reported somewhat similar scores. The perceived effectiveness of owner-managers of family and non-family firms in Brazil was 72 percent, while the equivalent perceived effectiveness for US family and non-family firm owner-managers was 76 percent.

Taken together, these findings suggest that although the Brazilian non-family firms are younger and smaller than their family firm counterparts, they do not suffer from 'liabilities of newness or smallness' (Aldrich and Auster, 1986) with regard to their comparative performance or perceived business effectiveness. In fact, the non-family firm owner-managers reported slightly higher 12-month firm performance and business effectiveness than the family firm owner-managers, although these differences were not significant. However, the family firm owner-managers did report greater satisfaction with their businesses than the non-family firms. Therefore, it could be that family firms, with relatively lower performance but higher satisfaction, may be stagnant yet content, as suggested in recent research (Miller, Steier, and Le Breton-Miller, 2003).

FAMILY VERSUS NON-FAMILY FIRM BUSINESS STRATEGIES

The strategies deployed by family and non-family firms may help us to understand why the relative youth and smaller size of the non-family firms do not appear to hurt perceived performance and business effectiveness—as well as whether the greater age and larger size of the family firms are encouraging stagnation. Given that significantly more family firms were headed by non-founders, it would not be surprising if the family firms displayed less entrepreneurship and growth orientation. The old adage, 'shirtsleeves to shirtsleeves in three generations' (Ward, 1997) captures the common perception that later generation family leaders may not be as effective in managing and growing the family firm as were their founders. Research comparing publicly held family and non-family firms has provided credence to this perception (Miller, Le Breton-Miller, Lester, and Cannella, 2007; Villalonga and Amit, 2006). In order to explore whether family and non-family firms in Brazil differ in regards to their strategy choices and orientations, we investigated their exploration versus exploitation and causation versus effectuation strategies as well as their orientations towards growth, entrepreneurialism and the long-term.

Exploration and exploitation are important to organizational success and survival, yet they entail very different knowledge processes (Floyd and Lane, 2000). While exploration involves the use of tacit knowledge to develop new technologies, innovations, and markets, exploitation involves the use of explicit knowledge bases to make incremental refinements to existing technologies, innovations, and markets (Lubatkin, Simsek, Ling, and Veiga, 2006). As such, exploration is intended to create something new and exploitation is intended to adapt to environmental changes or market needs. Although these two strategies are often depicted as opposites, more recent research has found that SMEs that are able to pursue both strategies, referred to as an ambidextrous orientation, accrue performance advantages (Lubatkin et al., 2006). Indeed, Sharma and Salvato (2011) argued that family firms should not only exploit already discovered opportunities, but also create new opportunities to avoid stagnation and decline. However, family firms often experience tension between innovating to exploit the changing environment and maintaining the firm's initial strategic direction (Eddleston, Kellermanns, and Zellweger, 2012).

Additionally, researchers have called for family businesses to intensify their strategic planning (Eddleston, Kellermanns, and Sarathy, 2008). Yet, results from recent research have questioned the benefits of strategic planning throughout a family firm's lifecycle (Eddleston, Kellermanns, Floyd, Crittenden, and Crittenden, 2013). Indeed, entrepreneurship scholars have begun to discriminate between different types of strategic planning processes and have proposed that different types may offer diverse benefits (Brinckmann, Grichnik, and Kapsa, 2010). In particular, it has been suggested that when strategic planning is linear, causal and projective, it can limit a firm's ability to adapt to environmental changes. This type of strategy process, referred to as causation, begins with a pre-determined goal and a given set of means, which are used to develop a specific, detailed plan (Sarasvathy, 2001).

In contrast, an effectuation strategy process calls for a flexible approach towards strategy development that encourages change and adaptation (Haveman, 1992; Mosakowski, 1997). This type of strategy process is seen as emergent and adaptive (Sarasvathy, 2001). Rather than beginning with a specific goal, the effectual strategy process starts with a given set of means and the goal is allowed to emerge over time as the firm evolves and

Table 5.2 Family versus non-family business strategies, orientations and SEW (Brazil sample)

Variables	α	Family		Non-family	
		Mean	S.D.	Mean	S.D.
Strategies					
Exploration	.72	5.81	0.91	5.61	1.03
Exploitation	.75	5.32	1.43	4.95	1.35†
Ambidexterity	.77	5.58	0.98	5.32	0.93†
Causation	.78	4.49	1.30	4.62	1.35
Effectuation	.74	5.14	1.04	5.31	1.04
Orientations					
Growth	.77	5.33	1.26	5.56	1.03
Entrepreneurial	.62	4.03	1.44	4.23	1.42
Long-term	.70	3.98	1.17	3.94	1.18
Socio-emotional wealth					
Family control	.83	4.46	1.46	3.01	1.39***
Identification	.72	6.03	0.94	5.88	0.89
Bonds	.70	5.58	0.96	5.53	0.91
Emotion	.80	5.86	1.07	5.61	1.24
Renewal	.70	3.98	1.17	3.94	1.18
Composite measure	.83	25.79	3.64	23.94	3.18***

Notes:
All scales are measured on a 7-point scale, except for the composite socio-emotional wealth measure (which could range from 5 to 35).
† $p \leq .10$, * $p \leq .05$, ** $p \leq .01$, *** $p \leq .001$ (two-tailed tests).

interacts with the environment (Sarasvathy, 2001). The main advantage of effectuation is that the strategy can be quickly implemented and adapted to capture arising opportunities. In her work on causation and effectuation, Sarasvathy (2001) argued that while entrepreneurs often have a tendency to favor one type of strategic process, some may actually use both processes, particularly as they become more experienced entrepreneurs.

Table 5.2 shows the degree to which these two sets of strategies are pursued by family and non-family firms in our sample. Exploration was measured with five items, including questions such as the degree to which a respondent agrees that the firm 'introduces new generations of products' to achieve its objective. Each question was rated on a 7-point Likert scale ranging from '1 = very unimportant' to '7 = very important' ($\alpha = .72$). Exploitation was measured with four items, using questions such as the firm should 'reduce production cost' and 'use new distribution channels,' again using a Likert scale to evaluate degree (α = .75). Ambidexterity is the joint pursuit of exploration and exploitation, measured by multiplying the items together (α = .77). Causation was measured by the average of four questions such as 'we designed and planned business strategies' using a 7-point Likert scale of 'strongly disagree' to 'strongly agree' (α = .78). Effectuation was captured using four questions, including 'we experimented with different products and/or business models,' using the same 7-point Likert scale (α = .74).

Family and non-family firms demonstrated rather high levels of exploration, exploitation, ambiguity and effectuation, with their average scores well above the scales' mean of 4.0. However, our results also showed that the family firms reported marginally significantly more exploitation than the non-family firms (5.32 versus 4.95). Further, although the two types of firms did not significantly differ in regards to exploration (5.81 versus 5.61), the family firms reported marginally more ambidexterity than the non-family firms (5.58 versus 5.32). In terms of causation and effectuation, the family and non-family firms reported similar levels, all of which were above the scales' midpoint of 4.0.

GROWTH, ENTREPRENEURIAL AND LONG-TERM ORIENTATIONS

Although there are many examples of family firms that have prospered over multiple generations, a very small percentage survive beyond three generations (Handler, 1994). Two key reasons that family firms fail to survive are their lack of investment in growth (Eddleston et al., 2008; 2013) and entrepreneurship (Kellermanns and Eddleston, 2006; Miller, Le Breton-Miller, and Scholnick, 2008). It is important for family firms to invest in growth and entrepreneurship in order to maintain their competitive advantage and market share. Because family firms often decline over time, a strong growth orientation may prevent stagnation (Miller et al., 2008) and an entrepreneurial orientation should revitalize the business. Furthermore, the need to be entrepreneurial is especially important for family firms given their desire to succeed across generations (Cruz and Nordqvist, 2012).

We investigated the growth and entrepreneurial orientations of the family and non-family firms in our sample. Growth orientation was measured using a 7-point Likert-type scale inspired by Cliff (1998), with seven items that assessed whether the owner-manager intends to expand the business or prefers to limit growth (α = .77). Entrepreneurial orientation was measured using three items, with a 7-point Likert-scale involving the dimensions of project rates of return, competitive positioning, and risk-taking ($\alpha = .62$). For growth orientation, both family and non-family firms reported mean values greater than 5.0, representing a desire for the firms to grow significantly. Regarding entrepreneurial orientation, both types of firms reported a high average level of entrepreneurial orientation (4.03 versus 4.23). These results suggest that family firms in Brazil are just as growth and entrepreneurial oriented as their non-family firm counterparts. This appears to contradict the common perception that family firms are stagnant and conservative in comparison with non-family firms.

A long-term orientation is also believed to contribute to a family firm's success (Zellweger, 2007). A long-term orientation allows a firm to put aside the pursuit of short-term gains in order to make patient investments in the firm's future. Scholars have suggested that a long-term orientation is often a resource for family firms as it allows them to pursue opportunities that their short-term oriented competitors reject (Sirmon and Hitt, 2003; Zellweger, 2007). To measure long-term orientation we used a 4-item measure from Eddleston et al. (2013). Two examples of items are: 'The firm is in business for the long run' and 'The incentives for our (middle) management are tied to the long-run performance of the firm.' All items were assessed with a 7-point Likert-type scale ($\alpha = .70$). Contrary to expectations, we found that family and non-family firms exhibited a similar degree of orientation towards the long-term (3.98 versus 3.94).

SOCIO-EMOTIONAL WEALTH

Socio-emotional wealth (SEW) was introduced by Gómez-Mejía, Haynes, Núñez-Nickel, Jacobson, and Moyano-Fuentes (2007) to explain how family firms often use a family based referent point when making decisions. Family firms are not only motivated by economic concerns, but also by the desires of the family, such as the need to maintain family control of the firm and to protect family wealth and employment opportunities. SEW has been used to explain family firm risk taking (Gómez-Mejía et al., 2007), diversification strategies (Gómez-Mejía, Makri, and Kintana, 2010), and innovation (Gómez-Mejía, Cruz, Berrone, and De Castro, 2011). SEW consists of five components: family control, identification, bonds, emotional attachment to the firm, and renewal (Berrone, Cruz, and Gómez-Mejía, 2012). Although scholars generally assume that SEW is unique to family firms (in other words, Berrone, Cruz, Gómez-Mejía, and Larraza-Kintana, 2010; Berrone et al., 2012), others have suggested that family-related and socio-emotional factors are important motivators for many business owners (Eddleston and Powell, 2008; 2012; Powell and

Eddleston, 2013). We therefore compared the SEW of family and non-family firms in Brazil.

Our measure of SEW consists of five multi-item scales that assess the FIBER (in other words, family control, identification, family bonds, emotional attachment, and renewal) dimensions of SEW conceptualized by Berrone et al. (2012). Consistent with other scales, the items are rated on 7-point Likert-type scales, which we averaged for each dimension. We also created a composite SEW measure by summing the five averaged dimensions to capture their cumulative effects. Table 5.2 shows the alphas for each dimension and the composite measure; as indicated, all are above .70.

Of the five SEW dimensions, only family control was found to be significantly higher for family firms than non-family firms (4.46 versus 3.01). This dimension of SEW captures the owner-manager's desire to keep the business under family control and to see the business passed on to the next generation. Although the family firms reported higher mean scores than the non-family firms on the other SEW dimensions, these differences were not significant. Thus, similar to family firm owner-managers, non-family firm owner-managers in Brazil are motivated by identification (in other words, 'I am committed to perpetuating a positive firm image'), bonds (in other words, 'In the business, employees are treated as if they are part of one family'), emotion (in other words, 'I am emotionally attached to the firm'), and renewal (in other words, 'The firm has the possibility to seize investment projects that take a longer time until pay back'). Regarding the composite measure, family firms were significantly higher than non-family firms (25.79 versus 23.94), likely due to their higher motivation for family control.

THE RELATIONSHIP BETWEEN STRATEGY, ORIENTATION, SEW AND PERFORMANCE

Now that we uncovered some differences between family and non-family firms in Brazil, as well as some unexpected similarities, we will explore how the variables related to strategy, orientation and SEW influence firm performance. Several controls were used in each model including industry, industry dynamism, firm size, firm age, family firm status, founder presence, owner-manager gender, owner-manager marital status, and owner-manager education level. Table 5.3 presents the aggregate results for the family and non-family firms combined.

Among the controls, we see in Model 1 that only manufacturing is significantly related to 12-month firm performance ($\beta = -.14$, $p < .10$). Turning to the main variables of interest—those for business strategies,

Table 5.3   Net associations with prior 12-month performance index (Brazil sample)

Variables	Performance					
	Model 1	Model 2	Model 3	Model 4	Model 5	Model 6
Controls						
Manufacturing	−.142†	−.179*	−.179*	−.178*	−.179*	−.178*
Services	−.055	−.027	−.03	−.022	−.003	−.023
Industry dynamism	.015	.035	.032	.03	.038	.03
Family firm	−.02	−.018	−.017	−.02	−.018	−.016
Logged company size	−.017	−.013	−.009	−.021	−.034	−.023
Company age	.01	.04	.037	.09	.095	.092
Founder	.103	.072	.073	.083	.083	.084
Owner-manager gender	−.049	−.051	−.052	−.036	−.053	−.034
Owner-manager married	−.015	.005	.005	−.003	.008	−.002
Owner-manager education	.005	−.045	−.049	−.04	−.022	−.042
Business Strategies						
Exploration			.047	.025	.024	.026
Exploitation			.021	.029	.037	.029
Causation		.092	.093	.073	.098	.072
Effectuation		.286***	.287***	.296***	.308***	.302***
Ambidexterity		.061†				
Orientations						
Growth				−.02	−.029	−.02
Entrepreneurial				.132†	.134†	.13†
Socio-emotional Wealth						
Family control					.012	
Identification					.061	
Bonds					−.032	
Emotion					−.012	
Renewal					−.079	
SEW (FIBER) Combined						−.019
Overall model *F*	.843	2.729***	2.518**	2.415**	1.895*	2.267**
R square	.039	.148	.147	.161	.079	.161
Observations	218	218	218	218	218	218

Notes:
Values in the table are standardized OLS regression coefficients (beta values).
† $p \leq .10$, * $p \leq .05$, ** $p \leq .01$, *** $p \leq .001$ (one-tailed tests).

orientations and SEW—several interesting patterns emerge. The addition of the business strategy variables increased the R^2 from .04 to .15. In Model 2, effectuation is strongly related ($\beta = .29$, $p < .001$) and ambidexterity is marginally related ($\beta = .06$, $p < .10$) to 12-month firm performance. However, exploration, exploitation and causation were not found to be significantly related to firm performance. These results contrast with those from the US sample, which showed exploration, causation and effectuation to be positively related to 12-month firm performance.

In regards to the orientation variables, only entrepreneurial orientation was found to be marginally positively related to 12-month firm performance for the Brazilian data. In comparison, all orientation variables (growth, entrepreneurial, long-term) were strongly, positively related to performance for the US firms. Additionally, while some of the SEW variables were shown to significantly predict US firm performance (specifically, identification, renewal, and the SEW composite measure), none of the variables were significant for the Brazilian sample.

Taken together, these results are not very robust in predicting the 12-month firm performance of Brazilian firms. While the R^2 for the US sample testing similar models reached .40, our R^2 only reached .16. The most consistent predictor of Brazilian firm performance proved to be effectuation. Perhaps the emerging market context of Brazil, with its transforming institutional environment and market reforms, make effectuation particularly important to firm success. If so, this would suggest that the ability to anticipate and adapt to change may distinguish the most successful firms in Brazil. This idea led us to wonder if different predictors influence the firm performance of family versus non-family firms.

In Table 5.4 we present the separate results for Brazilian family and non-family firms. Several interesting patterns emerge from these analyses, which may help explain the results in Table 5.3. First, we see that, for both family and non-family firms, effectuation is significantly positively related to 12-month firm performance. This suggests that the ability to adapt to change and develop emergent strategies is important to firm success in Brazil. However, effectuation was the only variable found to be significantly related to *both* family and non-family firm performance.

For family firms, an entrepreneurial orientation was positively related to firm performance, suggesting that family firms must invest in entrepreneurship if they are to improve their firm performance. This finding is in line with previous research that has found that innovation is positively related to family firm performance (Kellermanns, Eddleston, Sarathy, and Murphy, 2012). With regard to non-family firms, exploitation and growth orientation were shown to be positively related to firm performance. This suggests that non-family firms need to focus more on exploiting their capabilities and pursuing growth initiatives if they are to improve their firm performance.

Finally, in regards to SEW, similar to the results in Table 5.3, none of the SEW dimensions were found to be significantly related to family firm or non-family firm 12-month performance. These results suggest that, in

Table 5.4   Net associations with prior 12-month performance index: subsample comparison of family and non-family firms in Brazil

Variables	Family Model 1	Non-family Model 2	Family Model 3	Non-family Model 4	Family Model 5	Non-family Model 6
Controls						
Service industry	.026	−.1	.014	−.053	.017	.05
Industry dynamism	.049	−.033	.054	−.054	.054	−.056
Firm age	−.035	.1	.027	.129	.056	.097
Founder presence	.077	−.031	.092	−.007	.1	−.012
Business strategies						
Exploration	.006	.106	−.026	.068	−.024	.077
Exploitation	−.116	.205†	−.123	.23*	−.118	.25*
Causation	.126	.084	.067	.103	.07	.18†
Effectuation	.242*	.29*	.251**	.3**	.29**	.297*
Orientations						
Growth			−.087	.25*	−.108	.212*
Entrepreneurial			.207*	.027	.207†	.095
Socio-emotional wealth						
Family control					−.103	.16
Identification					.12	.202
Bonds					−.033	−.051
Emotion					−.076	−.046
Renewal					−.064	−.11
Overall model *F*	1.753†	3.21**	1.855†	3.464***	1.355	2.833***
R square	.113	.23	.147	.292	.165	.35
Observations	118	94	118	94	118	94

Notes:
Values in the table are standardized OLS regression coefficients (beta values); Note: Substituting the composite SEW variable for the individual FIBER components in Models 5 and 6 did not make the SEW component significant (Non-family Model #6, F= 3.215 (sig .000), R^2 = .299); Family Model # 5, F= 1.781, (sig .066), R^2 = .155).
† $p \leq .10$, * $p \leq .05$, ** $p \leq .01$, *** $p \leq .001$ (two-tailed tests).

Brazil, SEW does not play an influential role in predicting firm performance. Perhaps in an emerging market context where there is a high proportion of necessity entrepreneurs (GEM, 2013), an economic referent point takes precedence over any family-based or socio-emotional endowment. Further, in such a context, the ability of a firm to financially provide for the family may be the dominant referent point which thereby suggests that different sources of SEW may arise from business ownership in emerging markets. As such, rather than directly influence firm performance, perhaps SEW plays a greater role in predicting a firm's investment in expansion and strategic pursuits. In other words, perhaps these endowments motivate owner-managers to invest in growth and entrepreneurship, and to develop causal and effectual strategies. With these ideas in mind we therefore investigated how the SEW dimensions influence family and non-family firms' orientations and strategic processes.

EXPLORING SEW'S IMPACT ON STRATEGY AND ORIENTATION

Table 5.5 displays the impact of SEW on growth and entrepreneurial orientations as well as on causation and effectuation. Results are displayed for our full sample and the family and non-family subsamples. To save space and focus on our variables of interest, the controls used in Tables 5.3 and 5.4 are included in the analyses but not displayed. For growth orientation we found only one significant SEW dimension: renewal was found to negatively affect the full sample's growth orientation ($\beta = -.17$, $p < .05$) as well as that of family firms ($\beta = -.29$, $p < .01$). These results are surprising since renewal is associated with patient capital and long-term investments that are often assumed to sustain a family firm's performance (Sirmon and Hitt, 2003; Berrone et al., 2012). In contrast, our results suggest that for family firms in Brazil, greater emphasis on renewal is associated with a *lower* growth orientation. Perhaps these firms focus more on sustaining their current strategies rather than developing new avenues for growth. Indeed, the family firms in our study reported greater exploitation than the non-family firms.

Turning to entrepreneurial orientation, we found a couple of differences between family and non-family firms. While family control was negatively related to entrepreneurial orientation for both the family and non-family firms, bonds and emotion were found to be positively, albeit marginally, related to the entrepreneurial orientation of the family firms. Thus, while a greater desire to maintain family control of the firm inhibits the entrepreneurial orientation of both family and non-family firms in Brazil, strong bonds and emotional attachment to the business increase the entrepreneurial orientation of family firms. Additionally, the composite SEW measure was found to be negatively related to non-family firm entrepreneurial orientation. These results suggest that when family firm owner-managers place emphasis on their attachment to the business as opposed to their attachment to the family, entrepreneurship is encouraged. Further, for non-family firms, the results suggest that a strong SEW, and particularly family control, inhibits their entrepreneurial orientation.

The results also revealed differences among the SEW predictors of

Table 5.5   *The impact of SEW and the FIBER dimensions on orientations and strategy (Brazil sample)*

Variables	Growth Orientation			Entrepreneurial Orientation		
	Full Sample Model 1	Family Model 2	Non-family Model 3	Full Sample Model 4	Family Model 5	Non-family Model 6
Controls	Included	Included	Included	Included	Included	Included
SEW Composite	−.018	−.06	.098	−.088	.009	−.263*
Model *F*	1.867	1.215	1.325	6.262***	3.918**	2.626*
Family Control	−.09	−.068	−.09	−.174*	−.218*	−.278†
Identification	.111	.093	.103	.004	.003	.001
Bonds	.003	.04	−.033	.075	.148†	−.045
Emotion	.068	.084	.121	.028	.184†	−.147
Renewal	−.171*	−.293**	−.054	−.013	.021	−.015
FIBER Model *F*	2.403*	1.973*	1.114	4.18***	3.542***	1.966†
N	218	118	94	218	118	94

	Causation			Effectuation		
	Full Sample Model 7	Family Model 8	Non-family Model 9	Full Sample Model 10	Family Model 11	Non-family Model 12
Controls	Included	Included	Included	Included	Included	Included
SEW Composite	.02	.061	−.031	.303***	.385***	.195*
Model *F*	1.216	.806	.631	5.893***	4.378***	6.042***
Family Control	−.094	−.181†	−.03	.029	.144	−.006
Identification	−.164*	−.102	−.263*	.127	.068	.185†
Bonds	.127†	.153	.127	.219***	.116	.246*
Emotion	.052	.16	−.013	−.059	.023	−.191†
Renewal	.256***	.21*	.275*	.245***	.3**	.172†
FIBER Model *F*	3.607***	1.897†	2.36*	5.521***	3.011**	5.664
N	218	118	94	218	118	94

Note: Values in the table are standardized OLS regression coefficients (beta values); control variables include services industry, industry dynamism, company age and founder presence.

family and non-family firms' causation and effectuation. For the full sample, identification was negatively and bonds and renewal were positively related to causation. For family firms, while family control diminished their causation ($\beta = -.18$, p < .10), renewal increased it ($\beta = .21$, p < .05). In regards to non-family firms, while renewal also increased their causation ($\beta = .28$, p < .05), strong identification diminished it ($\beta = -.26$, p < .05). As such, while firms that emphasize renewal for the long-term are more likely to employ a causal strategy process, family firms that strongly value family control and non-family firms that place emphasis on identification are less likely to employ a causal strategy process.

Regarding effectuation, the SEW composite was shown to be positively related to the effectuation of the full sample ($\beta = .30$, $p < .001$), family firm sample ($\beta = .39$, $p < .001$), and non-family firm sample ($\beta = .20$, $p < .05$). Strong bonds and renewal were also shown to increase the effectuation of the full sample. For family firms, besides the SEW composite measure, only renewal was found to enhance effectuation. However, for non-family firms, all SEW dimensions except family control were found to significantly predict effectuation. While emotion was negatively related to non-family firm effectuation, identification, bonds and renewal were positively related to their effectuation.

Our results concerning the link between SEW and Brazilian firm orientations and strategies suggest that SEW indirectly affects family and non-family firm performance through its effect on growth orientation, entrepreneurial orientation, causation and effectuation. As such, although the socio-emotional referent point of Brazilian entrepreneurs may not directly affect firm performance, the dimensions of SEW play an important role in explaining their orientations and strategies. Most important, the SEW dimensions were often found to influence family and non-family firms in different ways. While some SEW dimensions enhanced family or non-family firm orientations and strategies, other SEW dimensions hampered the orientations and strategies of family or non-family firms.

DISCUSSION

Summary

Given Brazil's entrepreneurial spirit and family-focused culture, this chapter sought to explore whether differences exist in the performance, strategies and orientations of the country's family versus non-family firms. Although little empirical research on family firms in emerging markets exists, debates exist as to whether family firms have an advantage or disadvantage relative to non-family firms in such contexts (Banalieva, Eddleston, and Zellweger, in press). Our study revealed that Brazilian family and non-family firms are perceived by their owner-managers as exhibiting similar levels of 12-month firm performance. The relatively low levels of perceived performance reported by both types of owner-managers may help explain why they considered themselves to be only moderately effective and satisfied within the business sphere. The fact that Brazil is dominated by necessity entrepreneurs (GEM, 2013) who tend to own businesses that are quite small and young (as reflected by our data), suggests that more efforts need to be made to encourage entrepreneurs to seek entrepreneurial opportunities that can grow their businesses. Indeed, entrepreneurial orientation was found to be positively related to firm performance, especially for family firms. Additionally, effectuation was shown to consistently predict the performance of family and non-family firms. Conversely, in the US study causation was shown to enhance firm performance. Perhaps the emerging market context of Brazil, with its transforming institutional environment and market reforms, makes effectuation necessary to achieve strong firm performance.

Although there were few significant differences in the reported strategies, orientations and SEW of family and non-family firms, our study revealed that different factors contribute to the firm performance of family and non-family firms. While effectuation significantly contributed to family and non-family firm performance, for family firms a high level of entrepreneurial orientation was also needed. The importance of an entrepreneurial orientation to family firm success is in line with previous research that has called for these firms to invest in entrepreneurship in order to avoid stagnation and to ensure a strong, healthy firm for the next generation (Cruz and Nordqvist, 2012; Kellermanns and Eddleston, 2006). In comparison, for non-family firms, high levels of exploitation and growth orientation significantly contributed to their performance. Because the non-family firms tended to be smaller and younger, those that pursue an exploitation strategy and growth orientation may be best equipped to overcome liabilities of newness and smallness.

While the SEW dimensions were not significantly related to the Brazilian firms' performance or perceived business effectiveness, we did find that they are related to growth orientation, entrepreneurial orientation, causation and effectuation. These results suggest that SEW is a more distant and indirect influence on the performance of the Brazilian firms. Further, we found that different SEW dimensions affected the strategies and orientations of family and non-family firms. For family firms, renewal proved to be an important influence on growth orientation, causation, and effectuation. While renewal was negatively related to their growth orientation, it was positively related to causation and effectuation. For non-family firms, renewal was positively related to causation and effectuation. In addition, emotion, bonds and identification were related to non-family firm effectuation. Further, while identification was positively related to effectuation, it was negatively related to causation for non-family firms.

Our results also revealed that the SEW dimension of family control is not beneficial to family or non-family firms in Brazil. Family control was found to be negatively related to their entrepreneurial orientation and also the use of causation by family firms. Because entrepreneurial orientation is a significant contributor to family firm performance, these results suggest that the desire to maintain family control reduces a family firm's investment in entrepreneurship, which may thereby limit their performance. These findings support the notion that family firms can become stagnant and risk-averse over time, focusing more on wealth preservation than wealth generation as they age (Kellermanns and Eddleston, 2006). Therefore, for family firms in Brazil, emphasis should be placed on developing SEW bonds and emotions that contribute to entrepreneurial orientation and thus firm performance. Those family firms that nurture their entrepreneurial orientation and effectuation should, in turn, accrue performance advantages.

Implications

The little research on family firms in emerging economies has debated whether family firms have an advantage or disadvantage relative to non-family firms (Banalieva et al., in press; Khanna and Palepu, 2000; Miller et al., 2009; Morck and Yeung, 2003; Peng and Jiang, 2010). While our study on firms in Brazil failed to show that family firms have a significant advantage or disadvantage, it discovered that, in general, different factors affect the firm performance, orientations, and strategies of family and non-family firms. The only factor that was shown to contribute to both family and non-family firm performance was effectuation. Therefore, firms in Brazil should be encouraged to develop their effectual strategy process skills. The transitioning economy likely requires firms to quickly adapt to institutional changes and opportunities in order to remain competitive and hold on to market share (Banalieva et al., in press). Additionally, while family firms should be encouraged to enhance their entrepreneurial orientation in order to avoid stagnation, non-family firms should be encouraged to pursue exploitation strategies and additional avenues for growth. As such, those looking to further enhance the entrepreneurial spirit of Brazil need to recognize the distinctive needs and capabilities of family and non-family firms.

Limitations

As with most studies, our research has limitations that should be acknowledged. First, because we used a university to assist with the data collection, our sample is not necessarily representative of all business owners in Brazil. Second, our reliance on self-reported data is a limitation. For example, it would have been beneficial if we had been able to corroborate on certain variables through different sources, particularly firm performance. Third, the sample is drawn from entrepreneurs located in Sao Paulo, Brazil's largest and most economically dynamic city. A sample of Brazilian entrepreneurs drawn from less competitive regional economic environments in Brazil may provide different results.

Conclusion

Although we did not find that family firms in Brazil have an inherent advantage or disadvantage relative to non-family firms, our study discovered that different strategies and orientations distinguish the most successful family and non-family firms. The only factor that contributed to both family and non-family firm performance was effectuation, which is likely due to the transitioning economy of Brazil that requires rapid adaptation and opportunity assessment. Further, while the SEW dimensions did not directly influence family or non-family firm performance or perceived business effectiveness, they did contribute to growth orientation, entrepreneurial orientation, causation and effectuation. However, SEW dimensions affected family and non-family firm orientations and strategies in different ways. Therefore, whether family firms have an advantage or disadvantage relative to non-family firms in Brazil does not appear to be the right research question to explore. Rather, future research should focus on the distinctive needs of family and non-family firms in Brazil and ask why these firms are able to capitalize on and apply different capabilities to produce strong firm performance and business effectiveness.

NOTE

1. Firm performance relative to competitors was assessed by the mean of a 7-item scale, with each item rated from '1 = worse than competitors' to '7 = better than competitors'. The seven items consisted of sales growth, market share, profitability, return on sales, return on assets, return on equity, and cash flow.

REFERENCES

Aldrich, H. and E.R. Auster (1986), 'Even dwarfs started small: Liabilities of age and size and their strategic implications,' *Research in Organizational Behavior*, **8**, 165–186.
Banalieva, E.R., K.A. Eddleston, and T.M. Zellweger (in press), 'When do family firms have an advantage in transitioning economies? Toward a dynamic institution-based view.' *Strategic Management Journal*. DOI 10.1002/smj.2288 (first published online July 9, 2014).
Berrone, P., C. Cruz, and L.R. Gómez-Mejía (2012), 'Socioemotional wealth in family firms: theoretical dimensions, assessment approaches, and agenda for future research,' *Family Business Review*, **25** (3), 258–279.

Berrone, P., C. Cruz, L.R. Gómez-Mejía, and M. Larraza-Kintana (2010), 'Socioemotional wealth and corporate responses to institutional pressures: Do family-controlled firms pollute less?,' *Administrative Science Quarterly*, **55** (1), 82–113.

Brinckmann, J., D. Grichnik, and D. Kapsa (2010), 'Should entrepreneurs plan or just storm the castle? A meta-analysis on contextual factors impacting the business planning–performance relationship in small firms,' *Journal of Business Venturing*, **25** (1), 24–40.

Cliff, J.E. (1998), 'Does one size fit all? Exploring the relationship between attitudes towards growth, gender, and business size,' *Journal of Business Venturing*, **13** (6), 523–542.

Cruz, C. and M. Nordqvist (2012), 'Entrepreneurial orientation in family firms: A generational perspective,' *Small Business Economics*, **38** (1), 33–49.

Eddleston, K.A. and G.N. Powell (2008), 'The role of gender identity in explaining sex differences in business owners' career satisfier preferences,' *Journal of Business Venturing*, **23** (2), 244–256.

Eddleston, K.A., F.W. Kellermanns, and R. Sarathy (2008), 'Resource configuration in family firms: Linking resources, strategic planning and technological opportunities to performance,' *Journal of Management Studies*, **45** (1), 26–50.

Eddleston, K.A., F.W. Kellermanns, and T.M. Zellweger (2012), 'Exploring the entrepreneurial behavior of family firms: does the stewardship perspective explain differences?,' *Entrepreneurship Theory and Practice*, **36** (2), 347–367.

Eddleston, K.A., F.W. Kellermanns, S.W. Floyd, V.L. Crittenden, and W.F. Crittenden (2013), 'Planning for growth: Life stage differences in family firms,' *Entrepreneurship Theory and Practice*, **37** (5), 1177–1202.

Endeavor Brazil (2012). Retrieved from http://www.endeavor.org/network/ affiliates/brazil/1 (accessed August 1, 2014).

Fama, E.F. and M.C. Jensen (1983), 'Separation of ownership and control,' *Journal of Law and Economics*, **26** (2), 301–325.

Family Firm Institute (n.d.) http://www.ffi.org/?page=GlobalDataPoints (accessed February 14, 2015).

Floyd, S.W. and P.J. Lane (2000), 'Strategizing throughout the organization: Managing role conflict in strategic renewal,' *Academy of Management Review*, **25** (1), 154–177.

Gedajlovic, E., M. Carney, J.J. Chrisman, and F.W. Kellermanns (2012), 'The adolescence of family firm research: taking stock and planning for the future,' *Journal of Management*, **38** (4), 1010–1037.

GEM (2013), 'Global Entrepreneurship Monitor Report,' retrieved from http:// www.gemconsortium.org/docs/3106/gem-2013-global-report (accessed July 15, 2014).

GEM Brasil (2012), 'Global Entrepreneurship Monitor. Empreendedorismo no Brasil,' IBQP, Instituto Brasileiro de Qualidade e Produtividade, Curitiba,' retrieved from http://www.gemconsortium.org/docs/download/2806 (accessed January 20, 2014).

Gomes, L. (2013), 'Brazilian family firms reveal tips for success,' BBC News, February 26, retrieved from http://www.bbc.com/news/business-21412761 (accessed January 20, 2014).

Gómez-Mejía, L.R., M. Makri, and M.L. Kintana (2010), 'Diversification decisions in family-controlled firms,' *Journal of Management Studies*, **47** (2), 223–252.

Gómez-Mejía, L.R., C. Cruz, P. Berrone, and J. De Castro (2011), 'The bind that ties: Socioemotional wealth preservation in family firms,' *The Academy of Management Annals*, **5** (1), 653–707.

Gómez-Mejía, L.R., K.T. Haynes, M. Núñez-Nickel, K.J. Jacobson, and J. Moyano-Fuentes (2007), 'Socio-emotional wealth and business risks in family-controlled firms: Evidence from Spanish olive oil mills,' *Administrative Science Quarterly*, **52** (1), 106–137.

Handler, W.C. (1994), 'Succession in family business: A review of the research,' *Family Business Review*, **7** (2), 133–157.

Haveman, H.A. (1992), 'Between a rock and a hard place: Organizational change and performance under conditions of fundamental environmental transformation,' *Administrative Science Quarterly*, **37** (1), 48–75.

Jensen, M.C. and W.H. Meckling (1976), 'Theory of the firm: managerial behavior, agency costs and ownership structure,' *Journal of Financial Economics*, **3** (4), 305–360.

Kellermanns, F.W. and K.A. Eddleston (2006), 'Corporate entrepreneurship in family firms: A family perspective,' *Entrepreneurship Theory and Practice*, **30** (6), 809–830.

Kellermanns, F.W., K.A. Eddleston, R. Sarathy, and F. Murphy (2012), 'Innovativeness in family firms: A family influence perspective,' *Small Business Economics*, **38** (1), 85–101.

Kelley, D.J., C.G. Brush, P.G. Green, and Y. Litovski (2011), 'Global Entrepreneurship Monitor 2010 Women's Report,' GERA/GEM.

Khanna, T. and K. Palepu (2000), 'Is group affiliation profitable in emerging markets? An analysis of diversified Indian business groups,' *Journal of Finance*, **55** (2), 867–891.

Lubatkin, M.H., Z. Simsek, Y. Ling, and J.F. Veiga (2006), 'Ambidexterity and performance in small-to medium-sized firms: The pivotal role of top management team behavioral integration,' *Journal of Management*, **32** (5), 646–672.

Luo, X. and C.N. Chung (2005), 'Keeping it all in the family: The role of particularistic relationships in business group performance during institutional transition,' *Administrative Science Quarterly*, **50** (3), 404–439.

Miller, D., I. Le Breton-Miller, and B. Scholnick (2008), 'Stewardship vs. stagnation: An empirical comparison of small family and non-family businesses,' *Journal of Management Studies*, **45** (1), 51–78.

Miller, D., L. Steier, and I. Le Breton-Miller (2003), 'Lost in time: Intergenerational succession, change, and failure in family business,' *Journal of Business Venturing*, **18** (4), 513–531.

Miller, D., J. Lee, S. Chang, and I. Le Breton-Miller (2009), 'Filling the institutional void: The social behavior and performance of family vs. non-family technology firms in emerging markets,' *Journal of International Business Studies*, **40** (5), 802–817.

Miller, D., I. Le Breton-Miller, R.H. Lester, and A.A. Cannella Jr. (2007), 'Are family firms really superior performers?,' *Journal of Corporate Finance*, **13** (5), 829–858.

Morck, R. and B. Yeung (2003), 'Agency problems in large family business groups,' *Entrepreneurship Theory and Practice*, **27** (4), 367–382.

Mosakowski, E. (1997), 'Strategy making under causal ambiguity: Conceptual issues and empirical evidence,' *Organization Science*, **8** (4), 414–442.

Park, S., S. Li, and D. Tse (2006), 'Market liberalization and firm performance during China's economic transition,' *Journal of International Business Studies*, **37**, 127–147.

Peng M. and Y. Jiang (2010), 'Institutions behind family ownership and control in large firms,' *Journal of Management Studies*, **47** (2), 253–273.

Powell, G.N. and K.A. Eddleston (2013), 'Linking family-to-business enrichment and support to entrepreneurial success: Do female and male entrepreneurs experience different outcomes?,' *Journal of Business Venturing*, **28** (2), 261–280.

Rutherford, M.W., D.F. Kuratko, and D.T. Holt (2008), 'Examining the link between 'familiness' and performance: Can the F-PEC untangle the family business theory jungle?,' *Entrepreneurship Theory and Practice*, **32** (6), 1089–1109.

Sarasvathy, S.D. (2001), 'Causation and effectuation: Toward a theoretical shift from economic inevitability to entrepreneurial contingency,' *Academy of Management Review*, **26** (2), 243–263.

Schulze, W.S., M.H. Lubatkin, R.N. Dino, and A.K. Buchholtz (2001), 'Agency relationships in family firms: Theory and evidence,' *Organization Science*, **12** (2), 99–116.

Sharma, P. and C. Salvato (2011), 'Commentary: Exploiting and exploring new opportunities over life cycle stages of family firms,' *Entrepreneurship Theory and Practice*, **35** (6), 1199–1205.

Sirmon, D. G. and M.A. Hitt (2003), 'Managing resources: Linking unique resources, management and wealth creation in family firms,' *Entrepreneurship Theory and Practice*, **27** (4), 339–358.

Villalonga, B. and R. Amit (2006), 'How do family ownership, control and management affect firm value?,' *Journal of Financial Economics*, **80** (2), 385–417.

Ward, J.L. (1997), 'Growing the family business: Special challenges and best practices,' *Family Business Review*, **10** (4), 323–337.

Watson, S.R., A.M. Barreira, and T.C. Watson (2000), 'Perspectives on quality of life: The Brazilian experience,' in K.D. Keith and R.L Shalock (eds), *Cross-cultural Perspectives on Quality of Life*, Washington DC: AAMR, pp. 112–139.

Zellweger, T. (2007), 'Time horizon, costs of equity capital, and generic investment strategies of firms,' *Family Business Review*, **20** (1), 1–15.

6. Strategies and motives of family and non-family firms in India: unexpected differences and similarities

Ravi Sarathy, K. Kumar and Kimberly A. Eddleston

INTRODUCTION

There is much debate in regards to whether family firms have a competitive advantage over non-family firms (Miller, Le Breton-Miller, Lester, and Cannella, 2007; Villalonga and Amit, 2006). While some research portrays family firms as outperforming their non-family counterparts due to the family's strong commitment, social capital and long-term perspective (Miller, Le Breton-Miller, and Scholnick, 2008; Sirmon and Hitt, 2003), other research suggests that the tendency of family firms toward conservative strategies and risk aversion puts them at a disadvantage (Bertrand and Schoar, 2006; Morck and Yeung, 2003). Researchers also debate whether family firms have an advantage or disadvantage in emerging markets (Gedajlovic, Carney, Chrisman, and Kellermanns, 2012). While they may have an advantage in such contexts because of their family's social capital and stability (for example, Luo and Chung, 2013; Miller, Lee, Chang, and Le Breton-Miller, 2009), they could be ill-equipped to compete in such markets due to their resistance to change and emphasis on family control (for example, Bertrand, Mehta, and Mullainathan, 2002). This chapter explores the strategies and motives of privately held family and non-family firms in India, whether the strategies and motives of family firms vary from those of non-family firms—and, consequently, whether family firms possess a performance advantage relative to non-family firms.

FAMILY FIRMS IN INDIA

Family firms, unlike non-family firms, are motivated by both family and business goals, which may interact, overlap and possibly compete. Family firms thus provide a unique context to study a wide variety of organizational phenomenon including issues related to strategic management and entrepreneurship and attitudinal issues associated with their owners. Further, in emerging markets, with irregular growth, capital restraints and considerable unemployment, the family becomes an important resource for most privately held businesses, family and non-family firms alike. Indeed, 74 percent of entrepreneurs in India reported that they have received family support for their business (National Knowledge Commission, 2008) and only 16 percent believe that they could find someone outside of their family to be a trusted business partner (Yu and Tandon, 2012).

Because of institutional voids in India, such as an underdeveloped capital market, uneven application of laws, and a caste-based traditional society, kinship becomes an important basis for economic organization (Mandelbaum, 1948). In fact, India has the highest percentage of publicly held family firms in Asia (Asian Family Business Report, 2011). Family firms account for 70–80 percent of all businesses in India and 67 percent of listed businesses are family firms (Asian Family Business Report, 2011), generating 27 percent of overall employment in the country (KPMG, 2013), with public family firms alone accounting for half of all corporate jobs (Asian Family Business Report, 2011). Additionally, family firms contribute two-thirds of India's GDP and 90 percent of gross industry output (KPMG, 2013).

In a 2012 PricewaterhouseCoopers (PWC) study of executives from affluent family businesses, almost three-quarters felt that family firms in India were more entrepreneurial than their non-family firm counterparts. However, key obstacles to growth identified by the executives included volatile markets, government regulation and competition. Many successful family businesses in India face challenges in attracting non-family employees and in dealing with family conflicts and politics (PWC, 2013). Preliminary evidence suggests that publicly listed family firms underperform the broader market (Asian Family Business Report, 2011). Additionally, privately held family firms may struggle to grow when they lack expertise and suffer from family–business role conflict (Gill, Sharma, and Mand, 2011).

Further, given that the majority of entrepreneurs in India are 'necessity entrepreneurs' who were pushed into entrepreneurship because of a lack of employment (GEM, 2013), it is important to investigate whether socioemotional wealth (SEW) matters to them. SEW reflects the non-economic and emotional value associated with a firm that serves to meet the family's affective needs like identity, influence and control (Gómez-Mejía, Haynes, Núñez-Nickel, Jacobson, and Moyano-Fuentes, 2007). High levels of SEW could motivate family firms to behave in ways that would benefit the firm (Berrone, Cruz, and Gómez-Mejía, 2012). For example, the majority of family firms in India plan to pass the firm on to the next generation and 40 percent adopt a long-term view when making decisions (PWC, 2013). These findings suggest that family firms in India might highly value SEW.

However, the pursuit of SEW can be at odds with financial performance (Gómez-Mejía et al., 2007). Whether SEW contributes or detracts from family firm performance in India is not known, nor do we know if non-family firm entrepreneurs also value SEW. Because entrepreneurship is a relatively new phenomenon in India (Koster and Rai, 2008), most family firms are in the first generation, compared with European and US family firms which are in the fourth and fifth generations (Asian Family Business Report, 2011). Therefore, previous research that views family firms as stagnant and conservative (in other words, Ward, 2004) and willing to give up financial gains in order to maintain SEW (Gómez-Mejía et al., 2007) may not reflect the relatively young family firms in India. It is against this backdrop that we investigate the performance of family and non-family firms in this emerging market context, with particular emphasis on their strategies and their entrepreneurial and growth orientations.

METHODOLOGY AND SAMPLE CHARACTERISTICS

The data for this chapter were obtained from an online survey completed by a sample of 245 owner-managers heading firms within India over the period June 2012–2013. Respondents were participants at university entre-preneurship and incubator programs in Bangalore. There were 236 usable responses, though some of the tables show smaller sample sizes because of missing data. Respondents classified their enterprises as either family or non-family firms by answering the question: 'Do you consider this company to be a family business?' Due to missing data Table 6.1 reports data for 183 businesses, comprised of 80 and 103 considered to be family firms versus non-family firms, respectively.

While 51.7 percent of the family firms reported being in manufacturing, only 18.6 percent of the non-family firms did so. Across the entire sample, the average firm size was 148 employees and firm age was 14.15 years. Regarding family firms, 19 percent had 1 to 10 employees, 69 percent had 11 to 250 employees, 2 percent had 251 to 500 employees, and 10 percent had greater than 500 employees. In comparison, non-family firms reported

Table 6.1 Family versus non-family firm and owner-manager characteristics (India sample)

Variables	Family	Non-family
N	80	103
Number of full-time employees		
1 to 10	18.5%	34.0%
11 to 250	69.1%	55.0%
251 to 500	2.5%	6.9%
Greater than 500	9.9%	3.9%
Industry categories (%)		
Manufacturing	51.7%	18.6%***
Personal services	27.2%	51.2%***
Professional services	7.0%	7.75%
Other	14.0%	22.5%
Other attributes of the firms		
Number of states with operations	5.48	5.17
Number of countries with operations	2.62	2.34
Company age (years)	22.5	10.0***
Owner-manager characteristics (%)		
Male	75.3%	81.7%
Female	24.5%	18.3%
Married	74.0%	80.8%
Education (at least some university)	97.5%	98.0%
Founder	44.4%	85.6%***
Outcomes		
12-month average perceived firm performance (7-point scales)	4.74	4.83
5-year average perceived firm performance (7-point scales)	4.85	4.82
12-month average perceived firm performance (converted to 5-point scales)	3.39	3.45
5-year average perceived firm performance (converted to 5-point scales)	3.46	3.44
Perceived effectiveness in the business sphere (max of 10)	7.11	7.52
Perceived satisfaction with the business (converted from 100 to 10 point scale)	7.25	7.58

Note: † $p \le .10$, * $p \le .05$, ** $p \le .01$, *** $p \le .001$ (two-tailed tests).

the following: 34 percent had 1 to 10 employees, 55 percent had 11 to 250 employees, 7 percent had 251 to 500 employees, and 4 percent had greater than 500 employees. Family and non-family firms reported operating in a similar number of Indian states (5.48 versus 5.17, respectively) and countries (2.62 versus 2.34, respectively). However, family firms were significantly older than non-family firms (22.5 versus 10 years).

Seventy-five percent of the family firm owners and 82 percent of the non-family firm owners were male. The majority of owner-managers reported being married (74 percent family firms; 81 percent non-family firms), and almost all had at least some university education. Further, while the majority of non-family firm owner-managers were the founder of their business (86 percent), only 44 percent of the family firm owner-managers were founders. Thus, the family firms in our sample tended to be older than the non-family firms and more likely to be managed by a later-generation family member.

In regards to outcomes such as firm performance,[1] perceived business effectiveness, and satisfaction with the business, we see that the family and non-family firms did not significantly differ. The 12-month and 5-year perceived performance relative to peers are equally above average for family and non-family firms: approximately 4.80, which is slightly above the midpoint of the 7-point scale. While the owner-managers of non-family firms reported higher perceived effectiveness and satisfaction with the business (75 percent and 76 percent on a scale of 100 percent as 'completely satisfied') than family firms (71 percent and 73 percent), the difference was not significant. Thus, it appears that owner-managers of family firms and non-family firms are moderately effective and satisfied with their businesses. Given that family firms are significantly older and more likely to be owned and managed by a successor than a founder, why are there no significant differences in firm performance, owner-manager effectiveness or satisfaction?

FAMILY VERSUS NON-FAMILY FIRM BUSINESS STRATEGIES

The answer to the question above may lie in the firms' strategies as well as their growth and entrepreneurial orientations. While recent research on family firms has demonstrated the benefits of strategic planning to firm growth (Eddleston, Kellermanns, Floyd, Crittenden, and Crittenden, 2013) and corporate entrepreneurship (Kellermanns and Eddleston, 2006), little is known about the types of strategies family versus non-family firms pursue, particularly in emerging markets like India. Further, entrepreneurship scholars have questioned the value of formal strategic planning to new firms and small businesses (Brinckmann, Grichnik, and Kapsa, 2010). It has been suggested that strategic planning, when it is linear and projective, can limit a firm's ability to adapt to environmental changes. This type of strategy process, referred to as causation, begins with a pre-determined goal and a given set of means which are used to identify the optimal plan to achieve the goal (Sarasvathy, 2001).

In contrast, some researchers advocate for emergent and adaptive strategies that can quickly be implemented to capture arising opportunities (Mosakowski, 1997). A flexible approach toward strategy that allows for change and adaptation could heighten performance (Haveman, 1992; Mosakowski, 1997). The strategic planning process known as effectuation reflects this logic. Rather than beginning with a specific goal, the effectual strategy process starts with a given set of means and the goal is allowed to emerge over time as the firm evolves and interacts with the environment. In her work on causation and effectuation, Sarasvathy (2001) notes how most entrepreneurs have a tendency for each type of strategic process, although some may use both.

Drawing from effectuation theory, Sharma and Salvato (2011) discussed the need for family firms to not only exploit already discovered opportunities, but to also explore new opportunities. An exploitation strategy focuses on the pursuit of incremental and progressive innovations, often with the aim of improving efficiency or achieving market saturation. However, over time, a reliance on an exploitation strategy can hurt a firm's competitive advantage because competitors may introduce better products to the market. In contrast, an exploration strategy focuses on the development of radical innovations to create new technologies, products, and markets (Cohen and Levinthal, 1990). While an exploration strategy helps to develop a competitive advantage, it is also a risky strategy that does not always lead to success, especially in the short-term. Hence, firms might benefit from pursuing an ambidextrous strategy whereby both exploration and exploitation strategies are equally stressed (Benner and Tushman, 2003). Research indicates that long-lived family firms tend to pursue both exploitation and exploration strategies, thus suggesting that the pursuit of both strategies contributes to family firm survival (Bergfeld and Weber, 2011).

Table 6.2 shows the degree to which these two strategies are pursued by family and non-family firms in our sample. The measures for the sets of strategies were drawn from published research and utilized a 5-point Likert-type scale (from 1 = 'very unimportant' to 5 = 'very important'). Exploration was measured by questions such as the degree to which the firm 'introduces new generations of products' to achieve its objective.

Table 6.2   Family versus non-family business strategies, orientations and SEW (India sample)

Variables	α	Family		Non-family	
		Mean	S.D.	Mean	S.D.
Strategies					
Exploration	.79	3.81	0.81	3.99	0.77
Exploitation	.82	4.11	0.87	3.91	0.86
Ambidexterity	.84	15.89	3.10	15.77	2.74
Causation	.79	3.63	0.66	3.81†	0.68
Effectuation	.57	3.81	0.47	3.77†	0.52
Orientations					
Growth	.73	3.3	0.55	3.49*	0.50
Entrepreneurial	.73	4.22	1.02	4.66**	1.15
Long-term	.66	3.60	0.60	3.73	0.71
Socio-emotional wealth					
Family control	.87	3.31	0.79	2.38***	0.85
Identification	.84	4.40	0.65	4.47	0.63
Bonds	.79	3.74	0.63	3.86	0.65
Emotion	.86	3.85	0.82	3.86	0.85
Renewal	.65	3.68	0.66	3.76	0.77
Composite measure	.81	19.21	2.18	18.65†	3.83

Note: † $p \leq .10$, * $p \leq .05$, ** $p \leq .01$, *** $p \leq .001$ (two-tailed tests).

Exploitation was measured by questions such as the firm 'needs to improve existing products' or 'reduces production costs.' Ambidexterity was measured as the joint pursuit of exploration and exploitation.

Causation and effectuation were measured using a 5-point Likert-type scale that ranged from 'strongly disagree' to 'strongly agree.' Causation was measured by the average of four questions such as 'we designed and planned business strategies' and 'we did meaningful analysis to select target markets.' Effectuation was captured using four questions, including 'we experimented with different products and/or business models.' However, because the alpha for the effectuation scale was low (.57), a problem also identified in the US sample, we investigated alternative specifications. Unfortunately, we were not able to create a scale with a higher alpha. Below we rely on the averaged scores from the scales reported in Table 6.2, but caution the interpretation of the effectuation results.

Our results show that family and non-family firms do not significantly differ in their degree of exploitation, exploration and ambidexterity, with both reporting above-average means for these strategies. Turning to causation and effectuation we see that while non-family firms reported marginally higher causation (3.81 versus 3.63), family firms reported marginally higher effectuation (3.81 versus 3.77). As the non-family firms in our sample are significantly younger, they have had less experience running their businesses relative to the family firms, which may bias them towards using more analytical planning models in arriving at strategies, relative to the more mature family firms who may be more willing to rely on intuition.

GROWTH AND ENTREPRENEURIAL ORIENTATIONS

In order for family firms to survive through multiple generations, researchers have argued that they must pursue growth (Eddleston et al., 2013; Eddleston, Kellermanns, and Sarathy, 2008) and cultivate an entrepreneurial orientation (Miller et al., 2008). While several studies on publicly held family firms have shown that family firms have a performance *disadvantage* relative to non-family firms (Miller et al., 2007; Villalonga and Amit, 2006), researchers have questioned whether this would hold true for privately held family firms (Eddleston et al., 2013). For example, Le Breton-Miller, Miller, and Lester (2011) argued that privately held family firms may be more likely to invest in growth than their publicly held counterparts because of their closely-held structure which allows the reputation and accomplishments of the founding generation to accrue to later generations. Additionally, a strong growth orientation is expected to be especially important to family firms as growth is necessary to sustain an organization across generations. Jaffe and Lane (2004) argued that the typical family firm must grow 10–15 percent compounded annually to provide a financial inheritance to the next generation. Therefore, a growth orientation is necessary for family firms to sustain an expanding family and avoid the decline of the business.

It has also been argued that a strong entrepreneurial orientation is necessary for firms to prosper and survive (Cruz and Nordqvist, 2012). An entrepreneurial orientation helps a firm to stay competitive and to revitalize the business. The need to be entrepreneurial may be even more important for family firms given their desire to succeed across generations (Cruz and Nordqvist, 2012). However, because entrepreneurial projects involve much risk and can take years to generate a return, family firms can become reluctant to invest in entrepreneurship, because failure of an entrepreneurship strategy can place financial strain on the family and cause relationship problems among family members (Eddleston, Kellermanns, and Zellweger, 2012).

Accordingly, we investigated growth and entrepreneurial orientations. Growth orientation was measured using a scale inspired by Cliff (1998) that assessed whether the owner-manager intends to expand the business or prefers to limit growth. Entrepreneurial orientation was measured by averaging eight 5-point Likert-type items involving the dimensions of innovativeness, autonomy, and risk-taking. For growth orientation, non-family firms reported a significantly higher desire to grow than family firms (3.49 versus 3.30). Regarding entrepreneurial orientation, once again the non-family firms had a significantly higher mean than the family firms (4.66 versus 4.22), suggesting that non-family firms are more entrepreneurial than their family firm counterparts in India. These results support the contention in the literature that family firms become less entrepreneurial over time because they become risk averse and focus more on wealth preservation than wealth generation.

SOCIO-EMOTIONAL WEALTH

Socio-emotional wealth (SEW) is portrayed as being associated with positive valence and a source of motivation that inspires family firms to avoid harm and to demonstrate care for stakeholders (Cennamo, Berrone, Cruz, and Gómez-Mejía, 2012). SEW consists of five components—family control, identification, bonds, emotional attachment to the firm, and renewal (Berrone et. al. 2012). SEW helps explain why some family firms may place family needs above those of the firm; that is, why a family firm may pursue a strategy that ensures the maintenance of family control instead of one that would increase financial success (Gómez-Mejía et al., 2007). While research generally assumes that SEW is a unique motivator for family firms (in other words, Berrone et al., 2010; Cennamo et al., 2012), recent research suggests that family-related factors are important motivators for many business owners (Eddleston and Powell, 2012; Powell and Eddleston, 2013). We therefore compared the SEW of family and non-family firms in India.

Each dimension of SEW proposed by Berrone et al. (2012) was assessed by multiple items on a 5-point Likert-type scale, which were then averaged. We also created a composite SEW measure where we summed the dimensions to capture their cumulative effects. Table 6.2 shows the alphas for each dimension and the composite measure. All but that for renewal demonstrated an acceptable alpha above .70. Of the five SEW dimensions, only family control was found to be significantly higher for family firms than non-family firms (3.31 versus 2.38). This dimension of SEW captures the owner-managers' desire to keep the business under family control and to see the business passed on to future generations. Although the other SEW dimensions did not show a significant difference, it is interesting to note that the non-family firms reported higher mean scores than the family firms. Thus, similar to family firms, non-family firms in India are motivated by identification (in other words, 'I am committed to perpetuating a positive firm image'), bonds (in other words, 'In the business, employees are treated as if they are part of one family'), emotion (in other words, 'I am emotionally attached to the firm'), and renewal (in other words, 'The firm has the possibility to seize investment projects that take a longer time until pay back'). Regarding the composite measure, family firms were marginally higher than non-family firms (19.21 versus 18.65), likely due to their higher motivation for family control.

THE RELATIONSHIP OF STRATEGY, ORIENTATION AND SEW TO PERFORMANCE

We now explore how the variables related to strategy, orientation and SEW influence 12-month and 5-year firm performance. Only 12-month results are presented here, with extended results available from the authors. Several controls were used in each model including industry, number of states in which the firm operated, firm size, founder presence, and owner-manager gender, marital status, and education level. While we originally included an extended list of controls to mirror the US analyses, given our smaller sample size, we excluded controls that never approached significance. Further, because exploration was highly correlated with exploitation, and causation was highly correlated with effectuation, we ran two models where only exploration and causation were included so as to better assess the variables' impact on firm performance.

Among the controls, we see in Model 1 that the number of states in which the firm operates is marginally related to 12-month firm performance. However, once the strategy variables are added, this control is no longer significant. The presence of the founder was significant or marginally significant for half of the models, positively affecting 12-month firm performance. But once the orientation or SEW variables were entered, the founder effect was no longer significant. The one control that remained highly significant through all models was logged company size (in other words, number of employees).

Turning to the main variables of interest, while Model 3, which included all of the business strategies, improved the R^2 from .11 to .14, only causation was shown to be positively associated with 12-month performance. Further, when we replaced exploitation and effectuation with

Table 6.3   *Net associations with prior 12-month performance index (India sample)*

Variables	Model 1	Model 2	Model 3	Model 4	Model 5	Model 6
Controls						
Services	.030	.017	.009	.004	.015	.015
Industry dynamism	.007	−.001	.002	−.005	−.007	−.012
Number of states with operations	.119†	.103	.099	.083	.097	.086
Logged company size	.30***	.282***	.289***	.261***	.288***	.255***
Founder	.147*	.136†	.124†	.086	.143	.119
Owner-manager female	.020	.026	.025	.016	.019	.016
Owner-manager married	.031	.048	.046	.033	.034	.032
Owner-manager education	.006	.010	.009	.007	.010	.015
Business strategies						
Exploration		−.074	−.029	−.062	−.027	−.111*
Exploitation			−.111	−.108	.130†	
Causation		.135*	.120†	.087	.117†	.094
Effectuation			.060	.075	.030	
Orientations						
Growth orientation				.08		.093
Entrepreneurial orientation				.139*		.135*
Long-term orientation				.033		
Socio-emotional wealth						
Family control					.069	
Identification					.015	
Bonds					−.036	
Emotion					.09	
Renewal					.064	
SEW composite measure						.093
Overall model F	3.456***	3.334***	3.046***	2.993***	2.418**	3.34***
R square	.105	.125	.136	.164	.153	.158
Observations	244	244	244	244	244	244

Notes:
Values in the table are standardized OLS regression coefficients (beta values).
† $p \le .10$, * $p \le .05$, ** $p \le .01$, *** $p \le .001$ (two-tailed).

ambidexterity, we found that ambidexterity is significantly *negatively* related to 12-month performance, whether combined with causation and effectuation, with strategy variables, or with the SEW variables (results not included for space reasons).

Regarding the orientation variables, the results show that entrepreneurial orientation is positively significantly related to 12-month performance.

Firms within families

In reference to SEW, the individual dimensions and the composite measure are not significantly related to 12-month performance. However, when the composite measure is entered, exploration becomes *significantly* negatively related to 12-month performance.

Taken together, these results are not very robust in predicting 12-month firm performance. While the R^2 for the US sample testing similar models reached .40, our R^2 only reached .16. The most consistent predictor, besides company size, proved to be entrepreneurial orientation. This led us to wonder if different predictors influence the firm performance of family versus non-family firms in India, particularly given the interesting differences discovered through their mean comparisons in Table 6.2.

In Table 6.4 we present the separate results for family and non-family firms. Given the small sample size, we were careful not to include all of the

Table 6.4 Net associations with prior 12-month performance index – subsample comparison of family and non-family firms in India

Variables	Family Model 1	Non-family Model 2	Family Model 3	Non-family Model 4	Family Model 5	Non-family Model 6
Controls						
Firm size	.027	.292**	−.005	.331**	.043	.281**
States in which firm operates	−.01	.215*	.045	.229*	.001	.215*
Founder presence	−.147	.185*	−.143	.225*	−.131	.192*
Business strategies						
Exploration	−.032	−.099	−.045	−.047	−.049	−.102
Causation	.223*	.042	.244†	.099	.205	.031
Orientations						
Growth oriented	−.037	.137			−.039	.139
Entrepreneurial	.208†	.100			.207†	.103
Socio-emotional wealth						
Family control			−.136	.160†		
Identification			.163	−.060		
Bonds			−.056	−.057		
Renewal			.253*	.017		
SEW composite					.068	.046
Overall model *F*	1.328	4.535***	1.534	3.361***	1.191	3.964***
R square	.113	.249	.163	.243	.117	.250
Observations	80	103	80	103	80	103

Notes:
Values in the table are standardized OLS regression coefficients (beta values).
† $p \leq .10$, * $p \leq .05$, ** $p \leq .01$, *** $p \leq .001$ (two-tailed tests).

variables in any one model and allowed the results from Table 6.2 to guide which variables to include. Several interesting patterns emerged from these analyses that may help explain the inconsistent results in Table 6.3. First, while no controls were significant for family firms in predicting 12-month performance, three controls were highly significant for the non-family firms: firm size, number of states with operations, and founder presence. Additionally, when studying the other non-family firm models we see that these controls are the strongest predictors of non-family firm 12-month performance. The only other variable shown to be marginally significant is family control. This result suggests that those non-family firm owner-managers who are motivated to transfer their firms to the next generation, and thus become family firms, demonstrate marginally better performance than those non-family firms that do not.

For the family firm models, three variables appear to be associated with 12-month performance: causation, entrepreneurial orientation, and the SEW renewal dimension. Thus, these results suggest that family firms that utilize a causation business strategy, have an entrepreneurial orientation, and are motived by the need to renew their firm report the strongest 12-month performance. These results provide support for the contentions in the family business literature that formalized strategic planning (Eddleston et al., 2013), corporate entrepreneurship (Kellermanns and Eddleston, 2006; Eddleston et al., 2012) and a long-term orientation (Zellweger, 2007), distinguish the most successful family firms.

We also ran the same models to explore how business strategies, orientations and SEW are related to 5-year performance (tables available from authors). While the results for the non-family firms did not significantly change (only family control is related to performance), we found that exploration is positively related to family firm 5-year performance. This finding is interesting since the exploration coefficient was negative, although not significant, in the models predicting 12-month performance. This suggests that although an exploration strategy may take some time to gain a return, in the long run those family firms that pursue an exploration strategy have a performance advantage. Therefore, Sharma and Salvato's (2011) argument that family firms need to pursue exploration strategies to ensure that their competitive advantages extend over time appears to be supported.

EXPLORING SEW'S IMPACT ON STRATEGY AND ORIENTATION

Table 6.5 displays the impact of SEW on growth and entrepreneurial orientation as well as on causation and effectuation. To retain our focus on

Firms within families

Table 6.5   The impact of SEW and the FIBER dimensions on orientations and strategy (India sample)

Variables	Growth Orientation			Entrepreneurial Orientation		
	Full Model 1	Family Model 2	Non-family Model 3	Full Model 4	Family Model 5	Non-family Model 6
Controls	Included	Included	Included	Included	Included	Included
SEW Composite	.018	.099	−.005	−.016	.075	−.046
Model F	2.433*	4.847**	.781	5.402***	2.921*	.750
Family Control	−.155*	.045	−.141	−.099	−.054	−.078
Identification	.142†	.038	.216†	−.025	−.127	.035
Bonds	.035	.026	−.051	.023	.089	.003
Emotion	−.046	.018	−.121	.023	.083	−.013
Renewal	.064	−.012	.131	.116†	.173	.077
FIBER Model F	2.551*	2.279*	1.504	3.553***	2.052†	.526
N	236	80	103	236	80	103

Variables	Causation			Effectuation		
	Full Model 7	Family Model 8	Non-family Model 9	Full Model 10	Family Model 11	Non-family Model 12
Controls	Included	Included	Included	Included	Included	Included
SEW Composite	.198**	.264*	.251*	.344***	.465***	.26**
Model F	6.658***	4.753**	2.361†	9.753***	5.762***	3.098*
Family Control	−.050	−.026	−.064	.030	.124	−.115
Identification	.126†	.024	.222*	.097	.173	.076
Bonds	.192**	.312**	.132	.201**	.072	.319**
Emotion	.004	.121	−.047	.133†	.225†	.068
Renewal	.128*	.009	.223*	.136*	.282**	−.006
FIBER Model F	5.248***	3.38**	2.44*	5.715***	4.301***	2.517*
N	236	80	103	236	80	103

Notes:
Values in the table are standardized OLS regression coefficients (beta values).
† $p \leq .10$, * $p \leq .05$, ** $p \leq .01$, *** $p \leq .001$ (two-tailed tests).

the main covariates, the controls used in the previous tables have not been displayed. For the orientation variables, few SEW dimensions are shown to be significant. Regarding growth orientation, the full model indicates that family control is significantly negatively related, and identification is marginally positively related, to growth orientation. Although none of the SEW dimensions are significantly related to family firm growth orientation, identification is marginally positively related to non-family firm growth orientation. Combined, these results suggest that owner-managers who are strongly concerned with the firm's image and do not insist on passing the firm on to the next generation, report the strongest growth orientation. This pattern appears to be most evident for non-family firms.

In regards to entrepreneurial orientation, no SEW dimensions were found to be significant for family or non-family firms. In the full sample model, only renewal is marginally associated with entrepreneurial orientation. Therefore, in looking at the results for growth and entrepreneurial orientation, it can be inferred that SEW is not a strong motivator among Indian owner-managers. These results are in stark contrast to those obtained from the US sample.

The results for causation and effectuation are much stronger than those for the orientation variables. As such, SEW is significantly positively related to causation and effectuation for family and non-family firms. In reference to causation, the full sample shows identification, bonds and renewal to be significant. However, when the subsamples are investigated, we see that while bonds are positively related to family firm causation, identification and renewal are positively related to non-family firm causation. Thus, different SEW dimensions influence causation for family and non-family firms. Strong bonds motivate family firm owner-managers to employ a causation strategy process. In contrast, the importance of a positive firm image and long-term investments motivate non-family firm owner-managers to employ a causation strategy process. When we investigate the subsamples for effectuation, once again we find different dimensions to be associated with family and non-family firm strategy process. Renewal and emotion are significantly related to family firm effectuation, while bonds are significantly related to non-family firm effectuation.

Looking at the results for causation and effectuation together, we see that while bonds are related to family firm causation, they are related to non-family firm effectuation. Additionally, while renewal is associated with non-family firm causation, it is related to family firm effectuation. Therefore, not only do the factors associated with causation and effectuation differ for family and non-family firms in India, but factors that are associated with family firm causation are associated with non-family firm effectuation, and vice versa.

LINKING SEW TO PERCEIVED BUSINESS EFFECTIVENESS AND SATISFACTION

The SEW perspective suggests that family firms are motivated by the non-financial 'affective endowments' associated with firm ownership (Gómez-Mejía et al., 2007). In developing this perspective, Gómez-Mejía et al. (2007) drew from the behavioral agency model (Wiseman and Gómez-Mejía, 1998) to argue that firms make choices depending on the referent point of their dominant principles. SEW has therefore been used to explain the strategic choices of family firms, with the five dimensions of SEW reflecting the different referent points that motivate them. Although our analysis on firm performance did not find any of the SEW dimensions to be significant for the full sample, and for the family firm subsample only renewal was shown to be significant, research on SEW suggests that economic performance is not the only source of wealth that family firms seek. Therefore, given the importance of SEW to family firms and its portrayal as an 'endowment' and source of 'wealth' (Gómez-Mejía et al., 2007; Berrone et al., 2010; 2012), we investigate how SEW influences family and non-family firm owner-managers' perceived business effectiveness and satisfaction.

Table 6.6 shows that the SEW composite is significantly related to owner-managers' perceived business effectiveness and satisfaction for the full sample. When we look at the family and non-family subsamples, the SEW composite is only significantly related to non-family firm owner-managers' effectiveness and satisfaction, and is marginally related to family firm owner-managers' effectiveness. The examination of the SEW dimensions provides insight on these unexpected findings.

When we compare the family and non-family firm subsamples, we see

Table 6.6   The determinants of perceived effectiveness and business satisfaction among SMEs in India

Variables	Perceived Business Effectiveness			Business Satisfaction		
	Full	Family	Non-family	Full	Family	Non-family
Controls (incl performance)	Included	Included	Included	Included	Included	Included
SEW Composite	.213***	.200†	.289**	.210***	.158	.270**
Model *F*	7.046***	3.687**	2.748*	5.584***	1.801	2.981*
Family Control	.144*	.255†	.169†	.110	.158	.121
Identification	.143*	−.119	.367***	.173*	−.116	.403***
Bonds	.052	−.008	.109	.029	−.104	.117
Emotion	.041	.145	−.027	.063	.267†	−.073
Renewal	.018	−.073	.048	.057	−.090	.138
FIBER Model *F*	4.432***	2.523*	3.015**	3.967***	1.609	3.86***
N	236	80	103	236	80	103

Notes:
Values in the table are standardized OLS regression coefficients (beta values).
† $p \leq .10$, * $p \leq .05$, ** $p \leq .01$, *** $p \leq .001$ (two-tailed tests).

that while family control is marginally related to perceived business effectiveness for both family and non-family firms, identification is only significantly related to non-family firms' perceived effectiveness. This effect for non-family firms is particularly strong ($p < .001$), and it is interesting to note that the relationship is negative, although not significant, for family firms. In fact, when we compare the direction of the relationships for each of the SEW dimensions with perceived business effectiveness, we see that all but one (family control) are in the opposite direction for family and non-family firms.

Similarly, for business satisfaction the results show that all but one of the SEW dimensions (family control) are in the opposite direction for family and non-family firms. Only one of the SEW dimensions, emotion, is marginally significantly related to family firms' business satisfaction. In comparison, identification is significantly related to non-family firm owner-managers' business satisfaction ($p < .001$). Therefore, considering these results together it appears that identification is a strong source of perceived business effectiveness and satisfaction for non-family firm owner-managers. Further, our results from Table 6.5 demonstrate that identification is significantly related to non-family firms' growth orientation and causation. Our findings therefore suggest that identification is a key referent point for non-family firms in India.

In regards to family firms in India, our results suggest a more complex pattern whereby the dimensions of SEW appear to be related to different facets of the business. Specifically, while bonds are related to family firm causation, renewal and emotion are related to effectuation. And while family control is associated with family firms' perceived business effectiveness, emotion is related to business satisfaction. These results demonstrate the importance of decoupling the SEW construct. They also suggest that different SEW dimensions can become salient with different business processes and outcomes.

DISCUSSION AND CONCLUSION

In emerging markets, entrepreneurship can become an avenue of escape from unemployment, with India reporting one of the highest levels of 'necessity' entrepreneurship in the world (GEM, 2013). These necessity entrepreneurs provide subsistence for their families as well as employment for family members. Further, because of the strong kinship ties in India, approximately three-quarters of entrepreneurs receive some type of family support for their business (National Knowledge Commission, 2008). It is against this backdrop that we should consider our findings.

Our study suggests that there is no clear performance advantage for family firms in India. Two possible reasons exist: family firms are very heterogeneous (Chua, Chrisman, Steier, and Rau, 2012) so that not all of them obtain resources that lead to a competitive advantage, and non-family firms in India possess similar traits to those generally associated with family firms. More specifically, SEW seemed to matter more to non-family firms than to family firms. For example, the SEW dimension family control is positively associated with non-family firm performance but negatively related to family firm performance, even though the family firms reported significantly higher family control. Thus, SEW considerations are not unique to family firms (at least in India), and SEW helps to explain both family and non-family firm strategy process, perceived business effectiveness and business satisfaction.

Our results also show how the SEW dimensions influence family and non-family firms differently. For family firms, renewal is related to firm performance, bonds are related to causation, emotion and renewal are related to effectuation, family control is related to perceived business effectiveness, and emotion is related to business satisfaction. In comparison, for non-family firms, identification is the major driver of their SEW: it is related to growth orientation, causation, business effectiveness and business satisfaction. Additionally, for non-family firms, family control is related to firm performance and business effectiveness, renewal is related to causation, and bonds are related to effectuation. Interestingly, the variable associated with family firm causation (bonds), is associated with non-family firm effectuation, and while renewal is associated with non-family firm causation, it is associated with family firm effectuation.

In addition to the central role of the family in India, the age of the businesses may help explain some results. The non-family firms are on average only ten years old, whereas the family firms are on average 22.5 years old. Additionally, while 86 percent of the non-family firms are headed by their founder, only 45 percent of the family firms are. These differences may help explain why the non-family firms reported significantly higher growth and entrepreneurial orientation than the family firms. Being closer to their entrepreneurial roots and primarily headed by their founders may necessitate growth and entrepreneurship among the non-family firms. Conversely, because the family firms tended to be older and managed by a succeeding generation, their willingness to take risks associated with growth and entrepreneurship may wane. As family firms move beyond the first generation, they often stress wealth preservation over wealth generation, which promotes conservative behaviors.

Accordingly, the family firms that reported the strongest 12-month performance tended to have the highest entrepreneurial orientation.

Additionally, although family firms reported greater effectuation than non-family firms, those family firms that utilized a causation strategy process had stronger performance. Interestingly, while exploration was negatively related to family firm 12-month performance, it was positively related to 5-year performance. This finding lends support for research that has argued that family firms are able to make more patient investments that have a long payback period (Zellweger, 2007). Indeed, we found that family firms that scored higher on the renewal SEW dimension demonstrated the strongest performance.

In conclusion, while the owner-managers of the family and non-family firms reported similar levels of perceived performance, effectiveness and satisfaction, different factors were found to be influential across the two types of organizations. We found that *non*-family firms in India tend to be motived by SEW, with the family control dimension influencing their performance. Further, different SEW dimensions become salient for family versus non-family firms. Our results therefore highlight the importance of the family to entrepreneurship in India, and the need to further investigate how the family and business interact within the Indian entrepreneurship context.

NOTE

1. Firm performance relative to competitors was assessed by the mean of a 7-item scale, with each item rated from '1 = worse than competitors' to '7 = better than competitors'. The seven items consisted of sales growth, market share, profitability, return on sales, return on assets, return on equity, and cash flow.

REFERENCES

Asian Family Business Report. (2011), 'Asian Family Business Report 2011: Key trends, economic contribution and performance,' retrieved from http://www.scribd.com/doc/71428527/CS-Asian-Family-Report-2011 (accessed July 15, 2014).
Benner, M.J. and M.L. Tushman (2003), 'Exploitation, exploration, and process management: The productivity dilemma revisited,' *Academy of Management Review*, **28** (2), 238–256.
Bergfeld, M.M.H. and F.M. Weber (2011), 'Dynasties of innovation: Highly performing German family firms and the owners' role for innovation,' *International Journal of Entrepreneurship and Innovation Management*, **13** (1), 80–94.
Berrone, P., C. Cruz, and L.R. Gómez-Mejía (2012), 'Socio-emotional wealth in family firms: Theoretical dimensions, assessment approaches, and agenda for future research,' *Family Business Review*, **25** (3), 258–279.
Berrone, P., C. Cruz, L.R. Gómez-Mejía, and M. Larraza-Kintana (2010), 'Socioemotional wealth and corporate responses to institutional pressures: Do

family-controlled firms pollute less?' *Administrative Science Quarterly*, **55** (1), 82–113.

Bertrand, M. and A. Schoar (2006), 'The role of family in family firms,' *The Journal of Economic Perspectives*, **20** (2), 73–96.

Bertrand M., P. Mehta, and S. Mullainathan (2002), 'Ferreting out tunneling: An application to Indian business groups,' *Quarterly Journal of Economics*, **117**, 121–148.

Brinckmann, J., D. Grichnik, and D. Kapsa (2010), 'Should entrepreneurs plan or just storm the castle? A meta-analysis on contextual factors impacting the business planning–performance relationship in small firms,' *Journal of Business Venturing*, **25** (1), 24–40.

Cennamo, C., P. Berrone, C. Cruz, and L.R. Gómez-Mejía (2012), 'Socio-emotional wealth and proactive stakeholder engagement: Why family-controlled firms care more about their stakeholders,' *Entrepreneurship Theory and Practice*, **36** (6), 1153–1173.

Chua, J. H., J.J. Chrisman, L.P. Steier, and S.B. Rau (2012), 'Sources of heterogeneity in family firms: An introduction,' *Entrepreneurship Theory and Practice*, **36** (6), 1103–1113.

Cliff, J. E. (1998), 'Does one size fit all? Exploring the relationship between attitudes towards growth, gender, and business size,' *Journal of Business Venturing*, **13** (6), 523–542.

Cohen, W.M. and D.A. Levinthal (1990), 'Absorptive capacity: A new perspective on learning and innovation,' *Administrative Science Quarterly*, **35** (1), 128–152.

Cruz, C. and M. Nordqvist (2012), 'Entrepreneurial orientation in family firms: A generational perspective,' *Small Business Economics*, **38** (1), 33–49.

Eddleston, K.A. and G.N. Powell (2012), 'Nurturing entrepreneurs' work–family balance: A gendered perspective,' *Entrepreneurship Theory and Practice*, **36** (3), 513–541.

Eddleston, K.A., F.W. Kellermanns, and R. Sarathy (2008), 'Resource configuration in family firms: Linking resources, strategic planning and environmental dynamism to performance,' *Journal of Management Studies*, **45** (1), 26–50.

Eddleston, K.A., F.W. Kellermanns, and T.M. Zellweger (2012), 'Exploring the entrepreneurial behavior of family firms: Does the stewardship perspective explain differences?,' *Entrepreneurship Theory and Practice*, **36** (2), 347–367.

Eddleston, K.A., F.W. Kellermanns, S.W. Floyd, V.L. Crittenden, and W.F. Crittenden (2013), 'Planning for growth: When strategic and succession planning are most beneficial to the future of family firms,' *Entrepreneurship Theory and Practice*, **37** (5), 1177–1202.

Gedajlovic, E., M. Carney, J.J. Chrisman, and F.W. Kellermanns (2012), 'The adolescence of family firm research taking stock and planning for the future,' *Journal of Management*, **38** (4), 1010–1037.

GEM (2013), 'Global Entrepreneurship Monitor Report,' retrieved from http://www.gemconsortium.org/docs/3106/gem-2013-global-report (accessed July 15, 2014).

Gill, A., S.P. Sharma, and H.S. Mand (2011), 'Factors that affect Indian propensity to grow and expand small businesses,' *IUP Journal Of Entrepreneurship Development*, **8** (4), 79–88.

Gómez-Mejía, L.R., K.T. Haynes, M. Núñez-Nickel, K.J. Jacobson, and J. Moyano-Fuentes (2007), 'Socio-emotional wealth and business risks in family-controlled firms: Evidence from Spanish olive oil mills,' *Administrative Science Quarterly*, **52** (1), 106–137.

Haveman, H.A. (1992), 'Between a rock and a hard place: Organizational change and performance under conditions of fundamental environmental transformation,' *Administrative Science Quarterly*, **37** (1), 48–75.

Jaffe, D.T. and S.H. Lane (2004), 'Sustaining a family dynasty: Key issues facing complex multigenerational business- and investment-owning families,' *Family Business Review*, **17** (1), 81–98.

Kellermanns, F.W. and K.A. Eddleston (2006), 'Corporate entrepreneurship in family firms: A family perspective,' *Entrepreneurship Theory and Practice*, **30** (6), 809–830.

Koster, S. and S.K. Rai (2008), 'Entrepreneurship and economic development in a developing country: A case study of India,' *Journal of Entrepreneurship*, **17** (2), 117–137.

KPMG. (2013), 'Global Data Points,' retrieved from www.ffi.org/?page=global datapoints (accessed July 15, 2014).

Le Breton-Miller, I., D. Miller, and R.H. Lester (2011), 'Stewardship or agency? A social embeddedness reconciliation of conduct and performance in public family businesses,' *Organization Science*, **22** (3), 704–721.

Luo, X.R and C.N. Chung (2013), 'Filling or abusing the institutional void? Ownership and management control of public family businesses in an emerging market,' *Organization Science*, **24** (2), 591–613.

Mandelbaum, D.G. (1948), 'The family in India,' *Southwestern Journal of Anthropology*, 123–139.

Miller, D., I. Le Breton-Miller, and B. Scholnick (2008), 'Stewardship vs. stagnation: An empirical comparison of small family and non-family businesses,' *Journal of Management Studies*, **45** (1), 51–78.

Miller, D., I. Le Breton-Miller, R.H. Lester, and A.A. Cannella Jr. (2007), 'Are family firms really superior performers?,' *Journal of Corporate Finance*, **13** (5), 829–858.

Miller, D., J. Lee, S. Chang, and I. Le Breton-Miller (2009), 'Filling the institutional void: The social behavior and performance of family vs. non-family technology firms in emerging markets,' *Journal of International Business Studies*, **40** (5), 802–817.

Morck, R. and B. Yeung (2003), 'Agency problems in large family business groups,' *Entrepreneurship Theory and Practice*, **27** (4), 367–382.

Mosakowski, E. (1997), 'Strategy making under causal ambiguity: Conceptual issues and empirical evidence,' *Organization Science*, **8** (4), 414–442.

National Knowledge Commission. (2008), 'Entrepreneurship in India' retrieved from http://knowledgecommission.gov.in/downloads/documents/NKC_Entre preneurship.pdf (accessed July 15, 2014).

Powell, G.N. and K.A. Eddleston (2013), 'Linking family-to-business enrichment and support to entrepreneurial success: Do female and male entrepreneurs experience different outcomes?,' *Journal of Business Venturing*, **28** (2), 261–280.

PricewaterhouseCoopers (PWC) (2013), 'Family firm: The India perspective,' retrieved from www.pwc.in/. . ./family-business-survey/family-business-survey-2013.pdf (accessed July 15, 2014).

Sarasvathy, S.D. (2001), 'Causation and effectuation: Toward a theoretical shift from economic inevitability to entrepreneurial contingency,' *Academy of Management Review*, **26** (2), 243–263.

Sharma, P. and C. Salvato (2011), 'Commentary: Exploiting and exploring new opportunities over life cycle stages of family firms,' *Entrepreneurship Theory and Practice*, **35** (6), 1199–1205.

Sirmon, D.G. and M.A. Hitt (2003), 'Managing resources: Linking unique resources, management and wealth creation in family firms,' *Entrepreneurship Theory and Practice*, **27** (4), 339–358.

Villalonga, B. and R. Amit (2006), 'How do family ownership, control and management affect firm value?,' *Journal of Financial Economics*, **80** (2), 385–417.

Ward, J.L. (2004), *Perpetuating the Family Business: 50 Lessons Learned from Long Lasting, Successful Families in Business*, New York, USA: Palgrave Macmillan.

Wiseman, R. M. and L.R. Gómez-Mejía (1998), 'A behavioral agency model of managerial risk taking,' *Academy of Management Review*, **23** (1), 133–153.

Yu, D. and Y. Tandon (August 2012), 'India's big problem: Nurturing entrepreneurs,' retrieved from http://www.gallup.com/businessjournal/156143/India-Big-Problem-Nurturing-Entrepreneurs.aspx (accessed July 15, 2014).

Zellweger, T. (2007), 'Time horizon, costs of equity capital, and generic investment strategies of firms,' *Family Business Review*, **20** (1), 1–15.

7. Part I summary: the impact of SEW on family and non-family firms in developed versus emerging economies

P. Devereaux Jennings, Ravi Sarathy,
Kimberly A. Eddleston and Jennifer E. Jennings

The effect of business strategy on firm performance is generally considered to be determined by a firm's changing environment, industry rivalry, and a firm's unique resources and capabilities, with strategy seeking to position a firm within its competitive environment in a manner that leads to superior performance and sustainable competitive advantage (Barney, 1991; Porter 2008). When the firm in question is family owned-and-managed, however, additional goals and operating principles become salient (Salvato and Corbetta, 2014). Along with competitive advantage, family firms care about family centered, non-economic goals such as wealth preservation, family reputation, maintaining influence within the community, and developing a legacy for the next generation (Chrisman, Chua, and Litz, 2004; Chua, Chrisman, and Sharma, 1999; Miller and Le Breton-Miller, 2005).

Part I of this book has focused on this 'familiness' of owner-managed businesses using the well-known, currently popular concept of socio-emotional wealth (SEW), where SEW refers to 'non-financial aspects of the firm that meet the family's affective needs, such as identity, the ability to exercise family influence, and the perpetuation of the family dynasty' (Gómez-Mejía, Haynes, Núñez-Nickel, Jacobson, and Moyano-Fuentes, 2007: 106; see also Berrone, Cruz, and Gómez-Mejía, 2012). Measuring Berrone et al.'s (2012) proposed FIBER dimensions of SEW (in other words, family control, identification, bonds, emotion, and renewal), each country team was able to assess the separate and joint effects of these five dimensions on business orientations, business strategy, and, ultimately, business performance. Given that firms are embedded not only in families but also in country contexts (Carney and Gedajlovic, 2002; Fernandez and Nieto, 2014), each team also considered how those contexts may have impinged upon the findings for the owner-managed businesses in their sample. We now consider the overall pattern of results across the developed and emerging market contexts examined in our multi-country investigation: in other words, the United States, Switzerland and Germany, China, Brazil and India.

EMPHASIS UPON SEW BY COUNTRY CONTEXT AND TYPE OF FIRM

As noted in this book's introduction (Jennings, Eddleston, Jennings and Sarathy, Chapter 1), the first two guiding questions posed about SEW and its relationship to business strategy and performance were: (1) to what extent is SEW preservation and enhancement a motivation within owner-managed firms in general; and, (2) is the concern for the preservation and enhancement of SEW higher within family than non-family firms in particular? Figure 7.1 summarizes the cross-country findings related to these two questions. As indicated, this figure reports the means for both the composite SEW measure (in other words, the average of the FIBER dimensions) as well as the means for the composite measure absent the family control dimension, as some scholars have suggested that a concern about maintaining family control over the firm is quite distinct from the

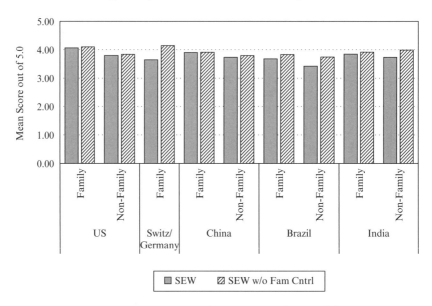

Figure 7.1   SEW composite scores by country and type of firm

other components (for example, Astrachan, Klein, and Smyrnios, 2002; Cliff and Jennings, 2005).

The findings reported in Figure 7.1 indicate that the scores for both measures of SEW are well above the scale's midpoint. In other words, SEW motivations were deemed by the 1372 owner-managers from the various countries to be important to at least some degree in their businesses. Notably, the highest scores were observed for SEW without the family control dimension in Germany, for both measures in the US, and for the measure without family control in India. This first set of results thus runs counter to our expectation that the emphasis placed upon SEW motivations within owner-managed enterprises would be higher within developing than developed economies due to the greater embeddedness of firms within families in the former than the latter contexts (cf., Gras and Nason, forthcoming; Gupta and Levenburg, 2010; Peredo and McLean, 2013; Zellweger, Nason, and Nordqvist, 2012).

Turning to the difference between family and non-family firms, our second question, we pooled the different means in the family versus non-family samples from the countries to see if there was a noticeable difference between them. Corroborating the findings presented visually in Figure 7.1, pooling revealed only marginal differences between the family and non-family firms on both the composite measure of SEW (3.82 for the family firms versus 3.67 for the non-family firms) as well as the measure without family control (3.98 versus 3.84, respectively). Although these findings are consistent with our overarching expectation, the differences are not as pronounced as current discourse about the unique nature of family firms seems to suggest. Why might that be?

One explanation might be that SEW is a broad concept that captures something akin to organizational culture; in other words, the pattern of deeper norms, values and attitudes within a firm (Martin, 1992). Like culture, then, SEW would be important to all types of firms, particularly if concern for maintaining family control were omitted from the construct and its measure. Indeed, a closer examination of the individual FIBER dimensions by country revealed that the highest dimension scores were routinely for identification and emotion, and the lowest for renewal and control. A second explanation might be our samples, which, with the exception of the Switzerland/Germany study, included mostly small and medium-sized enterprises (SMEs) headed by owner-managers who were also the founders. One might presume that SEW would be of greater relevance in such organizations than within larger firms that are no longer headed by their founders. Even if the size-SEW correlations within our samples did not show much evidence for this second explanation, a wider sample of family and non-family firms might do so. We thus encourage other researchers to explore such antecedents of SEW. Our primary concern is with the cross-country consequences of such motivations for business orientations, strategies and performance, to which we now turn.

CROSS-COUNTRY EFFECTS OF SEW ON ORIENTATIONS, STRATEGY AND PERFORMANCE

The second two questions guiding the analyses presented within the Part I chapters were: (3) to what extent do SEW motivations influence standard variables of interest to strategy scholars; and, (4) to what extent do SEW motivations impact firm performance? We begin with the second question; that is, whether there is any evidence of SEW's direct impact on business performance for family and non-family firms. We then explore the various indirect ways that SEW might influence firm performance through its effect upon strategic orientations and business strategies.

Figure 7.2 reports the average perceived performance scores as well as the direct effects of SEW on performance by country and type of firm. The average perceived performance scores are presented relative to the scale's midpoint of 3.0 = 'same as competitors.' Notably, all of the scores are positive but not all that high, meaning that the owner-managers, on the whole, perceived their firms to be performing just above average.[1] As indicated, the highest scores were reported by the owner-managers of family firms in Switzerland/Germany, non-family firms in India and China, and family firms in China. Indeed, the lowest perceived performance scores were reported for family firms in the US, which might be expected given that the US was just exiting the 2008–2011 'Great Recession' and was rebounding more slowly than these other nations.

The coefficients for the direct effects of SEW on perceived firm performance reported in Figure 7.2 correspond to the unstandardized betas from the regression models with the controls and covariates for the orientation and strategy variables. In general, only performance coefficients over 0.15 were statistically significant. Two observations warrant mention. First, and somewhat surprisingly, it appears that the direct effects of SEW on perceived firm performance are relatively low and non-significant in many country family and non-family firm subsamples. Non-family firms in the US and family firms in Germany and China are the exception. Second, contrary to what the family business literature would suggest (for example, Gómez-Mejía et al., 2007; Berrone et al., 2012), the direct effect of SEW upon perceived firm performance does not appear to be consistently higher within family than non-family firms. Indeed, in the US it is higher in the *non*-family firms. The claim that SEW should (and does) make a

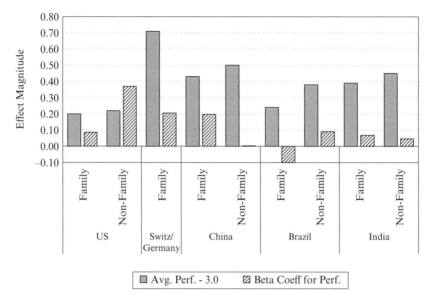

*Figure 7.2   Perceived firm performance and direct effect of SEW by
country and type of firm*

difference for firm performance, especially for family firms, needs further
exploration.

One avenue to explore is whether particular dimensions of SEW had
effects on performance, effects that were perhaps masked by using the
composite score. Each country team assessed the impact of the separate
FIBER dimension on performance. In the US family and non-family
samples, and in the India non-family sample, an emphasis on renewal
was positively associated with business performance. Renewal also had an
impact on performance in German family firms and in both Chinese family
and non-family businesses. Some other dimensions—especially bonds and
emotion—had selective influences on performance. Surprisingly, neither
identification nor family control made much difference in most analyses.

Another avenue to explore is whether SEW influences firm performance
indirectly through strategic orientations and business strategies. Displaying
all of these indirect effects would be far too complex for a single figure or
table. Instead, we briefly summarize the ways in which the composite SEW
measure affected orientations and strategies, and then offer a table of
direct effects for orientations and strategies on performance by country.
In the US, the overall measure of SEW had pervasive effects on orientation and strategies: SEW as a variable was significant and positive in

Firms within families

*Table 7.1   Direct effects of orientations and strategies on perceived firm
performance by country and type of firm*

	US		Switzerland/ Germany	China		Brazil		India	
	Family	Non-family	Family	Family	Non-family	Family	Non-family	Family	Non-family
Growth orientation	.186**	−.037				−.108	.212*	−.039	.139
Entrepreneurial orientation	.066	−.080	.177*	0.170	0.170*	.207†	.095	.207†	.103
Long-term orientation				0.236†	0.285**				
Exploration	.056	.043	.149†	0.239†	0.164†	−.024	.077	−.049	−.102
Exploitation	−.054	.007	.111	−0.138	−0.155	−.118	.25*		
Causation	.122	.253*		−0.004	0.085	.07	.18†	.205	.031
Effectuation	.180*	.117		−0.082	0.087	.29**	.297*		

Notes:
† p ≤ .10, * p ≤ .05, ** p ≤ .01, *** p ≤ .001 (two-tailed tests).

every model. Identification, bonds, and renewal, in particular, had strong effects. By contrast, in Germany, SEW primarily affected entrepreneurial orientation and the effect was primarily manifested (negatively) through family control and bonds. In Brazil, SEW primarily had an impact on entrepreneurial orientation and effectuation as a strategy. Identification, bonds, and renewal, in particular, made a difference for entrepreneurial orientation and effectuation. Finally, in India, while orientations were not affected, both entrepreneurial strategies—causation and effectuation— were affected. As in the US case, in India the primary dimensions that had an impact were identification, bonds, and renewal.[2] Therefore, overall, there is definitely a pattern of SEW influencing at least entrepreneurial orientation and certainly types of entrepreneurial strategy. This finding appears to be consistent with entrepreneurship research that has shown families to be a source of financial capital (Davidsson and Honig, 2003) and social capital for new ventures (Chang et al., 2009).

The effects of orientations and strategies, as the indirect links between SEW and performance, are displayed in Table 7.1. The reported values are the regression coefficients taken from the fully saturated models, along with their levels of significance. Some orientations (typically entrepreneurial and sometimes long-term) influence performance, as do some entrepreneurial strategies (particularly effectuation). Entrepreneurial orientations and entrepreneurial strategies, therefore, appear to be the routes through which SEW influences performance. In fact, given the lack of direct effects of the composite SEW measure in the US, Brazil and India, these indirect avenues are the primary routes for SEW's impact in these country contexts. In Brazil's case, a local saying about doing family business fits this pattern, '*dar um jeitinho,*' which means 'we will find a way.'

REFLECTIONS

Part I of this book has shown ample evidence, then, of the double embeddedness thesis. With respect to embeddedness at the *family* level, the constituent chapters have demonstrated that the orientations, strategies and (in some cases) the performance of owner-managed firms are indeed influenced by SEW considerations. This finding is consistent with other empirical studies that have adopted such a theoretical lens (for example, Berrone, Cruz, Gómez-Mejía, and Larraza-Kintana, 2010; Gómez-Mejía et al., 2007; 2010), yet extends existing work by explicitly measuring the SEW construct. The Part I chapters further extend extant work by assessing and demonstrating the independent and differential effects of the constituent FIBER components conceptualized by Berrone et al. (2012). In keeping with the suppositions of these scholars, it appears that the affective components of SEW matter a great deal for strategic orientations and business strategies. Identification, bonds and renewal, in particular, often exerted direct and indirect effects on perceived firm performance.

In the case of embeddedness at the *country* level, the Part I chapters reveal that SEW motivations and the SEW-performance relationship are indeed sensitive to national context. To our knowledge, no researchers as yet have conducted a systematic, multi-country analysis of SEW and its effects. Our cross-country results are intriguing. Even though the US, Switzerland and Germany are considered to be developed market nations and China, Brazil and India to be emerging market economies (Khanna and Palepu, 2013), China appears to be more similar to the US and Switzerland/Germany than to its two other compatriots. The findings for Brazil and India may be attributable to the higher incidence of necessity entrepreneurship and subsistence-type family enterprises within these countries. Necessity entrepreneurship is known to require different types of financial, human and social capital, in part due to the institutional voids in the countries where it occurs (Bruton, Ahlsrom, and Li, 2010; Jennings, Greenwood, Lounsbury, and Suddaby, 2013). As such, future researchers may want to specify a different set of control variables and re-theorize some of the mechanisms that affect performance for necessity versus opportunity-driven owner-managers (Stenholm, Acs, and Wuebker, 2013).

LIMITATIONS AND NEXT STEPS

Many limitations pertaining to the study's overall design (including its cross-sectional nature, the limited sample of countries and the self-reported data from the owner-managers) will be reviewed in the final chapter of this book (see Jennings, Eddleston, Jennings, and Sarathy, Chapter 14). One limitation that we wish to raise here, specific to the Part I chapters, pertains to the size and complexity of the firms, and thus the types of strategies that we were not able to examine. Because the samples consisted primarily of SMEs, the analyzed firms were not large and complex enough to be diversified. In the US sample, for example, only 25 firms (8 percent) were in more than one industry category, and only 7 (2 percent) were in more than two. In spite of diversification's importance as a family business strategy (Gómez-Mejía et al., 2010; Villalonga and Amit, 2006), we could not assess its effects. Nevertheless, in their review of family business strategies, Salvato and Corbetta (2014) report that the vast majority of family businesses, being SMEs, have, in fact, niche strategies. We encourage others to examine diversification in larger firms and to do so in conjunction with the sets of strategies examined here.

A second limitation pertinent to Part I is its lack of focus on social innovation and sustainability as types of performance outcomes. Today, these outcomes, along with environmental performance, are considered highly legitimate by many firms and countries (McWilliams and Siegel, 2006; 2011). A handful of studies have recently proposed and partially demonstrated that family businesses may be better stewards of the natural environment (Berrone et al., 2010), better at addressing internal social injustices within firms (Cruz, Firfiray, and Gómez-Mejía, 2011), and better community citizens (Gómez-Mejía et al., 2007). Part I of this book only partly engages with this burgeoning conversation, by examining factors often associated with social sustainability; for example, very small firm size, family involvement and the positive treatment of firm members through the development of identity, bonds and emotional resources. Part II of this book explores social sustainability issues more explicitly, by considering whether enterprising is necessarily 'good' for families. More specifically, the chapters in Part II examine the work–family strategies and experiences of business owner-managers in developed versus developing economies—and the implications for their psychological well-being.

NOTES

1. In addition, the reported standard deviations indicate that a quarter of firms in most countries were doing below average.
2. The China team did not report these particular analyses.

REFERENCES

Astrachan, J.H., S.B. Klein, and K.X. Smyrnios (2002), 'The F-PEC scale of family influence: A proposal for solving the family business definition problem,' *Family Business Review*, **15** (1), 45–58.

Barney, J. (1991), 'Firm resources and sustained competitive advantage,' *Journal of Management*, **17** (1), 99–120.

Berrone, P., C. Cruz, and L.R. Gómez-Mejía (2012), 'Socioemotional wealth in family firms: Theoretical dimensions, assessment approaches, and agenda for future research,' *Family Business Review*, **25** (3), 258–279.

Berrone, P., C. Cruz, and L.R. Gómez-Mejía (2014), 'Family-controlled firms and stakeholder management: A socioemotional wealth preservation perspective,' in L. Melin, M. Nordqvist, and P. Sharma (eds), *The SAGE Handbook of Family Business*, London: Sage Publications, pp. 179–195.

Berrone, P., C. Cruz, L.R. Gómez-Mejía, and M. Larraza-Kintana (2010), 'Socioemotional wealth and corporate responses to institutional pressures: Do family-controlled firms pollute less?,' *Administrative Science Quarterly*, **55** (1), 82–113.

Bruton, G.D., D. Ahlstrom, and H.L. Li (2010), 'Institutional theory and entrepreneurship: Where are we now and where do we need to move in the future?,' *Entrepreneurship Theory and Practice*, **34** (3), 421–440.

Carney, M. and E. Gedajlovic (2002), 'The co-evolution of institutional environments and organizational strategies: The rise of family business groups in the ASEAN region,' *Organization Studies*, **23** (1), 1–29.

Chang, E.P., E. Memili, J.J. Chrisman, F.W. Kellermanns, and J.H. Chua (2009), 'Family social capital, venture preparedness, and start-up decisions: A study of Hispanic entrepreneurs in New England,' *Family Business Review*, **22** (3), 279–292.

Chrisman, J.J., J.H. Chua, and R.A. Litz (2004), 'Comparing the agency costs of family and non-family firms: Conceptual issues and exploratory evidence,' *Entrepreneurship Theory and Practice*, **28** (4), 335–354.

Chua, J.H., J.J. Chrisman, and P. Sharma (1999), 'Defining the family business by behavior,' *Entrepreneurship Theory and Practice*, **23** (4), 19–40.

Cliff, J.E. and P.D. Jennings (2005), 'Commentary on the multidimensional degree of family influence construct and the F-PEC measurement instrument,' *Entrepreneurship Theory and Practice*, **29** (3), 341–347.

Cruz, C., S. Firfiray, and L.R. Gómez-Mejía (2011), 'Socioemotional wealth and human resource management (HRM) in family-controlled firms,' *Research in Personnel and Human Resources Management*, **30**, 159–217.

Davidsson, P. and B. Honig (2003), 'The role of social and human capital among nascent entrepreneurs,' *Journal of Business Venturing*, **18** (3), 301–331.

Fernandez, Z. and M.J. Nieto (2014), 'Internationalization of family firms,' in

L. Melin, M. Nordqvist, and P. Sharma (eds), *The SAGE Handbook of Family Business*, London: Sage Publications, pp. 403–422.

Gómez-Mejía, L.R., M. Makri, and M.L. Kintana (2010), 'Diversification decisions in family-controlled firms,' *Journal of Management Studies*, **47** (2), 223–252.

Gómez-Mejía, L.R., C. Cruz, P. Berrone, and J. De Castro (2011), 'The bind that ties: Socioemotional wealth preservation in family firms,' *The Academy of Management Annals*, **5** (1), 653–707.

Gómez-Mejía, L.R., K.T. Haynes, M. Núñez-Nickel, K.J. Jacobson, and J. Moyano-Fuentes (2007), 'Socio-emotional wealth and business risks in family-controlled firms: Evidence from Spanish olive oil mills,' *Administrative Science Quarterly*, **52** (1), 106–137.

Gras, D. and R.S. Nason (forthcoming), 'Bric by bric: The role of the family household in sustaining a venture in impoverished Indian slums,' *Journal of Business Venturing*.

Gupta, V. and N. Levenburg (2010), 'A thematic analysis of cultural variations in family businesses: The CASE project,' *Family Business Review*, **23** (2), 155–169.

Jennings, P.D., R. Greenwood, M.D. Lounsbury, and R. Suddaby (2013), 'Institutions, entrepreneurs, and communities: A special issue on entrepreneurship,' *Journal of Business Venturing*, **28** (1), 1–9.

Kellermanns, F.W., K.A. Eddleston, and T.M. Zellweger (2012), 'Extending the socioemotional wealth perspective: A look at the dark side,' *Entrepreneurship Theory and Practice*, **36** (6), 1175–1182.

Khanna, T. and K. Palepu (2013), *Winning in Emerging Markets: A Road Map for Strategy and Execution*, Boston, MA: Harvard Business Press.

Martin, J. (1992), *Cultures in Organizations: Three Perspectives*, Oxford, UK: Oxford University Press.

McWilliams, A. and D.S. Siegel (2011), 'Creating and capturing value strategic corporate social responsibility, resource-based theory, and sustainable competitive advantage,' *Journal of Management*, **37** (5), 1480–1495.

McWilliams, A., D.S. Siegel, and P.M. Wright (2006), 'Corporate social responsibility: Strategic implications,' *Journal of Management Studies*, **43** (1), 1–18.

Miller, D. and I. Le Breton-Miller (2005), *Managing for the Long Run: Lessons in Competitive Advantage from Great Family Businesses*, Boston, MA: Harvard Business Press.

Peredo, A.M. and M. McLean (2013), 'Indigenous development and the cultural captivity of entrepreneurship,' *Business and Society*, **52** (4), 592–620.

Porter, M.E. (2008), 'The five competitive forces that shape strategy,' *Harvard Business Review*, **86** (1), 25–40.

Salvato, C. and G. Corbetta (2014), 'Strategic content and process in family business,' in L. Melin, M. Nordqvist, and P. Sharma (eds), *The SAGE Handbook of Family Business*, London: Sage Publications, pp. 295–320.

Stenholm, P., Z.J. Acs, and R. Wuebker (2013), 'Exploring country-level institutional arrangements on the rate and type of entrepreneurial activity,' *Journal of Business Venturing*, **28** (1), 176–193.

Villalonga, B. and R. Amit (2006), 'How do family ownership, control and management affect firm value?,' *Journal of Financial Economics*, **80** (2), 385–417.

Zellweger, T.M., R.S. Nason, and M. Nordqvist (2012), 'From longevity of firms to transgenerational entrepreneurship of families: Introducing family entrepreneurial orientation,' *Family Business Review*, **25** (2) 136–155.

PART II

Family influences upon business owner-managers in diverse country contexts

8. The work–family interface strategies and experiences of US owner-managers: implications for satisfaction and perceived effectiveness

Jennifer E. Jennings and
P. Devereaux Jennings

INTRODUCTION

This chapter focuses upon the work–family interface (WFI) strategies, experiences and outcomes of enterprising families in the United States. Enterprising families are family households comprised of at least one individual who is involved in owning and managing a business (Heck and Trent, 1999). Despite their use of different definitions, methodologies and data sources, several groups of researchers have produced relatively similar estimates of the proportion of US households engaged in entrepreneurial activity since the 1980s. Utilizing data collected from the nation's tri-annual Survey of Consumer Finances (SCF), for instance, Kennickell and Shack-Marquez (1992) estimated the proportion at 14.2 percent in 1983. Using primary data obtained from their own household survey, Heck and Trent (1999) estimated the proportion at 10.0 percent in 1997. Based upon data provided by the subsequent tri-annual SCF, Bucks, Kennickell and Moore (2006) estimated the proportion at 11.5 percent in 2004. And most recently, Jennings, Breitkreuz, and James (2013) combined census data with the rates of entrepreneurial activity provided by the Global Entrepreneurship Monitor (GEM) to estimate the proportion at 10.5 percent in 2010.

At first glance these incidence rates might seem surprising low—especially considering how the US is typically portrayed within the popular press as one of the most entrepreneurial countries in the world (as noted by Shane, 2008). Given the size of the country's population, however, the proportions nevertheless equate to a very large number of households engaged in entrepreneurial activity. Moreover, given the extensive policy interest and government funding devoted to fostering and supporting entrepreneurship, the number and proportion of enterprising families within the US is bound to increase in the future. At present, however, very little is known about these families, in general, or, more specifically, whether business ownership is 'good' for their members (cf. Jennings et al., 2013; Olson, Zuiker, Danes, Stafford, Heck, and Duncan, 2003).

This chapter offers a rare glimpse into the characteristics of business-owning households within the US, based upon data collected from an online survey completed in the fall of 2012 by a stratified sample of 309 owner-managers across the country. After reporting basic demographic data on the participating business owners and their households, we present descriptive information on the extent to which they consider themselves to be effective and satisfied with respect to various aspects of their lives. We then present details on their WFI strategies and experiences. This is followed by a set of multivariate analyses that sheds light on the factors associated with these indicators of personal well-being within and across the family and business domains. In sum, this chapter offers not only a portrait of enterprising households in the US today—but also unique insight into the family, business and WFI characteristics that enable some business owners in this country to feel highly effective and satisfied with various aspects of their lives.

DATA COLLECTION

As noted within the most recent GEM report, 'the topic of well-being has been gaining presence rapidly in social sciences and economics' (Amoró and Bosma, 2014: 62). As yet, however, few publicly accessible datasets on entrepreneurs contain measures of their personal well-being (the 2013 GEM study is a notable exception in this regard)—let alone detailed information on their household characteristics and WFI strategies and experiences. We therefore conducted a primary data collection effort to obtain such information, administering a custom-designed survey to owner-managers across the United States. Although we designed the survey ourselves, we contracted its implementation to Qualtrics, one of the world's leading suppliers of online survey administration services. We requested that Qualtrics use their network of affiliated panel providers to secure responses from owner-managers of small and medium-sized enterprises (SMEs) across a variety of industries and geographic regions within the US, stratified by firm size as follows: micro (0–10 employees), small (11–250 employees), and medium (251–500 employees). We also requested responses from roughly equivalent proportions of males and females in order to facilitate future gender-based comparisons. Owner-managers from 309 separate SMEs completed the survey.

DEMOGRAPHIC CHARACTERISTICS OF THE BUSINESS OWNERS AND THEIR HOUSEHOLDS

Of the 309 owner-managers who participated in the US-based study, 158 (51.1 percent) indicated that they were male and 149 (48.2 percent) indicated that they were female (two values were missing). It is important to note that these almost-equivalent proportions are due to the study's stratified design, which over-sampled firms headed by women so that there would be a sufficient number available for potential subsample analyses. According to *The State of Women-Owned Business Report* prepared by American Express OPEN/Womenable, the estimated proportion of majority female-owned firms in the US was 30.0 percent in 2012. Notably, however, the estimated proportion of firms that are either majority women-owned or equally owned by a man and a woman—46.0 percent—is very close to the percentage of female participants in our sample.

Of the 307 participants who provided information on their highest education level, almost half (46.0 percent) indicated that they had completed a bachelor's degree at a college or university. Approximately one in five had either earned only a high school diploma (19.7 percent) or obtained a master's or doctorate degree (18.8 percent). The remaining 14.9 percent reported that they had completed an apprenticeship program after high school. On balance, then, the majority of the business owners in the US sample were quite highly educated.

Two-thirds (66.0 percent) of the participating owner-managers indicated that they had a spouse or marital-like partner. Less than half (44.2 percent) had children under the age of 18 living in their households. The number of children ranged from zero to six, with most respondents mentioning only one (16.6 percent) or two (16.6 percent). Single-parent households constituted 8.4 percent of the sample.

We were fortunate in being able to obtain personal and household income data from all but two and three of the participants, respectively. Measured by ten ordinal categories, both types of income data ranged from less than $25,000 USD to over $1 million USD. The means of $60,000–$74,999 USD for personal income and $75,000–$99,000 USD for household income were highly similar and the two variables were highly correlated (Spearman's *rho* = .84, *p* ≤ .001), which suggests that many of the owner-managers in the US sample were the primary (if not sole) economic providers for their families. Notably, fewer than one in three of the participants (29.3 percent) reported personal incomes over $100,000 USD and fewer than four in ten (37.9 percent) reported household incomes over this amount.

The fact that the majority of the respondents reported personal and household income levels below the $100,000 USD level is partially attributable to the study's stratified design of over-sampling female business owners. As noted in Jennings and Brush's (2013) recent review of the women's entrepreneurship literature, research consistently demonstrates that businesses headed by women tend to be smaller than those headed by men, consequently generating lower levels of income for their owners. Indeed, our analysis revealed not only significant and positive correlations between the two income measures and indicators of business size,[1] but also significant and negative correlations between the business size indicators and the owner-manager's sex when coded 1 = female, 0 = male.[2]

KEY INDICATORS OF PERSONAL WELL-BEING: PERCEIVED EFFECTIVENESS AND SATISFACTION

The income data summarized above could have been included in this section on outcomes in the family domain, as it is clearly an important economic outcome for those engaged in entrepreneurial activity. Indeed, several conceptual and empirical studies of the relationship between business ownership and household financial wealth already exist (see, for example, Carter, 2011; Haynes, Onochie, and Musje, 2007; Loscocco and Leicht, 1993). As noted by Rindova, Barry, and Ketchen (2009), however, considerable research indicates that entrepreneurship is not pursued solely (or even primarily) for economic gain. Thus, following calls for a more holistic approach to the conceptualization and measurement of outcomes associated with business ownership (Amoró and Bosma, 2014; Davidsson, 2004; Shane, 2012)—especially when considering the impact upon families (Jennings et al., 2013; Stafford, Duncan, Danes, and Winter, 1999)—in this section we focus upon key *non*-economic outcomes. More specifically, we report findings for perceived effectiveness and satisfaction within and across the domains of family and business.

For the *separate indicators of perceived effectiveness*, we asked the respondents to report how effective they considered themselves to date: (1) as a family member, (2) as a business owner-manager, and (3) in balancing the various aspects of their lives. Following Waismel-Manor, Moen, and Sweet (2002), each of the three items was rated on a scale ranging from 0 to 100. To assess the extent to which the respondents possessed *concurrent perceptions of effectiveness* within and across the family and business domains, we created a composite measure as follows. Following Jennings, Jennings and Sharifian (forthcoming), we first recoded each of the three constituent items dichotomously, assigning respondents a value of 1 if they reported a score of at least 80 out of 100 on the item, 0 if not. We then summed the three dichotomous measures and recoded the aggregate score such that a sum of 0 was deemed to reflect 'low concurrent perceived effectiveness,' sums of 1 or 2 were deemed to reflect 'moderate concurrent perceived effectiveness,' and a sum of 3 was deemed to reflect 'high concurrent perceived effectiveness.'

A parallel procedure was adopted to create the *separate indicators of perceived satisfaction* as well as the *concurrent satisfaction measure*. The aggregate ordinal measures of concurrent effectiveness and concurrent satisfaction were highly and significantly correlated (Spearman's *rho* = .72, $p \leq .001$). Table 8.1 summarizes the findings.

The findings reported in the top half of Table 8.1 provide insight into the question: 'To what degree to owner-managers in the US consider themselves *effective* within and across the domains of family and business?' The results presented in the first three rows alone suggest that the answer to this question is: 'To a fairly high degree.' As indicated, the majority of the respondents (68.6 percent, 59.5 percent, and 52.4 percent respectively) reported a score of at least 80 out of 100 on the separate indicators of perceived effectiveness as a family member, business owner and in balancing the two roles. The findings for the composite measure are also revealing. Although the majority were coded as reporting either a low (18.8 percent) or moderate (42.7 percent) level of concurrent effectiveness within and across the family and business domains, a substantial proportion (38.2 percent) were coded as expressing a high level of concurrent perceived effectiveness (in other words, scores of at least 80 out of 100 on each of the three constituent items).

The findings reported in the bottom half of Table 8.1 offer insight into the question: 'To what extent are owner-managers in the US *satisfied* within and across the domains of family and business?' As in the above case, the results suggest that the answer is: 'To a fairly great extent.' As indicated, on each of the separate indicators of perceived satisfaction, the majority of the respondents reported a score at or above 80 out of 100. Moreover, although the majority, in total, were coded as expressing either a low (22.0 percent) or moderate (37.2 percent) level of concurrent satisfaction within and across the family and business domains, once again a substantial proportion (40.1 percent) was deemed to exhibit a high level of

*Table 8.1   Perceived effectiveness and satisfaction within and across family
             and business domains (US sample)*

Indicators and Levels of Composite Measures	N	Mean/%	S.D.	Min	Max	% with Score ≥ 80
Perceived Effectiveness						
Separate Constituent Indicators						
Perceived effectiveness as a family member	309	80.19	19.32	0	100	68.6%
Perceived effectiveness as a business owner	309	77.06	18.66	3	100	59.5%
Perceived effectiveness in balancing family and business	308	74.29	21.24	0	100	52.4%
Levels of Composite Measure						
Low concurrent perceived effectiveness	58	18.8%				
Moderate concurrent perceived effectiveness	132	42.7%				
High concurrent perceived effectiveness	118	38.2%				
Perceived Satisfaction						
Separate Constituent Indicators						
Perceived satisfaction as a family member	308	78.39	22.00	0	100	66.0%
Perceived satisfaction as a business owner	308	76.20	21.20	1	100	58.3%
Perceived satisfaction in balancing family and business	309	73.12	22.81	0	100	52.1%
Levels of Composite Measure						
Low concurrent perceived satisfaction	68	22.0%				
Moderate concurrent perceived satisfaction	115	37.2%				
High concurrent perceived satisfaction	124	40.1%				

concurrent perceived satisfaction (in other words, scores of at least 80 out of 100 on each of the three constituent items).

In sum, approximately 4 in 10 of the business owners who participated in the US study considered themselves to be highly and concurrently *effective* within and across the family and business domains. Likewise, an almost identical proportion considered themselves to be highly and contemporaneously *satisfied* within and across the two domains. The implication, of course, is that approximately 6 in 10 did not perceive themselves to be highly and simultaneously effective or satisfied as family members, business owners and in balancing the two roles. The remainder of this chapter is dedicated to exploring the factors associated with these indicators of personal well-being.

WFI EXPERIENCES AND STRATEGIES

We are especially interested in factors at the intersection of the family and business domains. Considerations of how business owners experience and manage these overlapping spheres are central within several prominent models of family enterprise (for example, Gersick, Davis, McCollom Hampton, and Lansberg, 1997; Lansberg, 1983; Stafford et al., 1999). Attention to WFI considerations is also evident in conceptual frameworks depicting relationships between family factors and entrepreneurial processes and outcomes (for example, Aldrich and Cliff, 2003; Jennings and McDougald, 2007). These interface considerations are also starting to appear with increased frequency within empirical work in the entrepreneurship literature (for example, Eddleston and Powell, 2012; Jennings, Hughes, and Jennings, 2010; McGowan, Redeker, Cooper, and Greenan, 2012; Powell and Eddleston, 2013; Shelton, 2006).

Cognizant of the debate about whether work and family roles and commitments are depleting versus enhancing (Powell, 2011), we adopt an agnostic stance in this chapter. We start by presenting data on the degree of family-to-business conflict *and* enrichment experienced by the US business owners in our sample. We then provide descriptive information on a number of strategies for managing the work–family interface. Guided primarily by Jennings and McDougald's (2007) framework, these consist of: (1) individual-level strategies regarding time distribution, segmentation versus integration, and identification with the business; and, (2) household-level considerations such as the instrumental support provided by family members as well as the traditionalism and fairness in the division of domestic labor. We conclude with a multivariate regression analysis to assess which of these strategies are most strongly related to experienced family-to-business conflict and/or enrichment. Our descriptive findings and multivariate regression results are presented in Tables 8.2 and 8.3, respectively.

Family-to-Business Conflict and Enrichment

Family-to-business conflict was measured by the mean of a 6-item, Likert-type scale (α = .92). Three of the items, adapted from Netemeyer,

Table 8.2 Work–family interface experiences and strategies (US sample)

Variables	α	Mean	S.D.	Min	Max	% with Score
Family-to-business conflict	.92	2.63	0.98	1	5	≥ 4 (agree) = 13.3%
Family-to-business enrichment	.94	3.82	0.81	1	5	≥ 4 (agree) = 55.0%
Time devoted to the family sphere	n/a	16.47	11.86	0	90	≥ 20 hrs/wk = 38.5%
Time devoted to the business sphere	n/a	43.06	10.03	1	100	≥ 40 hrs/wk = 65.4%
Segmentation of family and business roles	.86	3.11	0.96	1	5	≥ 4 (agree) = 26.5%
Identification with the business	.92	4.21	0.64	1	5	≥ 4 (agree) = 70.2%
Instrumental support from family members	.92	3.46	1.02	1	5	≥ 4 (agree) = 40.5%
Traditionalism in division of household labor	.89	3.19	0.69	1	4	≥ 3.5 (mainly F) = 43.7%
Fairness in division of household labor	n/a	3.32	0.81	1	4	≥ 4 (very fair) = 50.5%

Table 8.3 Determinants of family-to-business conflict and enrichment (US sample)

Variables	Family-to-Business Conflict		Family-to-Business Enrichment	
	Model 1	Model 2	Model 3	Model 4
Individual and household-level control variables				
Female	0.01	−0.05	0.09	0.06
Education level	0.04	0.05	0.01	−0.05
Married or marital-like relationship	−0.16*	−0.11†	0.11†	0.02
Number of children in household	0.07	0.02	0.06	0.09
Household income	0.11	0.05	−0.08	−0.02
Firm-level control variables				
Founder-led firm	−0.09	−0.08	0.00	0.03
Family firm	0.07	0.02	0.07	−0.07
Firm age	−0.18**	−0.16*	−0.01	0.02
Firm size	0.12†	0.12†	0.09	0.07
Firm performance	0.06	0.08	0.14*	0.07
High-growth orientation	−0.08	−0.09	0.18**	0.08
Manufacturing firm	0.09	0.06	0.15*	0.05
General service firm	0.09	0.07	0.03	0.03
Professional service firm	0.03	−0.04	−0.08	−0.04
WFI strategies and experiences				
Time devoted to the family sphere		0.05		0.12*
Time devoted to the business sphere		0.00		−0.16**
Segmentation of family and business roles		−0.02		0.18**
Identification with the business		0.05		−0.01
Instrumental support from family members		0.03		0.48***
Traditional division of household labor		−0.12		0.03
Fairness in the division of household labor		−0.31***		0.07
Overall model *F*	1.63†	2.35***	2.97***	7.74***
R squared	.08	.17	.14	.40

Notes:
Values in the table are standardized OLS regression coefficients (beta values).
† $p \leq .10$, * $p \leq .05$, ** $p \leq .01$, *** $p \leq .001$ (two-tailed tests).

Boles, and McMurrian (1996), tapped behavioral conflict. An example is: 'Household/family commitments interfere with my ability to perform business-related duties.' The other three items, developed specifically for this study, tapped affective conflict, with an example being: 'I feel frustrated when my household/family responsibilities interfere with my work.' Each item was rated from '1 = strongly disagree' to '5 = strongly agree.' The findings reported in Table 8.2 indicate that most of the business owners in the US sample were not experiencing a high degree of family-to-business conflict. The sample mean of 2.63, for example, is below the scale's mid-point of '3 = neither agree nor disagree.' Moreover, in only 13.3 percent of the cases was the respondent's score at or above '4 = agree.'

Family-to-business enrichment was measured by the mean of a 6-item, Likert-type scale (α = .94) adapted from Carlson, Kacmar, Wayne, and Grzywacz (2006). As in the above case, three of the items tapped perceived behavioral enrichment, an example being: 'My involvement in my family requires me to be as focused as possible at work, which helps make me a better businessperson.' Likewise, the other three items tapped perceived affective enrichment. An example here is: 'My involvement with my family makes me cheerful and this helps me be a better businessperson.' Each item was rated from '1 = strongly disagree' to '5 = strongly agree.' The findings reported in Table 8.2 indicate that the majority of the business owners in the US sample experienced a high degree of family-to-business enrichment. The sample mean of 3.82, for example, is very close to the scale value of '4 = agree'; moreover, 55.0 percent of the respondents scored at or above this value.

Individual-level Strategies

Time devoted to the family sphere was measured by a single item—the number of hours that the respondent estimated spending per week on household-related tasks. Although there are recognized weaknesses in this measure, such as susceptibility to overestimation and discrepancy between marital partners (Yodanis, 2005), it has nevertheless been used in previous studies of entrepreneurship and the WFI (for example, Cliff, 1998; Jennings et al., 2010; Loscocco and Leicht, 1993). As indicated in Table 8.2, participants in the US study estimated spending 16.47 hours per week, on average, on household-related tasks. Over one-third (38.5 percent) reported that they dedicated at least 20 hours to such tasks in a typical week.

Time devoted to the business sphere was measured by a parallel item, the number of hours that the respondent estimated spending per week on business-related tasks, which has also been used in other studies of entrepreneurship and the WFI (for example, Jennings et al., 2010,; Powell and Eddleston, 2013). As indicated in Table 8.2, participants in the US study estimated spending 43.06 hours per week, on average, in the business sphere. Indeed, almost two-thirds (65.4 percent) were actively involved with their business on at least a full-time basis, putting in 40 hours or more during a typical week.

Segmentation was measured by the mean of three items ($\alpha = .86$) adapted from several WFI studies (Carlson, Kacmar, and Williams, 2000; Kreiner, 2006; Powell and Greenhaus, 2010). An illustrative item is, 'In reality, I often leave household/family issues behind when I'm at work.' The phrase 'In reality' was inserted at the beginning of each item to help focus the respondent on their experienced rather than preferred degree of segmentation between family and business roles. Each item was rated from '1 = strongly disagree' to '5 = strongly agree.' As indicated in Table 8.2, the sample mean ended up being very close to the scale's midpoint of '3 = neither agree nor disagree.' Approximately one-quarter of the participants (26.5 percent) could be deemed as enacting a segmentation strategy, with scores at or above the value of '4 = agree.'

An owner-manager's degree of *identification* with his/her business was measured by the mean of a 12-item, Likert-type scale ($\alpha = .92$) adapted from O'Reilly and Chatman (1986), as suggested by Berrone, Cruz, and Gómez-Mejía (2012). An example is: 'If I were describing myself, the firm would likely be something I would mention.' Each item was rated from '1 = strongly disagree' to '5 = strongly agree.' The findings reported in Table 8.2 indicate that the majority of the business owners in the US sample identified very highly with their firms. Not only did the sample mean of 4.21 fall above the scale value of '4 = agree,' but a large percentage of the respondents (70.2 percent) scored at or above this value.

Household-level Considerations

We measured the *instrumental support provided by family members* for the respondent's role of business owner by the mean of a 5-item, Likert-type scale ($\alpha = .92$) developed by Powell and Eddleston (2013). Illustrative items include: 'The members of my family who do not officially work in the business can be counted on to help out if something unexpected happens in this business' and 'The members of my family who do not officially work in the business often give me useful feedback and ideas concerning this business.' Each item was rated from '1 = strongly disagree' to '5 = strongly agree.' The findings reported in Table 8.2 indicate that many of the business owners in the US sample experienced a high level of instrumental support from the members of their families. Not only did the sample mean of 3.46 fall above the scale's midpoint, but 40.5 percent of the respondents had a score at or above the scale value of '4 = agree.'

We measured *traditionalism in the division of household labor* by the mean of a 4-item scale (α = .89) that Yodanis (2005) developed for capturing the distribution of housework. The respondent indicated who was responsible for four tasks (shopping for groceries, deciding what to have for dinner, doing the laundry and caring for the sick) by checking one of the following responses: '4 = always or usually the woman,' '3 = equally,' '2 = always or usually the man' or '1 = a third person (hired help).' As indicated in Table 8.2, the sample mean ended up being very close to the value of '3 = equally.' A sizeable proportion of the respondents (43.7 percent), however, could be deemed as living in a traditional household given that their scores fell at or above 3.5.

Perceived fairness in the division of household labor was measured by the respondent's response to the follow-up question, 'How fair do you feel that this division of household labor is for yourself?,' which was adapted from Milkie and Peltola (1999). The response categories ranged from '1 = very unfair' to '4 = very fair.' The findings reported in Table 8.2 reveal that many of the business owners in the US sample considered the division of labor in their households to be fair. Not only did the sample mean of 3.32 fall above the value of '3 = somewhat fair,' but just over half of the participants (50.5 percent) perceived the division of labor in their households to be very fair.

Determinants of Family-to-Business Conflict and Enrichment

In this subsection we investigate which of the above-noted set of individual-level strategies and household-level considerations are most strongly associated with the extent of family-to-business conflict and enrichment reported by the business owners. We examine these associations net of standard demographic characteristics pertaining to the owner-managers and their households as well as key characteristics of their firms.[3] The results of our multivariate ordinary least squares (OLS) analysis are presented in Table 8.3.

The findings summarized within Models 1 and 2 of Table 8.3 reveal surprisingly few statistically significant relationships for family-to-business *conflict*. Beyond the significant control variables of marital status, firm age and firm size, perceived fairness in the division of household labor emerged as the only other significant covariate. As indicated by its negative coefficient, business owners in the US who perceived greater fairness in the way that tasks were divided within their households also tended to report lower levels of family-to-business conflict.

In contrast, the findings reported in Models 3 and 4 of Table 8.3 reveal quite a few statistically significant associations for family-to-business *enrichment*. Although none of the control variables remained significant in the full model, four of the seven work–family interface variables were so. More specifically, business owners in the US who reported a higher level of family-to-business enrichment tended to spend more time in the family sphere and to devote fewer hours to the business sphere—and to report greater segmentation between the two domains as well as more instrumental support from family members. As indicated by the standardized beta coefficients, the most influential of these was the instrumental support variable. Combined, the entire set of variables explained 40.0 percent of the variance in perceived family-to-business enrichment.

FACTORS ASSOCIATED WITH PERCEIVED EFFECTIVENESS AND SATISFACTION

Having explored the factors associated with family-to-business conflict and enrichment, we turn now to investigating their relationships' perceived effectiveness and satisfaction. In each case we focus upon the composite measure of the outcome variable; in other words, the degree to which a business owner considers him/herself to be concurrently effective or concurrently satisfied within and across the family and business domains. Given that these composite measures consisted of three ordinal levels (low, moderate and high), the models were estimated by multinomial logistic regression. We ran three models for each outcome measure: (1) a baseline model of controls; (2) a model with the controls plus the block of WFI experience and strategy variables included; and (3) a full model containing all of these variables plus family-to-business conflict and enrichment. Two columns of estimates corresponding to the moderate and high outcome levels are provided for each model (the low level was selected as the holdout referent category). The complete set of models appears in Tables 8.4 and 8.5. In the interest of brevity we focus below upon the findings for a high level of each outcome variable.

As indicated in Table 8.4, two of the control variables were consistently and positively associated with a high level of *concurrent effectiveness*. Notably, one was in the family sphere (number of children) and the other was in the business sphere (firm performance). Several of the WFI strategy and experience variables exhibited significant associations. More specifically, business owners in the US who reported a high level of concurrent effectiveness also reported spending fewer hours on household tasks, a higher degree of identification with their business and

Table 8.4 *Factors associated with composite measure of perceived effectiveness (US sample)*

Variables	Model 1		Model 2		Model 3	
	Mod	High	Mod	High	Mod	High
Control variables						
Female	0.91*	0.84*	0.75	1.08†	0.83	1.19
Education level	0.09	0.15	0.05	0.09	0.08	0.20
Married or marital-like relationship	0.22	0.38	0.02	0.13	-0.17	-0.16
Number of children in household	0.34†	0.35†	0.34	0.42†	0.32	0.42†
Household income	-0.14	-0.12	-0.07	-0.04	-0.05	-0.02
Founder-led firm	0.30	1.32*	0.49	1.35†	0.37	0.96
Family firm	0.21	0.12	-0.18	-0.38	-0.01	-0.27
Firm age	0.02	0.02	0.02	0.02	0.02	0.01
Firm size	0.00	0.00	0.00	0.00	0.00	0.00
Firm performance	0.55***	0.82***	0.48**	0.69***	0.51**	0.82***
High-growth orientation	0.03	0.04	0.02	0.01	0.02	-0.02
Manufacturing firm	0.33	-0.22	0.14	-0.35	0.26	-0.18
General service firm	-0.12	-0.47	-0.25	-0.67	-0.11	-0.67
Professional service firm	-0.30	-0.93	-0.15	-0.63	-0.01	-0.71

WFI strategies and experiences				
Time devoted to the family sphere	−0.04*	−0.04*	−0.04*	−0.03†
Time devoted to the business sphere	0.01	0.01	0.01	0.01
Segmentation of family and business roles	−0.18	−0.34	−0.23	−0.35
Identification with the business	0.61†	0.89**	0.45	0.76*
Instrumental support from family members	0.41†	0.52*	0.37	0.45†
Traditional division of household labor	0.49	−0.08	0.48	−0.33
Fairness in the division of household labor	0.40	0.40	0.39	0.01
Family-to-business conflict and enrichment				
Family-to-business conflict			−0.30	−1.09***
Family-to-business enrichment			0.20	0.42
−2LL Chi-square	51.91**	83.90***	108.32***	
Nagelkerke R-square	.19	.30	.39	

Notes:
Values in the table are unstandardized multinomial logistic regression coefficients.
† $p \leq .10$, * $p \leq .05$, ** $p \leq .01$, *** $p \leq .001$ (two-tailed tests).

143

Table 8.5   *Factors associated with composite measure of perceived satisfaction (US sample)*

Variables	Model 1		Model 2		Model 3	
	Mod	High	Mod	High	Mod	High
Control variables						
Female	0.28	0.01	−0.21	0.12	−0.37	0.03
Education level	−0.08	0.06	−0.19	−0.08	−0.11	0.05
Married or marital-like relationship	0.24	0.47	0.18	0.41	−0.01	0.12
Number of children in household	0.29†	−0.14	0.37†	0.01	0.38	−0.04
Household income	−0.12	−0.00	−0.05	0.08	0.05	0.20
Founder-led firm	0.40	1.71**	0.72	1.91**	0.84	1.99**
Family firm	0.53	0.10	0.36	−0.18	0.78	0.08
Firm age	0.02	0.02	0.01	0.02	0.00	0.00
Firm size	0.00	0.00	0.00	0.00	0.00	0.00
Firm performance	0.59***	0.94***	0.67***	0.96***	0.80***	1.21***
High-growth orientation	0.00	0.05	−0.00	0.03	0.02	0.02
Manufacturing firm	−0.73	−1.04*	−1.25*	−1.40*	−1.16	−1.27†
General service firm	−0.45	−0.77†	−0.50	−0.88†	−0.21†	−0.73
Professional service firm	−0.13	−0.62	−0.14	−0.30	−0.22	−0.47

WFI strategies and experiences				
Time devoted to the family sphere	−0.03†	−0.03	−0.03	−0.02
Time devoted to the business sphere	0.02	0.01	0.02	0.02
Segmentation of family and business roles	−0.20	−0.25	−0.16	−0.13
Identification with the business	0.82*	1.16**	0.65†	1.08**
Instrumental support from family members	0.25	0.37†	0.29	0.26
Traditional division of household labor	0.75†	0.12	0.83*	−0.08
Fairness in the division of household labor	0.39	0.74**	0.35	0.47
Family-to-business conflict and enrichment				
Family-to-business conflict			−0.96***	−1.50***
Family-to-business enrichment			0.17	0.72*
−2LL Chi-square	73.04	123.68***	157.39***	
Nagelkerke R-square	.26	.42	.51	

Notes:
Values in the table are unstandardized multinomial logistic regression coefficients.
† $p \leq .10$, * $p \leq .05$, ** $p \leq .01$, *** $p \leq .001$ (two-tailed tests).

greater instrumental support from family members. Moreover, those who reported a high degree of family-to-business conflict were less likely to report a high level of concurrent effectiveness within and across the family and business domains.

As indicated in Table 8.5, several of the controls in the business domain (but none of those in the family domain) were consistently associated with a high level of *concurrent satisfaction*. These consisted of founder-led firms (positively associated), firm performance (positively associated) and manufacturing firms (negatively associated). Of the WFI strategy and experience variables, identification with the business was consistently and positively associated with high concurrent satisfaction. Perceived fairness in the division of household labor exhibited a positive association in the reduced model but did not remain significant in the full model. This was because family-to-business conflict and enrichment both emerged as highly significant. More specifically, US business owners who reported a high level of concurrent satisfaction within and across the family and business domains tended to report lower levels of family-to-business conflict and higher levels of family-to-business enrichment.

DISCUSSION

Summary

If we were asked to sketch a quick portrait of the WFI strategies, experiences and outcomes of business owner-managers in the US based upon our survey findings, what features would we emphasize? One would certainly be the relatively high levels of personal well-being reported within and across the family and business domains. Indeed, sizeable proportions (approximately 40.0 percent in each case) expressed a high level of concurrent effectiveness and/or a high level of concurrent satisfaction. Sizeable proportions also expressed low levels of family-to-business conflict (approximately 32.0 percent) and/or high levels of family-to-business enrichment (approximately 55.0 percent).

We would also call attention to the lack of significant associations between these variables and their household income levels, which were not very high on average (less than 40.0 percent had household incomes over $100,000 USD). Instead, our analysis indicates that the following factors tend to be associated with both a high level of effectiveness and a high level of satisfaction: stronger firm performance, higher levels of identification with the business and lower levels of family-to-business conflict. Interestingly, those who experienced greater family-to-business enrichment tended to report a high level of perceived satisfaction—but not perceived effectiveness—within and across the family and business spheres.

Implications

These findings possess implications for several strands of related discourse within the family business, entrepreneurship and WFI literatures. Most fundamentally, they lend additional empirical support to substantiate calls within the family business literature to supplement research on family enterprises with that on enterprising *families* (James, Jennings, and Breitkreuz, 2012; Jennings et al., 2013; Sharma, 2004; Stafford et al., 1999; Zahra and Sharma, 2004). Consistent with an important sub-theme evident within many of these calls, the heterogeneous demographic characteristics, WFI experiences/strategies and non-economic outcomes evident in our study offer illustrative evidence in support of the more specific plea for greater attention to the *diversity* inherent within business-owning families—even among those within a single country setting.

The findings also provide support for the family embeddedness view of entrepreneurship (Aldrich and Cliff, 2003). Rather than demonstrating how entrepreneurial processes and outcomes are influenced by family factors, however, our analysis joins other empirical studies (for example, Olson et al., 2003; Eddleston and Powell, 2012) in demonstrating how factors in both the business and household spheres—and at their intersection—influence outcomes for family members who are also owner-managers. By doing so, our findings cast further doubt on the 'atomistic actor' portrayal of enterpreneurs that has traditionally permeated much of the mainstream entrepreneurship literature.

The findings presented in this chapter also possess implications for an even more specific debate within the WFI literature. This is the dispute between proponents of the conflict versus enrichment perspectives. Consistent with studies of non-entrepreneurs (for example, Ohlott, Graves, and Ruderman, 2004; Powell and Greenhaus, 2010; Rothbard, 2001), our analysis demonstrates that the intersection between work and family for business owner-managers is more realistically characterized as a combination of the two perspectives. Although certain factors are associated with increased family-to-business conflict, others are associated with enhanced family-to-business enrichment. Combined with the fact the conflict and enrichment measures themselves were negatively but not significantly correlated ($r = -.07$, n.s.), and with the fact that time devoted to the family sphere did not detract from time devoted to the business sphere ($r = .18, p \leq .001$), our study thus lends support for Powell and Eddleston's call for a more 'positive view of the linkages between work and family to entrepreneurship' (Powell and Eddleston, 2013: 261).

Limitations

It is important to consider the preceding summary and implications in light of the study's limitations. One pertains to the fact that the sample is not necessarily representative of all business owners in the US. This is attributable to two factors. The first was our reliance upon a third-party company (Qualtrics) for the administration of the survey, which meant that we were not privy to the sampling frame. The second was the stratified design, which resulted in an over-sampling of female-led firms and those with greater than 10 employees. The latter aspect, however, likely contributed to a higher proportion of businesses deemed to be family firms by the respondents than might have otherwise been the case.

A second limitation is the reliance upon self-reported data from the business owners. Although such individuals are clearly well-qualified to provide information on their firms and households, it would have been ideal if we had been able to corroborate certain variables through different sources. This is especially so for the time use, division of domestic labor and firm performance data.

Related to the preceding point, the ideal design for shedding insight into the implicit overarching question of whether entrepreneurship is 'good' for family members would have involved collecting data from household members in addition to the business owner. The recent study by Marchisio, Mazzola, Sciascia, Miles, and Astrachan (2010) offers a nice template in this regard. An alternative would have been to ask the respondents to assess their family's functioning, as in Olson et al.'s (2003) investigation. At one point we had considered including such a question but unfortunately this was dropped due to concerns about its potentially sensitive nature and the overall length of the survey.

Conclusion

Given the above-noted limitations, this study can offer only suggestive and partial insight into the question of whether business ownership is beneficial for family members in the US. If the yardstick for measuring potential benefits is limited to indicators of the owner-manager's personal well-being, then we would respond as follows. In the US, owning and managing a company is 'good' for those who not only head high-performing firms but also for those who identify highly with their organization and those who divide household tasks fairly so that they are not negatively affected by a high level of family-to-business conflict. We are certain, however, that Jennings and her colleagues (2013) had broader outcomes in mind when they called for greater research on the timely and important issue of whether entrepreneurship necessarily benefits families. Hopefully this chapter will encourage others to contribute to the development of a much more comprehensive answer. As a direct follow-up to this study, for instance, future researchers could examine the extent to which the higher perceived effectiveness and satisfaction of business owners translates into stronger relationships with specific family members and greater family well-being in general.

ACKNOWLEDGEMENTS

The data collection for this chapter was supported by SSHRC grant number 410-2009-0321. The authors would like to thank Stephanie Cornforth for her excellent research assistance.

NOTES

1. The Spearman *rho* values were as follows: .55 ($p \leq .001$) between personal income and number of full-time equivalent employees; .66 ($p \leq .001$) between personal income and total revenues; .47 ($p \leq .001$) between household income and number of full-time equivalent employees; and .60 ($p \leq .001$) between household income total revenues.
2. The Spearman *rho* values were −.12 ($p \leq .05$) for female business owner and number of full-time equivalent employees and −.19 ($p \leq .05$) for female business owner and total revenues.
3. The firm-level controls consisted of the following variables from the US chapter in Part I (see Jennings, Jennings, and Joo, Chapter 2): *founder-led firm* (coded 1 if the respondent indicated that s/he had founded the focal business, 0 if not); *family firm* (coded 1 if the respondent considered the business to be a family firm, 0 if not); *firm age* (measured by subtracting the company's founding year from 2012); *firm size* (measured by the number of full-time equivalent employees currently employed by the firm, excluding the respondent); *firm performance* (measured by a 7-item Likert-type scale assessing the company's performance relative to competitors during the year prior to the survey, $\alpha = .95$); *high-growth orientation* (measured by an 8-item Likert-type scale assessing the respondent's attitudes towards business expansion, $\alpha = .77$); and, dummy variables for *manufacturing, general service* and *professional service* firms (with those classified as 'other' as the holdout).

REFERENCES

Aldrich, H.E. and J.E. Cliff (2003), 'The pervasive effects of family on entre-preneurship: Toward a family embeddedness perspective,' *Journal of Business Venturing*, **18** (5), 573–596.

Amoró, J.E. and N. Bosma (2014). 'Global Entrepreneurship Monitor 2013 global report.' Retrieved from http://www.gemconsortium.org/docs/download/3106 (accessed February 23, 2015).

Berrone, P., C. Cruz, and L.R. Gómez-Mejía (2012), 'Socioemotional wealth in family firms: Theoretical dimensions, assessment approaches, and agenda for future research,' *Family Business Review*, **25**, 258–279.

Bucks, B., A. Kennickell, and K. Moore (2006), 'Recent changes in US family finances: Evidence from the 2001 and 2004 Survey of Consumer Finances,' *Federal Reserve Bulletin*, **2006**, A1–A35.

Carlson, D.S., K.M. Kacmar, and L.J. Williams (2000), 'Construction and initial validation of a multidimensional measure of work–family conflict,' *Journal of Vocational Behavior*, **56**, 249–276.

Carlson, D.S., K.M. Kacmar, J.H. Wayne, and J.G. Grzywacz (2006), 'Measuring the positive side of the work–family interface: Development and validation of a work–family enrichment scale,' *Journal of Vocational Behavior*, **68**, 131–164.

Carter, S. (2011), 'The rewards of entrepreneurship: Exploring the incomes, wealth, and economic well-being of entrepreneurial households,' *Entrepreneurship Theory and Practice*, **35**, 39–55.

Cliff, J.E. (1998), 'Does one size fit all? Exploring the relationship between attitudes between growth, gender and business size,' *Journal of Business Venturing*, **13**, 523–542.

Davidsson, P. (2004), *Researching Entrepreneurship*. Boston: Springer.

Eddleston, K. and G. Powell (2012), 'Nurturing entrepreneurs' work–family balance: A gendered perspective,' *Entrepreneurship Theory and Practice*, **36**, 513–541.

Gersick, K., J. Davis, M. McCollom Hampton, and I. Lansberg (1997), *Generation to Generation: Life Cycles in Family Business*. Boston: Harvard University Press.

Haynes, G.W., J.I. Onochie, and G. Musje (2007), 'Is what's good for the business, good for the family: A financial assessment,' *Journal of Family and Economic Issues*, **28**, 395–409.

Heck, R.K.Z. and E.S. Trent (1999), 'The prevalence of family business from a household sample,' *Family Business Review*, **12**, 209–224.

James, A.E., J.E. Jennings, and R.S. Breitkreuz (2012), 'Worlds apart? Re-bridging the distance between family science and family business research,' *Family Business Review*, **25**, 87–108.

Jennings, J.E. and C.G. Brush (2013), 'Research on women entrepreneurs: Challenges to (and from) the broader entrepreneurship literature?,' *The Academy of Management Annals*, **7**, 661–713.

Jennings, J.E. and M.S. McDougald (2007), 'Work–family interface experiences and coping strategies: Implications for entrepreneurship research and practice,' *Academy of Management Review*, **32**, 747–750.

Jennings, J.E., R.S. Breitkreuz, and A.E. James (2013), 'When family members are also business owners: Is entrepreneurship good for families?,' *Family Relations*, **62**, 472–489.

Jennings, J.E., K.D. Hughes, and P.D. Jennings (2010), 'The work–family interface strategies of male and female entrepreneurs: Are there any differences?,' in C.G. Brush, A. de Bruin, E.J. Gatewood, and C. Henry (eds), *Women Entrepreneurs and the Global Environment for Growth*. Cheltenham, UK and Northampton, MA, USA: Edward Elgar Publishing, pp. 163–186.

Jennings, J.E., P.D. Jennings, and M. Sharifian (forthcoming), 'Living the dream? Assessing the "entrepreneurship as emancipation" perspective in developed region,' *Entrepreneurship Theory and Practice*. DOI: 10.1111/etap.12106.

Kennickell, A. and J. Shack-Marquez (1992), 'Changes in US family finances from 1983 to 1989: Evidence from the Survey of Consumer Finances,' *Federal Reserve Bulletin*, **1992**, 1–18.

Kreiner, G.E. (2006), 'Consequences of work–home segmentation or integration: A person–environment fit perspective,' *Journal of Organizational Behavior*, **27**, 485–507.

Lansberg, I. (1983), 'Managing human resources in family firms: The problem of institutional overlap,' *Organizational Dynamics*, **Summer**, 29–38.

Loscocco, K. and K.T. Leicht (1993), 'Gender, work–family linkages, and economic success among small business owners,' *Journal of Marriage and Family*, **55**, 875–887.

Marchisio, G., P. Mazzola, S. Sciascia, M. Miles, and J. Astrachan (2010), 'Corporate venturing in family business: The effects on the family and its members,' *Entrepreneurship and Regional Development*, **3–4**, 349–377.

McGowan, P., C.L. Redeker, S.Y. Cooper, and K. Greenan (2012), 'Female entrepreneurship and the management of business and domestic roles: Motivations, expectations and realities,' *Entrepreneurship and Regional Development*, **24**, 53–72.

Milkie, M.A. and P. Peltola (1999), 'Playing all the roles: gender and the work–family balancing act,' *Journal of Marriage and the Family*, **61**, 476–490.

Netemeyer, R.G., J.S. Boles, and R. McMurrian (1996), 'Development and validation of work–family conflict and family–work conflict scales,' *Journal of Applied Psychology*, **81**, 400–410.

Ohlott, P.J., L.M. Graves, and M.N. Ruderman (2004), 'Commitment to family roles: Effects on managers' work attitudes and performance,' Paper presented at the Academy of Management Meeting, New Orleans.

Olson, P., V. Zuiker, S. Danes, K. Stafford, R. Heck, and K. Duncan (2003), 'The impact of the family and the business on family business sustainability,' *Journal of Business Venturing*, **18**, 639–666.

O'Reilly, C. and J. Chatman (1986), 'Organizational commitment and psychological attachment: The effects of compliance, identification, and internalization on prosocial behavior,' *Journal of Applied Psychology*, **71**, 492–499.

Powell, G.N. (2011), *Women and Men in Management*. Los Angeles: Sage Publications.

Powell, G.N. and K.A. Eddleston (2013), 'Linking family-to-business enrichment and support to entrepreneurial success: Do female and male entrepreneurs experience different outcomes?,' *Journal of Business Venturing*, **28**, 261–280.

Powell, G.N. and J.H. Greenhaus (2010), 'Sex, gender, and the work-to-family interface: Exploring negative and positive interdependencies,' *Academy of Management Journal*, **53**, 513–534.

Rindova, V., D. Barry, and D.J. Ketchen (2009), 'Entrepreneuring as emancipation,' *Academy of Management Review*, **34**, 477–491.

Rothbard, N.P. (2001), 'Enriching or depleting? The dynamics of engagement in work and family roles,' *Administrative Science Quarterly*, **46**, 655–684.

Shane, S.A. (2008), *The Illusions of Entrepreneurship: The Costly Myths that Entrepreneurs, Investors, and Policy Makers Live By*. New Haven, CT and London: Yale University Press.

Shane, S. (2012), 'Reflections on the 2010 *AMR* decade award: Delivering on the promise of entrepreneurship as a field of research,' *Academy of Management Review*, **37**, 10–20.

Sharma, P. (2004), 'An overview of the field of family business studies: Current status and directions for the future,' *Family Business Review*, **27**, 1–36.

Shelton, L.M. (2006), 'Female entrepreneurs, work–family conflict, and venture performance: New insights in the work–family interface,' *Journal of Small Business Management*, **44**, 285–297.

Stafford, K., K. Duncan, S. Danes, and M. Winter (1999), 'A research model of sustainable family businesses,' *Family Business Review*, **12**, 197–208.

Waismel-Manor, R., P. Moen, and S. Sweet (2002), 'Managing and thriving: What factors predict dual-earner middle-class couples feeling highly successful in their jobs, families and balancing both?' BLCC Working Paper #02-20.

Yodanis, C. (2005), 'Divorce culture and marital gender equality: A cross-national study,' *Gender and Society*, **19**, 644–659.

Zahra, S. and P. Sharma (2004), 'Family business research: A strategic reflection,' *Family Business Review*, **17**, 331–346.

9. The family-to-business strategies and experiences of owner-managers in Switzerland and Germany: implications for personal well-being

Philipp Sieger, Melanie Ganter and Thomas Zellweger

INTRODUCTION

The primary purpose of this chapter is to shed light on the family-to-business strategies, experiences and outcomes of 'enterprising families' in Switzerland and Germany; that is, of family households comprised of at least one individual who is involved in owning and managing a business. The second objective is to place our regional findings in an international context, particularly by comparing them with those obtained from a similar study conducted in the US.

The significance of entrepreneurs and family businesses for German-speaking economies is widely recognized in academia and in practice. A recent Global Entrepreneurship Monitor (GEM) report, for example, revealed that approximately 18 percent of the national workforce in Switzerland and 16 percent in Germany were engaged in entrepreneurial activities in 2012 (Xavier, Kelly, Kew, Herrington, and Vorderwülbecke, 2012). Moreover, national studies reveal that family businesses are the prevailing organizational form, constituting approximately 90 percent of all firms in these two countries (Frey, Halter, Klein, and Zellweger, 2004; Gottschalk et al., 2011).

Despite this dominant role of entrepreneurship in general, and family businesses in particular, little is known about the effect of business ownership on family life, or vice versa, within these two countries. This is surprising given that a large-scale European study conducted in 2010 revealed that 31 percent of Swiss and 28 percent of German respondents reported work–family balance as a major reason for considering an entrepreneurial career (Amway-GmbH and LMU-Entrepreneurship-Center,

2010). This chapter therefore seeks to explore whether entrepreneurial activities are actually 'good' for owner-managers of enterprising families (Jennings, Breitkreuz, and James, 2013) in Switzerland and Germany.

We first present basic demographic information on the owner-managers who participated in our study, including key details about their households. We then present descriptive data on the degree to which these owner-managers perceive themselves to be effective and satisfied with their family–work interface. Subsequently, we share detailed insights into their family-to-business strategies and experiences by investigating their relationships with both family-to-business conflict and enrichment. This is followed by multinomial logistic regression analyses that seek to shed light on whether and how all of these factors are associated with indicators of personal well-being; in other words, perceived effectiveness and satisfaction within and between the family and business domains. Comparisons are also made with the findings from the initial study conducted in the US.

METHODOLOGY

To construct our initial sampling frame, we used the Amadeus/Bureau van Dijk database to identify large and long-living family firms within Switzerland and Germany. We decided to focus on owner-managers of the largest family-owned and governed firms in these countries to complement insights from our US colleagues, who over-sampled small, owner-managed firms. Hence, to be included in our sample, at least 25 percent of the firm's equity had to be held by a single family and the company had to have at least EUR 80 million in revenues. Our specially developed questionnaire was entered into a survey software program; an email invitation was then sent to the identified family firm owners in the spring of 2012. A second online survey that included an extended set of questions about their family-to-business strategies and experiences was sent to the same business owners in 2013. Third, given the underrepresentation of women in our initial sample, we sent the same survey to additional female business owners in Switzerland and Germany in 2014 that we identified by collaborating with numerous associations for women entrepreneurs. Depending on the nature of the survey question, the sample size available for analysis ranges from approximately 100 to 373 respondents.

DEMOGRAPHIC CHARACTERISTICS OF THE BUSINESS OWNERS AND THEIR HOUSEHOLDS

Of the 373 participants in total, 199 (53.4 percent) indicated that they were male and 174 (46.6 percent) indicated that they were female. The proportion of female respondents is thus very similar to that reported in the US sample (48.2 percent). The respondents ranged from 25 to 78 years of age, with a mean and median both around 52 years. Of the participants who revealed their educational background, almost half held a college or university degree (48.2 percent) and approximately 1 in 10 (9.8 percent) had obtained a doctorate. Only 20.7 percent had completed an apprenticeship program or vocational training. In line with the US sample, the clear majority (72.2 percent) indicated that they are married. More than half (51.9 percent) had at least one child under the age of 18 living in their household. The number of children ranged from one to five and most had either one (26.2 percent) or two (14.8 percent) children.

We were only able to obtain personal and household income data from a small proportion of our overall sample (n = 101). This might be due to cultural differences as private financial information is regarded as very confidential for most business owners in Germany and Switzerland. Moreover, given the large size of the sampled firms, the respective owner-managers might be especially reluctant to reveal this private information. Measured by six ordinal categories, both types of income data ranged from less than 25,000 EUR to over 1 million EUR. The category that was selected most often for both the personal and household levels was EUR 250,000 to EUR 499,000. At the individual level, 33.7 percent of all respondents chose that category; at the household level, it was 21.7 percent. While the total means and standard deviations differ considerably, the two variables were significantly correlated (Spearman's *rho* = .55, p < 0.01). We thus confirm the US finding that owner-managers are often the primary economic provider of their families. Interestingly, and in sharp contrast to the US sample, only 7.5 percent of the respondents reported a personal income of less than 100,000 EUR. Referring to household income, the corresponding share is 5.0 percent. In the US sample these percentages amounted to 70.7 percent and 62.1 percent, respectively. Our results therefore provide further evidence that private income is dependent on firm size as we deliberately over-sampled owner-managers in large family firms.

KEY INDICATORS OF PERSONAL WELL-BEING: PERCEIVED EFFECTIVENESS AND SATISFACTION

Having outlined the economic implications of owning and managing a family run enterprise, a topic that has received ample attention in the literature (see, for example, Carter, 2011; Haynes, Onochie, and Muske, 2007; Loscocco and Leicht, 1993), this chapter explores the non-economic outcomes of business ownership (Rindova, Barry, and Ketchen, 2009) and in particular the impact of the latter upon families (Jennings et al., 2013; Stafford, Duncan, Dane, and Winter, 1999). More specifically, we report findings for perceived effectiveness and satisfaction within and across the domains of family and business of those owner-managers who answered the corresponding questions in our survey. These indicators are similar to, yet expand upon, the indicators of psychological well-being used within the most recent GEM study (Amoró and Bosma, 2014).

In line with the US sample we used three *separate indicators of perceived effectiveness*, asking the participants to indicate their current perceived effectiveness (1) as a family member, (2) as a business owner-manager, and (3) in balancing the various aspects of their lives. Inspired by Waismel-Manor, Moen and Sweet (2002), each of the three items was rated on a scale ranging from 0 to 100. More specifically, we offered respondents 11 options to choose from (anchored at 0, 10, 20, up to 100). To evaluate the degree to which the owner-managers possessed *concurrent perceptions of effectiveness* within and across the family and business domains, we used a composite measure that was developed in two steps. First, we recoded each of the three constituent items dichotomously, assigning respondents a value of 1 if they reported a score of at least 80 out of 100 on the item, 0 if not (Jennings, Jennings, and Sharifian, forthcoming). Second, we then summed the three dichotomous measures and recoded the aggregate score such that a sum of 0 was deemed to reflect 'low concurrent perceived effectiveness,' sums of 1 or 2 were deemed to reflect 'moderate concurrent perceived effectiveness,' and a sum of 3 was deemed to reflect 'high concurrent perceived effectiveness.' A parallel procedure was adopted to create the three *separate indicators of perceived satisfaction* as well as the *concurrent satisfaction measure*. We tested the correlation of the aggregate ordinal measures of concurrent effectiveness and concurrent satisfaction and found that they were highly and significantly correlated (Spearman's *rho* = .64, $p < .001$). Table 9.1 summarizes the findings.

The results depicted in the upper half of Table 9.1 shed light on the degree to which owner-managers in Switzerland and Germany consider themselves effective within and across the domains of family and business.

Table 9.1   Perceived effectiveness and satisfaction within and across family and business domains (Swiss/German sample)

Indicators and Levels of Composite Measures	N	Mean	S.D.	Min	Max	% with Score ≥ 80
Perceived Effectiveness						
Separate Constituent Indicators						
Perceived effectiveness as a family member	149	72.01	19.49	0	100	53.7
Perceived effectiveness as a business owner	152	80.07	13.35	0	100	71.1
Perceived effectiveness in balancing family and business	152	67.76	22.85	0	100	46.7
Levels of Composite Measure						
Low concurrent perceived effectiveness	18	11.7%				
Moderate concurrent perceived effectiveness	94	61%				
High concurrent perceived effectiveness	42	27.3%				
Perceived Satisfaction						
Separate Constituent Indicators						
Perceived satisfaction as a family member	154	78.96	19.24	10	100	68.8
Perceived satisfaction as a business owner	153	79.48	17.16	20	100	66.7
Perceived satisfaction in balancing family and business	152	70.53	24.49	0	100	51.2
Levels of Composite Measure						
Low concurrent perceived satisfaction	22	14.3%				
Moderate concurrent perceived satisfaction	70	45.5%				
High concurrent perceived satisfaction	62	40.3%				

Interestingly we find that while the vast majority of respondents perceive themselves to be highly effective in the business domain (71.1 percent reported a score of at least 80 out of 100), participants assessed their own effectiveness as a family member as well as their effectiveness in balancing the two domains much lower (53.7 percent and 46.7 percent reported a score of at least 80 out of 100). The latter numbers are also lower than those for the US (68.6 percent and 52.4 percent, respectively). Based on these findings it can be assumed that business owners in Switzerland and Germany primarily focus their attention on business matters and in turn might accept a loss in effectiveness—especially in the family domain. The findings for the composite measure show an interesting related pattern. On the one hand, the share of Swiss and German owner-managers who fall into the 'high' concurrent effectiveness category is considerably smaller than in the US (27.3 percent compared with 38.2 percent). On the other hand, the share of owner-managers in the 'low' category is smaller as well (11.7 percent compared with 18.8 percent in the US). Consequently, the 'moderate' group is much larger in Switzerland and Germany than in the US (61 percent compared with 42.7 percent). As a whole, the Swiss and German owner-managers seem to be more 'normally distributed' than US owner-managers.

The findings reported in the lower half of Table 9.1 provide insights into the question: 'To what extent are owner-managers in Switzerland and Germany satisfied within and across the domains of family and business?' In contrast to the effectiveness measures, business owner-managers perceive themselves to be highly satisfied within both domains. Particularly for the first two indicators (in other words, perceived satisfaction as a family member and as a business owner), the majority of the respondents (68.8 percent and 66.7 percent, respectively) reported a score at or above 80 out of 100. These figures are particularly noteworthy when compared with the US findings, which showed that the American respondents rated themselves slightly lower on these satisfaction scales (66 percent and 58.3 percent respectively). Combined with the insights generated above it seems that German and Swiss owner-managers, despite being less effective in the family domain, seem to be more satisfied in both their business and familial roles in comparison to their American counterparts.

In sum, the majority of the business owners who participated in the German and Swiss study considered themselves to be highly effective in the business domain; however, they scored lower on concurrent perceived effectiveness across different domains. In contrast, a majority of respondents consider themselves to be highly and contemporaneously satisfied within and across the two domains. In the following parts of this chapter we will explore the factors that influence these indicators of personal well-being.

FAMILY-TO-BUSINESS EXPERIENCES AND STRATEGIES

Seeking to explore the factors that determine personal well-being as expressed by levels of perceived effectiveness and satisfaction, we focus on aspects at the intersection of the family and business domains. Exploring the nature and effect of this intersection is particularly valuable as recent research points to the centrality of the work–family interface for entre-preneurial outcomes (Aldrich and Cliff, 2003; Jennings and McDougald, 2007) and thus highlights the need to further investigate work–family dynamics (for example, Eddleston and Powell, 2012; McGowan, Redeker, Cooper, and Greenan, 2012; Shelton, 2006).

Given the ongoing debate on whether the co-existence of work and family commitments are impeding or enhancing (Powell, 2011), this section adopts a neutral approach. We thus start by presenting data on the degree of family-to-business conflict *and* enrichment as experienced by our sampled Swiss and German owner-managers. In a subsequent step we provide descriptive information on various strategies for managing the work–family interface. Based on Jennings and McDougald's (2007) frame-work we focus on: (1) individual-level strategies regarding time distribu-tion, segmentation versus integration, and identification with the business; and, (2) household-level considerations by investigating the instrumental support provided by family members, traditionalism in the division of household labor, and the perceived fairness of the same distribution.

Family-to-Business Conflict and Enrichment

Family-to-business conflict was measured by the mean of a 6-item, Likert-type scale ($\alpha = .74$). Three of the items, which were adapted from Netemeyer, Boles, and McMurrian (1996), measured behavioral conflict. An example is: 'Household/family commitments interfere with my ability to perform business-related duties.' The remaining three items investigated affective conflict and were specifically developed for this study, an example being: 'I feel frustrated when my household/family responsibilities inter-fere with my work.' Each item was rated from '1 = strongly disagree' to '5 = strongly agree.' The findings reported in Table 9.2 indicate that a large majority of owner-managers in the Swiss and German sample were not experiencing a high degree of family-to-business conflict. The sample mean of 2.19, for example, is below the scale's midpoint of 3 and below the mean of the US sample (which was 2.63). Relatedly, we note that only 3.4 percent of our respondents exhibit an overall family-to-business con-flict level of 4 or higher.

Table 9.2 Family-to-business experiences and strategies (Swiss/German sample)

Variables	α	Mean	S.D.	Min	Max	% with Score
Family-to-business conflict	0.74	2.19	0.85	1	5	≥ 4 (agree) = 3.4%
Family-to-business enrichment	0.91	3.66	0.96	1	5	≥ 4 (agree) = 49%
Time devoted to the family sphere	n/a	13.82	11.1	0	50	≥ 20 hrs/wk = 15.9%
Time devoted to the business sphere	n/a	45.84	16.05	4	90	≥ 40 hrs/wk = 73.4%
Segmentation of family and business roles (actual)	0.89	3.1	1.12	1	5	≥ 4 (agree) = 31.8%
Identification with the business	0.71	5.65	1.08	1.33	7.00	≥ 6 (agree) = 47.7%
Instrumental support from family members	0.86	3.14	1.15	1	5	≥ 4 (agree) = 31.4%
Traditionalism in the division of household labor[a]	n/a	1.66	0.57	1	3.5	= 1 (woman) = 21.2%
Perceived fairness in the division of household labor	n/a	3.08	0.78	1	4	= 4 (very fair) = 30.6%

Note:

a   Given that this scale is conceptualized as formative rather than reflective in nature (Yodanis, 2005), it is not meaningful to calculate Cronbach's alpha.

Family-to-business enrichment was measured by the mean of a 6-item, Likert-type scale ($\alpha = .91$) adapted from Carlson, Kacmar, Wayne, and Grzywacz (2006). As in the above case, three of the items investigated the perceived behavioral enrichment, an example being: 'My involvement in my family requires me to be as focused as possible at work, which helps make me a better businessperson.' Likewise, the other three items measured perceived affective enrichment. An example here is: 'My involvement with my family makes me cheerful and this helps me be a better businessperson.' Each item was rated from '1 = strongly disagree' to '5 = strongly agree.' The results depicted in Table 9.2 reveal that the majority of the sampled business owners from Switzerland and Germany experienced a high degree of family-to-business enrichment. This is evidenced by the sample mean of 3.66 which is close to the scale value of 4 (which corresponds to 'agree'); furthermore, 49 percent of the respondents scored at or above this value.

Individual-level Strategies

Time devoted to the family sphere was measured by a single item—the number of hours that the respondent estimated spending per week on household-related tasks. Although there are recognized weaknesses in this measure, such as susceptibility to over-estimation and discrepancy between marital partners (Yodanis, 2005), it has nevertheless been used in previous studies of entrepreneurship and the work–family interface (Cliff, 1998; Loscocco and Leicht, 1993). As indicated in Table 9.2, participants in the Swiss and German study estimated spending 13.82 hours per week, on average, on household-related tasks. This is lower than the US sample that reported an average of 16.47 hours. Moreover, only 15.9 percent of German and Swiss participants (as compared with 38.5 percent of US respondents) indicated that they dedicated at least 20 hours per week to family-related tasks.

Time devoted to the business sphere was measured by a parallel item— the number of hours that the respondent estimated spending per week on business-related tasks. This measure has been used in other studies of entrepreneurship and the work–family interface (for example, Jennings, Hughes, and Jennings, 2010; Jennings et al., 2013; Powell and Eddleston, 2013). As reported in Table 9.2, participants in the Swiss and German study estimated spending 45.84 hours per week, on average, in the business sphere. In fact, 73.4 percent were actively involved with their business on at least a full-time basis, putting in 40 hours or more during a typical week. Working hours thus seem to be longer in Germany and Switzerland than in the United States (43.06 hours on average, 65.4 percent $\geq$ 40 hrs/wk).

Segmentation was measured by the mean of three items ($\alpha = .89$)

adapted from several work–family interface studies (Carlson, Williams, and Kacmar, 2000; Powell and Greenhaus, 2010). An illustrative item is: 'In reality, I often leave household/family issues behind when I'm at work.' The phrase 'In reality' was inserted at the beginning of each item to help focus the respondent on their experienced rather than preferred degree of segmentation between family and business roles. Each item was rated from '1 = strongly disagree' to '5 = strongly agree.' As indicated in Table 9.2, the sample mean of 3.1 is very close to the scale's midpoint of 3. Almost one third of the participants (31.8 percent) can be assumed to enact a segmentation strategy as those respondents scored at or above the value of '4 = agree.'

The owner-manager's degree of *identification* with his/her business was measured by the mean of a 7-item, Likert-type scale ($\alpha = .71$) adapted from O'Reilly and Chatman (1986) and based on the suggestions by Berrone, Cruz, and Gómez-Mejía (2012). An example is: 'If I were describing myself, the firm would likely be something I would mention.' In contrast to our previous measures, the corresponding items were rated from '1 = strongly disagree' to '7 = strongly agree.' The findings indicated in Table 9.2 reveal that the majority of the business owners in the Swiss and German sample identified very highly with their firms. The sample mean is 5.65 (on a 1 to 7 scale), with 47.7 percent of the respondents indicating a value of 6 or higher.

Household-level Considerations

The *instrumental support provided by family members* for the respondent's role of business owner was measured by a 5-item, Likert-type scale ($\alpha = .86$) developed by Powell and Eddleston (2013). Example items include: 'The members of my family who do not officially work in the business can be counted on to help out if something unexpected happens in this business' and 'The members of my family who do not officially work in the business often give me useful feedback and ideas concerning this business.' Each item was rated from '1 = strongly disagree' to '5 = strongly agree.' The findings reported in Table 9.2 indicate that many of the sampled business owners in Germany and Switzerland experienced a moderate to high level of instrumental support from the members of their family. Similar to the US survey, the sample mean of 3.14 falls slightly above the scale's midpoint and 31.4 percent of the respondents (slightly more than in the US sample) had a score at or above the scale value of '4 = agree.'

We measured *traditionalism in the division of household labor* by the mean of a 4-item formative scale from Yodanis (2005). Respondents indicated the member of their household who was responsible for four tasks (shopping for groceries, deciding what to have for dinner, doing the laundry and caring for the sick) by checking one of the following responses: '1 = always or usually the woman,' '2 = equally,' '3 = always or usually the man,' or '4 = a third person (hired help).' As indicated in Table 9.2, the sample mean of 1.66 is in between the values for the woman and an equal distribution of household tasks. Interestingly, the largest group of respondents (21.2 percent) indicated '1' for all four questions. This shows that a sizeable proportion of the respondents seem to live in a 'traditional' household, similar to the findings from the US.

Perceived fairness in the division of household labor was measured by the respondent's response to the question, 'How fair do you feel that this division of household labor is for yourself?' (adapted from Milkie and Peltola, 1999). The response categories ranged from '1 = very unfair' to '4 = very fair.' The Swiss and German owner-managers tend to view the division of labor in their households as fair. The mean of 3.08 is slightly above the value of '3 = somewhat fair'; 30.6 percent perceived the distribution as 'very fair' (with 51 percent assessing it as somewhat fair). This is in line with the US findings.

Determinants of Family-to-Business Conflict and Enrichment

In this section we explore whether the above-mentioned household considerations as well as individual-level strategies are associated with the degree of family-to-business conflict and enrichment indicated by owner-managers. To assess this, we also control for different demographic characteristics of the owner-managers, their households, and their firms.[1] The results of our multivariate ordinary least squares (OLS) regressions are presented in Table 9.3.

Referring to family-to-business conflict, our analyses show that marital status is the only (marginally) significant control variable. Of the family-to-business strategies and experiences, the time devoted to the family sphere exhibits a significant and positive relationship with family-to-business conflict. Hence, the more time owner-managers spend in the family domain, the higher their family-to-business conflict. Also, owner-managers who perceive that the division of labor in their household is fair tend to report a lower level of family-to-business conflict (as indicated by the negative and significant coefficient). The latter was also found within the US sample.

Referring to family-to-business enrichment, we note that the number of children living in the household is positively associated with the level of enrichment. Of our independent variables, only instrumental support from family members is significantly related to enrichment (positively). This is in

Table 9.3 Determinants of family-to-business conflict and enrichment (Swiss/German sample)

	Family-to-business Conflict		Family-to-business Enrichment	
Individual and household-level control variables				
Female	.030	.022	−.131	−.069
Education level	.070	.046	−.022	−.027
Married or marital-like relationship	−.163†	−.155†	.016	.019
Number of children in household	.140	.103	.218*	.197*
Household income	−.155	−.111	.087	.059
Firm-level control variables				
Founder-led firm	−.004	−.005	−.095	−.050
Self-perception as family firm	.062	.085	−.032	−.031
Firm age	−.141	−.123	.185	.155
Firm size	−.019	−.028	−.071	−.067
Firm performance	−.105	−.027	.147	.119
High-growth orientation	−.049	−.112	−.108	−.049
Manufacturing firm	.025	.008	.080	.060
Service firm	−.102	−.070	−.104	−.118
Family-to-business strategies and experiences				
Time devoted to the family sphere		.229*		−.001
Time devoted to the business sphere		.156		−.121
Segmentation of family and business roles		−.134		−.058
Identification with the business		.009		.053
Instrumental support from family members		−.007		.188*
Traditional division of household labor		.058		.071
Fairness in the division of household labor		−.240*		.095
Overall model F	*1.628†*	*1.183**	*1.912**	*1.897**
R squared	*0.151*	*0.269*	*0.173*	*0.253*

Notes:
Standardized OLS regression coefficients shown; N = 133.
† p < 0.10; * p<0.05; ** p<0.01.

line with the US findings, as this variable was found to have the strongest effect on enrichment among the US owner-managers.

FACTORS ASSOCIATED WITH PERCEIVED EFFECTIVENESS AND SATISFACTION

Having explored potential antecedents of family-to-business conflict and enrichment we now investigate their relationships with perceived effectiveness and satisfaction as indicators of personal well-being. For each indicator (in other words, effectiveness and satisfaction) we use the corresponding composite measure that describes if the respondent can be classified into the low, moderate, or high category of effectiveness (or satisfaction). As these variables consist of three ordinal levels, we apply multinomial logistic regression where one category is selected as the comparison baseline (in our case, the 'low' category) and the other categories are compared with that base category separately. For each dependent variable, we estimated three different models: one with the control models, one where we added the work–family interface strategy and experience variables, and a full model where we added the conflict and enrichment variables. The results appear in Table 9.4 (perceived effectiveness) and Table 9.5 (perceived satisfaction).

As indicated in Table 9.4, several control variables have a significant relationship with a high(er) level of perceived effectiveness. Gender has a very strong effect: female owner-managers have a systematically higher level of perceived effectiveness than males. Moreover, the age of the firm is marginally significant in several models; hence, perceived effectiveness seems to be higher amongst owner-managers of the older firms. Out of our family-to-business strategies and experiences variables, identification is found to have a significant and positive relationship with perceived effectiveness. The relevance of identification is also confirmed in the US context. Also, fairness in the household task distribution is marginally and positively significant when comparing the moderate level of perceived effectiveness to the low level. This suggests that higher fairness in the distribution of household tasks is associated more with the 'moderate' category of perceived effectiveness than with the 'low' category. Neither family-to-business conflict nor enrichment, however, exhibit a significant relationship with perceived effectiveness.

In contrast to our models pertaining to perceived effectiveness, gender (being female) is not a significant control variable in Table 9.5; hence, the level of satisfaction seems to be unaffected by gender. In general, significant control variables can hardly be found; only firm size is significantly and negatively related to perceived satisfaction in two of our models. Referring to our family-to-business strategy and experience variables, we find that the time devoted to the family sphere is significantly and negatively related to perceived satisfaction in the two models that compare the moderate to the low satisfaction category. While strong support for the identity variable can be found in the US sample, our analysis fails to show a significant relationship. However, an interesting pattern can be observed for the household labor variables: while a traditional division of household labor exhibits negative coefficients in all models, fairness in the division of

Table 9.4 Factors associated with composite measure of perceived effectiveness (Swiss/German sample)

| | Perceived Effectiveness (composite measure) | | | | | |
	Mod	High	Mod	High	Mod	High
Control variables						
Female	1.797†	1.971*	4.143*	5.134**	6.103**	7.476*
Education level	.508†	.177	.417	.036	.454	.005
Married or marital-like relationship	−.133	−.265	−.090	−.038	−.338	−1.097
Number of children in household	−.134	−.191	−.342	−.624	−.695	−1.006†
Household income	.000	.000	.000	.000	.000*	.000
Founder-led firm	.068	−.591	1.672	1.289	2.539	2.932
Self-perception as family firm	−.144	−.811	−.848	−.941	−1.005	−.057
Firm age	.019	.023†	.021	.028	.037†	.040†
Firm size	.000	.000	.000	.000	.000	.000
Firm performance	.172	.321	.109	.359	.163	.564
High-growth orientation	.339	.346	.525	.703	.483	.555
Manufacturing firm	−.501	.180	−1.639	−.546	−1.668	−.340
Service firm	1.807	1.123	2.375	1.570	3.526†	2.683

Family-to-business strategies and experiences

Time devoted to the family sphere	.007	.014	.010	.056
Time devoted to the business sphere	-.033	-.050	-.061	-.055
Segmentation of family and business roles	-.367	-.429	-.224	-.461
Identification with the business	.508	.931†	.993	1.508*
Instrumental support from family members	.354	.299	.461	.382
Traditional division of household labor	-.728	-1.530	-1.191	-2.419
Fairness in the division of household labor	.793	.645	1.436†	.564
Family-to-business conflict and enrichment				
Family-to-business conflict			.826	-1.161
Family-to-business enrichment			-.472	-.287
-2 Log Likelihood	246.884	181.927	144.892	
Chi square	32.341	50.837	83.319***	
Pseudo R² (Nagelkerke)	0.226	0.386	0.571	

Notes:
Unstandardized multinomial logistic regression coefficients shown; base category = low effectiveness; N = 133.
† $p < 0.10$; * $p < 0.05$; ** $p < 0.01$.

Table 9.5 Factors associated with composite measure of perceived satisfaction (Swiss/German sample)

	Perceived Satisfaction (composite measure)					
	Mod	High	Mod	High	Mod	High
Control variables						
Female	−.955	−1.232	−.931	−1.497	.131	−.971
Education level	.324	−.153	.337	−.068	.148	−.354
Married or marital-like relationship	−.354	−.283	−.560	−.336	−1.075	−1.382
Number of children in household	.045	−.051	.265	.009	.286	−.060
Household income	.000	.000	.000	.000	.000	.000
Founder-led firm	−.638	−1.234	−.967	−.964	−1.033	−.738
Self-perception as family firm	−.558	−.687	−.870	−.535	−.819	−.177
Firm age	.005	.011	.003	.010	.007	.009
Firm size	−.001**	.000	−.001*	.000	−.001	.000
Firm performance	.431	.512†	.258	.460	.353	.564
High-growth orientation	.023	−.214	.077	−.161	.024	−.344
Manufacturing firm	.413	.721	1.075	1.438	1.399	1.534
Service firm	.014	.256	.488	.627	.690	1.034

Family-to-business strategies and experiences

Time devoted to the family sphere	-.092*	-.041	-.104*	-.008
Time devoted to the business sphere	-.036	-.062*	-.041	-.055
Segmentation of family and business roles	.103	.594	.107	.557
Identification with the business	.214	.295	.424	.376
Instrumental support from family members	-.363	-.370	-.399	-.619
Traditional division of household labor	-.651	-1.656†	-.941	-2.450*
Fairness in the division of household labor	1.190*	1.154†	1.354*	.806
Family-to-business conflict and enrichment				
Family-to-business conflict			-.570	-2.255***
Family-to-business enrichment			-.002	.712
-2 Log Likelihood	*276.797*	*200.645*		*166.627*
Chi square	*32.024*	*59.121**		*91.264****
Pseudo R² (Nagelkerke)	*0.217*	*0.42*		*0.583*

Notes:
Unstandardized multinomial logistic regression coefficients shown; base category = low effectiveness; N = 133.
† $p < 0.10$; * $p < 0.05$; ** $p < 0.01$.

those tasks is positively associated with satisfaction. Lastly, our analyses reveal that family-to-business conflict is significantly and negatively related to satisfaction when comparing the high to the low satisfaction category. This is consistent with the US findings.

DISCUSSION

Summary

Our initial glimpse into family-to-business strategies of owners of large family businesses in Switzerland and Germany has revealed several novel insights. Importantly, the majority of owner-managers seem to be satisfied with their work and family life, with 68.8 percent reporting a satisfaction level of at least 80 (on a scale from 0 to 100) for the family sphere and 66.7 percent for the business sphere. However, Swiss and German owner-managers perceive themselves to be not very effective in the family domain (only 53.7 percent report high levels of corresponding perceived effectiveness). One reason for this might be the limited time spent on family commitments: an average of only 13.82 hours per week. Moreover, Swiss and German owner-managers scored very low on family-to-business conflict (sample mean of 2.19, range: 1–5) and felt rather enriched by the overlap of family and business matters (sample mean of 3.66, range: 1–5). Family-to-business conflict, in turn, was found to be increased by the amount of time devoted to the family sphere, and to be reduced by the perceived fairness in the distribution of household tasks. Family-to-business enrichment, in turn, was enhanced by instrumental support from family members. A high level of identification with the business was revealed as a factor that enhances the level of perceived effectiveness in our multinomial logistic regressions. Lastly, perceived satisfaction was found to be affected by several factors; for instance, it was reduced by a traditional division of labor in the household and by a higher level of family-to-business conflict.

Implications

Our study's exploratory results offer intriguing and important insights relevant for the family business, entrepreneurship and work–family interface literatures. Family business scholars have recently called for a shift in focus away from organizational level analyses to an increased attention on business-owning families (for example, James, Jennings, and Breitkreuz, 2012; Sharma, 2004; Zellweger, Nason, and Nordqvist, 2012). Zellweger et al. (2012), for instance, provide initial evidence that families often

engage in portfolio entrepreneurship and pursue trans-generational investment strategies. However, such family internal strategy-making and intra-
familial dynamics remain undetected if one solely focuses on the family
business as organization. Our study adds to this emerging focus on business families by revealing their strategies to juggle and align the family and
business domains. In doing so, we contribute to the emerging literature on
the family and the professional logic that can co-exist within business families (cf. Greenwood, Díaz, Li, and Lorente, 2010; Miller, Le Breton-Miller,
and Lester, 2011). A central question within this research stream, deriving
from institutional theory (for example, Greenwood, Raynard, Kodeih,
Micelotta, and Lounsbury, 2011; Kraatz and Block, 2008; Pache and
Santos, 2010), is whether family and professional logics compete with or
re-enforce each other. This question is also reflected in the conflict versus
enrichment perspectives of the work–family interface literature. Here, we
offer interesting insights. On the one hand, the time devoted to the family
sphere leads to greater family-to-business conflict (see Table 9.3). On the
other hand, familial support enhances family-to-business enrichment, supporting the enrichment perspective. Overall, in line with the US findings
and related research (for example, Powell and Greenhaus, 2010; Rothbard,
2001), we conclude that the intersection between work and family in
Switzerland and Germany is best described as a combination of conflict
and enrichment.

Our findings also contribute to recent research on non-economic goals
and endowments of business owners (Berrone et al., 2012; Gómez-Mejía,
Cruz, Berrone, and De Castro, 2011; Gómez-Mejía, Haynes, Núñez-
Nickel, Jacobson, and Moyano-Fuentes, 2007) by shedding light on the
level and factors of personal well-being related to the work–family interface. Past studies on non-economic goals have primarily centered on family
internal goals concerning firm matters such as exerting influence and
control over the firm, securing transgenerational succession, and protect-
ing ties to stakeholders (Berrone et al., 2012). Our study helps to reveal a
more holistic set of non-economic goals by focusing on the effect of family
life on business ownership and vice versa.

Revealing the two-sided relationship between family and working life
in the context of entrepreneurial activity provides further evidence for
the family embeddedness view of entrepreneurship (Aldrich and Cliff,
2003) while simultaneously supporting studies that stress the effect of
entrepreneurial activity on family life (Eddleston and Powell, 2012; Olson
et al., 2003). As such, our study provides initial hints as to whether entrepreneurship contributes to personal well-being in terms of feeling satisfied and effective in both one's business and family lives. Our findings
for Swiss and German owner-managers reveal, for instance, that strong

family-to-business conflict leads to lower levels of satisfaction. Referring to personal well-being in general, we offer additional valuable insights as we find that being female is associated with a higher level of perceived effectiveness, but does not affect the level of satisfaction. Put differently, female owner-managers feel more effective but not happier than male owner-managers.

Limitations

The implications of our study need to be reflected in light of the study's limitations. First, our sample is not representative of business owners in Switzerland and Germany because we deliberately focused on owner-managers of the largest family-controlled firms in German-speaking economies. Therefore, the proportion of high earners is higher than national averages. In that sense, our sample differs considerably from that of the US study, which, while providing additional insights, also limits the comparability of results.

A second limitation is the reliance upon self-reported data from owner-managers. While owner-managers are clearly able to provide accurate information on their business activities as well as their private life, alternative data sources for triangulation would have enhanced this study's insights. In addition, it would have been beneficial for this study to have multiple respondents from one household in order to triangulate the owner-managers perception of the family-to-business interface with those of his/her family members (cf. Marchisio, Mazzola, Sciascia, Miles, and Astrachan, 2010).

Conclusion

Our study's insights serve as important initial indications of whether business ownership is beneficial for family members in Switzerland and Germany. Our findings point to high levels of concurrent satisfaction within and across family and business domains associated with business ownership. This satisfaction is strongly driven by a low perception of conflict between the two domains. Our study's results also reveal a positive relationship of familial support and the individual's perception of enrichment between the two spheres. If we were to give one recommendation derived from our study's findings, we would advise business owners in Switzerland and Germany to spend more hours in the family sphere. While too much time devoted to familial commitments might plant the seed for family-to-business conflict, the increased time spent in this domain is likely to heighten an owner-manager's perceived effectiveness as a family member and to enhance the instrumental support received from family members for the business, thereby potentially promoting even greater family-to-business enrichment.

NOTE

1. The firm-level controls consisted of the following variables that are very similar to those used in the US chapter: *founder-led firm* (coded 1 if the respondent indicated that s/he had founded the focal business, 0 if not); *self-perception as family firm* (coded 1 if the respondent considered the business to be a family firm, 0 if not); *firm age* (measured by subtracting the company's founding year from 2014); *firm size* (measured by the number of full-time equivalent employees currently employed by the firm, excluding the respondent); *firm performance* (measured by a 4-item Likert-type scale assessing the company's performance relative to competitors in the last three years in the dimensions growth of sales, growth of market share, growth of profitability, and return on equity, $\alpha = .85$); *high-growth orientation* (measured by an 3-item Likert-type scale assessing the respondent's attitudes towards business expansion, $\alpha = .74$); and, dummy variables for *manufacturing* and *service* firms (with those classified as 'other' as the holdout).

REFERENCES

Aldrich, H.E. and J.E. Cliff (2003), 'The pervasive effects of family on entrepreneurship: toward a family embeddedness perspective,' *Journal of Business Venturing*, **18**(5), 573–596.

Amoró, J.E. and N. Bosma (2014), 'Global Entrepreneurship Monitor: 2013 Global Report,' Global Entrepreneurship Research Association (GERA).

Amway-GmbH and LMU-Entrepreneurship-Center. (2010), *Zukunft Selbstständigkeit: Eine europäische Studie der Amway GmbH und des LMU Entrepreneurship Center*. Puchheim, Germany.

Berrone, P., C. Cruz, and L.R. Gómez-Mejía (2012), 'Socioemotional wealth in family firms: Theoretical dimensions, assessment approaches, and agenda for future research,' *Family Business Review*, **25**(3), 258–279.

Carlson, D.S., L.J. Williams, and K.M. Kacmar (2000), 'Construction and initial validation of a multidimensional measure of work–family conflict,' *Journal of Vocational Behavior*, **56**(2), 249–276.

Carlson, D.S., K.M. Kacmar, J.H. Wayne, and J.G. Grzywacz (2006), 'Measuring the positive side of the work–family interface: Development and validation of a work–family enrichment scale,' *Journal of Vocational Behavior*, **68**(1), 131–164.

Carter, S. (2011), 'The rewards of entrepreneurship: Exploring the incomes, wealth, and economic well-being of entrepreneurial households,' *Entrepreneurship Theory and Practice*, **35**(1), 39–55.

Cliff, J.E. (1998), 'Does one size fit all? Exploring the relationship between attitudes towards growth, gender, and business size,' *Journal of Business Venturing*, **13**(6), 523–542.

Eddleston, K.A. and G.N. Powell (2012), 'Nurturing entrepreneurs' work–family balance: A gendered perspective,' *Entrepreneurship Theory and Practice*, **36**(3), 513–541.

Frey, U., F. Halter, S. Klein, and T. Zellweger (2004), *Family Business in Switzerland:*

Significance and Structure. Paper presented at the FBN 15th World Conference, Copenhagen, DEN.

Gómez-Mejía, L.R., C. Cruz, P. Berrone, and J. De Castro (2011), 'The bind that ties: Socioemotional wealth preservation in family firms,' *Academy of Management Annals*, **5**(1), 653–707.

Gómez-Mejía, L.R., K.T. Haynes, M. Núñez-Nickel, K.J.L. Jacobson, and J. Moyano-Fuentes (2007), 'Socioemotional wealth and business risks in family-controlled firms: Evidence from Spanish olive oil mills,' *Administrative Science Quarterly*, **52**(1), 106–137.

Gottschalk, S., M. Niefert, G. Licht, A. Hauer, D. Keese, and M. Woywode (2011), *Die volkswirtschaftliche Bedeutung der Familienunternehmen*. München, Germany: Stiftung Familienunternehmen.

Greenwood, R., A.M. Díaz, S.X. Li, and J.C. Lorente (2010), 'The multiplicity of institutional logics and the heterogeneity of organizational responses,' *Organization Science*, **21**(2), 521–539.

Greenwood, R., M. Raynard, F. Kodeih, E.R. Micelotta, and M. Lounsbury (2011), 'Institutional complexity and organizational responses,' *The Academy of Management Annals*, **5**(1), 317–371.

Haynes, G.W., J.I. Onochie, and G. Muske (2007), 'Is what's good for the business, good for the family: A financial assessment,' *Journal of Family and Economic Issues*, **28**(3), 395–409.

James, A.E., J.E. Jennings, and R.S. Breitkreuz (2012), 'Worlds apart? Rebridging the distance between family science and family business research,' *Family Business Review*, **25**(1), 87–108.

Jennings, J.E. and M.S. McDougald (2007), 'Work–family interface experiences and coping strategies: Implications for entrepreneurship research and practice,' *Academy of Management Review*, **32**(3), 747–760.

Jennings, J.E., R.S. Breitkreuz, and A.E. James (2013), 'When family members are also business owners: Is entrepreneurship good for families?,' *Family Relations*, **62**(3), 472–489.

Jennings, J.E., K. Hughes, and P.D. Jennings (2010), 'The work–family interface strategies of male and female entrepreneurs: Are there any differences?.' In C.G. Brush, A. De Bruin, E.J. Gatewood, and C. Henry (eds), *Women Entrepreneurs and the Global Environment for Growth* (pp. 163–186). Cheltenham, UK and Northampton, MA: Edward Elgar Publishing.

Jennings, J.E., P.D. Jennings, and M. Sharifian. (forthcoming), 'Living the dream? Exploring the "entrepreneurship as emancipation" notion in a developed region,' *Entrepreneurship Theory and Practice*. DOI is 10.1111/etap.12106.

Kraatz, M.S. and E.S. Block (2008), 'Organizational implications of institutional pluralism.' In Royston Greenwood, Christine Oliver, Roy Suddaby, and K. Sahlin-Andersson (eds), *The Sage Handbook of Organizational Institutionalism* (Vol. 840). London: Sage Publications.

Loscocco, K.A. and K.T. Leicht (1993), 'Gender, work–family linkages, and economic success among small business owners,' *Journal of Marriage and the Family*, **55**(4), 875–887.

Marchisio, G., P. Mazzola, S. Sciascia, M. Miles, and J. Astrachan (2010), 'Corporate venturing in family business: The effects on the family and its members,' *Entrepreneurship and Regional Development*, **22**(3–4), 349–377.

McGowan, P., C.L. Redeker, S.Y. Cooper, and K. Greenan (2012), 'Female entrepreneurship and the management of business and domestic roles: Motivations, expectations and realities,' *Entrepreneurship and Regional Development*, **24**(1–2), 53–72.

Milkie, M.A. and P. Peltola (1999), 'Playing all the roles: Gender and the work–family balancing act,' *Journal of Marriage and the Family*, **61**(2), 476–490.

Miller, D., I. Le Breton-Miller, and R.H. Lester (2011), 'Family and lone founder ownership and strategic behaviour: Social context, identity, and institutional logics,' *Journal of Management Studies*, **48**(1), 1–25.

Netemeyer, R., J.S. Boles, and R. McMurrian (1996), 'Development and validation of work–family conflict and family–work conflict scales,' *Journal of Applied Psychology*, **81**(4), 400–410.

Olson, P.D., V.S. Zuiker, S.M. Danes, K. Stafford, R. Heck, and K.A. Duncan (2003), 'The impact of the family and the business on family business sustainability,' *Journal of Business Venturing*, **18**(5), 639–666.

O'Reilly, C.I. and J.A. Chatman (1986), 'Organizational commitment and psychological attachment: The effects of compliance, identification, and internalization of prosocial behavior,' *Journal of Applied Psychology*, **71**(3), 492–499.

Pache, A.C. and F. Santos (2010), 'When worlds collide: The internal dynamics of organizational responses to conflicting institutional demands,' *Academy of Management Review*, **35**(3), 455–476.

Powell, G.N. (2011), *Women and Men in Management*. Los Angeles: Sage Publications.

Powell, G.N. and K.A. Eddleston (2013), 'Linking family-to-business enrichment and support to entrepreneurial success: Do female and male entrepreneurs experience different outcomes?,' *Journal of Business Venturing*, **28**(2), 261–280.

Powell, G.N. and J.H. Greenhaus (2010), 'Sex, gender, and decisions at the family–work interface,' *Journal of Management*, **36**(4), 1011–1039.

Rindova, V., D. Barry, and D.J. Ketchen (2009), 'Entrepreneuring as emancipation,' *Academy of Management Review*, **34**(3), 477–491.

Rothbard, N.P. (2001), 'Enriching or depleting? The dynamics of engagement in work and family roles,' *Administrative Science Quarterly*, **46**(4), 655–684.

Sharma, P. (2004), 'An overview of the field of family business studies: Current status and directions for the future,' *Family Business Review*, **17**(1), 1–36.

Shelton, L.M. (2006), 'Female entrepreneurs, work–family conflict, and venture performance: New insights into the work–family interface,' *Journal of Small Business Management*, **44**(2), 285–297.

Stafford, K., K.A. Duncan, S. Dane, and M. Winter (1999), 'A research model of sustainable family businesses,' *Family Business Review*, **12**(3), 197–208.

Waismel-Manor, R., P. Moen, and S. Sweet (2002), 'Managing and thriving: What factors predict dual-earner middle-class couples feeling highly successful in their jobs, families and balancing both?' BLCC Working Paper, Number 02-20.

Xavier, S.R., D. Kelly, J. Kew, M. Herrington, and A. Vorderwülbecke (2012), 'Global Entrepreneurship Monitor 2012,' Global Report (http://www. gemconsortium. org/docs/download/2645).

Yodanis, C. (2005), 'Divorce culture and marital gender equality a cross-national study,' *Gender and Society*, **19**(5), 644–659.

Zellweger, T., R.S. Nason, and M. Nordqvist (2012), 'From longevity of firms to transgenerational entrepreneurship of families: Introducing family entrepreneurial orientation,' *Family Business Review*, **25**(2), 136–155.

10. The work–family interface of business owner-managers in China

Li Tian and Yanfeng Zheng

INTRODUCTION

One of the fast-growing emerging economies, China has achieved miraculous progress in terms of economic and social welfare development over the past few decades. At least part of this progress can be attributed to the evolution in the state's orientation towards entrepreneurship, which shifted from one of strict prohibition, to one of tolerance then accommodation, and now to one of encouragement (Peng, 2004). As elucidated by Puffer, McCarthy and Boisot, although the economic reforms initiated in 1978 'were in certain respects a response to a bottom-up entrepreneurial dynamic,' 'most of the reform measures adopted since that time have been favorable to the development of an entrepreneurial climate' (Puffer et al., 2010: 451). Puffer and her colleagues further noted that the public's perceptions of the entrepreneurial function have shifted dramatically as a result; indeed, as documented within the most recent Global Entrepreneurship Monitor (GEM) report (Amoró and Bosma, 2014), it is estimated that 69.6 percent of China's population aged 18–64 consider entrepreneurship to be a good career choice.

Indicative of this increasingly positive orientation towards business enterprising, 'by 2005 China had 24 million private companies and was registering a 15–20% annual growth in their number' (Puffer et al., 2010: 452). In 2010, the small and medium-sized enterprise (SME) sector was estimated to account for 75 percent of new job creation in the country (Puffer et al., 2010) and close to 94 million families were estimated to be involved in either starting new businesses or owning and managing established enterprises (Jennings, Breitkreuz, and James, 2013). In 2013, 14 percent of adults between the ages of 18 and 64 in the country were estimated to be involved in early stage entrepreneurial activity, with another 11 percent engaged in established business ownership; notably, both of these estimates are higher than the respective rates of 12.7 percent and 7.5 percent for the United States (Amoró and Bosma, 2014).

Despite the increasing prominence and contributions of privately held firms to the Chinese economy, very little is known about such organizations and their owner-managers. This is especially so with respect to how these individuals manage the domains of work and family—a topic of increasing interest within the general entrepreneurship literature (see for example, Eddleston and Powell, 2012; Jennings, Hughes, and Jennings, 2010; Jennings and McDougald, 2007; McGowan, Redeker, Cooper, and Greenan, 2012; Powell and Eddleston, 2013). Using data collected via an online survey completed by 300 owner-managers across 29 provinces or equivalent regions of mainland China, this chapter offers a rare glimpse into the work–family interface (WFI) strategies invoked by Chinese business owners and the effects of these strategies on their psychological well-being.

The organization of this chapter is as follows. We start by describing our study's methodology, sample, and basic demographic characteristics of the business owners and their households. Following this, we present information on key indicators of personal well-being; specifically, on the extent to which business owners in China consider themselves to be effective and satisfied with respect to various aspects of their lives. We then present details on their strategies for managing the work–family interface and their experienced work–family conflict and enrichment. This is followed by a series of multivariate analyses that shed light on the factors associated with the psychic outcomes of perceived effectiveness and satisfaction. In sum, this chapter offers unique descriptive data on business owners and their households in China—as well as a sense of the business, family and work–family interface characteristics that enable some to feel more effective and satisfied with various aspects of their lives than others.

METHODOLOGY AND SAMPLE

Our data was collected primarily through a professional survey service company that had access to family business associations, financial institutions, and other related agencies. We provided the company with the survey items, which were converted into an online questionnaire that launched in October 2012 and closed at the end of January 2013. For those respondents who preferred a paper survey, we mailed the same survey to them. The sampling frame of potential participants was stratified by geographic region, industry, and other firm characteristics (for example, firm size). The survey was sent to 353 owner-managers (243 via online, 110 via mail). We received 300 complete surveys, which corresponds to a high response rate of approximately 85 percent. We validated the responses by contacting a random sample of 10 percent of all respondents.

The sampled firms come from 29 provinces or central governed cities in mainland China—including Beijing, Shanghai, Tianjin and Chongqing— and cover a broad range of industries such as manufacturing, personal services and professional services. The ages of the firms range from 1 to 33 with a median of 6. The average firm employed 80 full-time employees but the median is only 17. The sampled firms had average sales in 2012 of 9.34 million RMB (the median is 1 million RMB). Of the 300 respondents, 107 considered their organizations to be family firms (35.7 percent) while 193 (or 64.3 percent) did not.

DEMOGRAPHIC CHARACTERISTICS OF THE BUSINESS OWNERS AND THEIR HOUSEHOLDS

Of the 300 owner-managers who participated in the China-based study, 202 (67.3 percent) indicated that they were male and 98 (32.7 percent) indicated that they were female. This gender distribution is similar to that reported in the Chinese Panel Study of Entrepreneurial Dynamics project (Zhang, Yang, Au, and Reynolds, 2011), which showed that among all nascent entrepreneurs in mainland China in that year, 70.1 percent were male and 29.9 percent were female.

With respect to education, almost all of the participants possessed at least a high school diploma. Indeed, only 12.0 percent indicated that this was their highest educational degree. Approximately one-third (34.0 percent) had completed some form of apprenticeship program, 46.0 percent had earned a bachelor's degree, and 0.6 percent possessed a master's or doctorate.

The vast majority of the participating owner-managers (81.3 percent) indicated that they had a spouse or marital-like partner. Close to 70 percent (69.3 percent) of the participants reported having at least one child under the age of 18 living in their households. The number of children ranged from zero to eight, with most respondents mentioning only one (55.7 percent) or two (12.3 percent). Single-parent households constituted 4.3 percent of the sample; of these, there was an almost even distribution between male and female entrepreneurs (51.8 percent versus 48.2 percent, respectively).

We were able to obtain personal and household income data from all respondents. This data was measured by eight ordinal categories ranging from 'less than 100,000 RMB' to 'over 10 million RMB.' The means for both personal and household income were 200,000–500,000RMB, which suggests that many of the owner-managers in the China sample were the primary (if not sole) economic providers for their families. Notably, only 0.3 percent of the participants reported personal incomes over 10,000,000 RMB and only 2.0 percent reported household incomes over this amount.

The national statistic bureau's survey for the year 2012 showed that the annual salaries of the Chinese working population employed by non-private and private organizations were 46,769 RMB and 26,752 RMB, respectively (Chinese Statistic Yearbook, 2013). As such, the household incomes of a typical Chinese family (two working adults and one child), should roughly be 93,538 RMB and 53,504 RMB respectively. Thus, in comparison with the Chinese working population as whole, Chinese business owners create more wealth for themselves as well as for their families via their entrepreneurial endeavors.

OUTCOMES IN THE FAMILY DOMAIN

The income data reported above represents an economic outcome for those involved in business ownership. As noted by Rindova, Barry, and Ketchen (2009), however, considerable research has shown that economic gain is not the only (or even the primary) motivation for entrepreneurship. Thus, following recent calls for a more holistic approach to the conceptualization and measurement of outcomes associated with business ownership (Amoró and Bosma, 2014; Jennings and Brush, 2013; Jennings and McDougald, 2007; Guest, 2002)—especially when considering the impact upon families (Jennings et al., 2013)—we present a few key *non*-economic outcomes in this section. Specifically, we report findings for perceived effectiveness and satisfaction across the family and business domains.

To measure *perceived effectiveness*, we asked the respondents to report how effective they considered themselves to date: (1) as a business owner-manager, (2) as a family member, and (3) in balancing the various aspects of their lives. Following Waismel-Manor, Moen, and Sweet (2002), each of the three items was rated on a scale ranging from 0 to 100. To assess the extent to which the respondents possessed *concurrent perceptions of effectiveness* across the business and family domains, we created a composite measure as follows. First, we recoded each of the three constituent items dichotomously, assigning respondents a value of '1 = highly effective' if they reported a score of at least 80 out of 100 on the item, 0 if not. Following Jennings, Jennings, and Sharifian (forthcoming), we then summed the three dichotomous measures and recoded the aggregate score such that a sum of 0 was deemed to reflect 'little concurrent perceived effectiveness,' sums of 1 or 2 were deemed to reflect 'partial concurrent perceived effectiveness,' and a sum of 3 was deemed to reflect 'full concurrent

Firms within families

Table 10.1   Perceived effectiveness and satisfaction (China sample)

	Perceived Effectiveness	
	Low effectiveness (score < 80/100)	High effectiveness (score ≥ 80/100)
Perceived effectiveness as a business owner	33.0%	67.0%
Perceived effectiveness as a family member	54.3%	45.7%
Perceived effectiveness in balancing business and family roles	47.3%	52.7%

Concurrent perceived effectiveness in balancing business and family roles		
Little (0 of the above scored high) 21%	Partial (1–2 of the above scored high) 44.3%	Full (all 3 of above scored high) 34.7%

	Perceived Satisfaction	
	Low satisfaction (score < 80/100)	High satisfaction (score ≥ 80/100)
Perceived satisfaction as a business owner	34.3%	65.7%
Perceived satisfaction as a family member	49.7%	50.3%
Perceived satisfaction in balancing the business and family roles	48.3%	51.7%

Concurrent perceived satisfaction in balancing business and family roles		
Little (0 of the above scored high) 23.3%	Partial (1–2 of the above scored high) 39.3%	Full (all 3 of above scored high) 37.3%

perceived effectiveness.' A parallel procedure was adopted for *perceived satisfaction*. Table 10.1 summarizes the findings.

The findings reported in the top half of Table 10.1 provide insight into the question: 'To what degree do owner-managers in the China consider themselves *effective* across the domains of business and family?' The results presented in the first three rows alone suggest that the answer to this question is: 'To a fairly high degree.' To be concrete, 67.0 percent, 45.7 percent and 52.7 percent of the respondents considered themselves to be highly effective on the separate indicators of perceived effectiveness as a business owner, family member and in balancing the two roles. The findings for the composite measure are also revealing. Although the majority were coded as reporting either little (21.0 percent) or only partial (44.3 percent) concurrent effectiveness across the business and family domains, a substantial proportion (34.7 percent) were coded as expressing full concurrent perceived effectiveness (in other words, scores of at least 80 out of 100 on each of the three constituent items).

The findings reported in the bottom half of Table 10.1 offer insight into the question: 'To what extent are owner-managers in China *satisfied* across the domains of business and family?' As in the above case, the results suggest that the answer is: 'To a relatively great extent.' As indicated, on each of the separate indicators of perceived satisfaction, 65.7 percent, 50.3 percent and 51.7 percent of the respondents reported a score at or above 80 out of 100. Moreover, although the majority were coded as expressing either little (23.3 percent) or only partial (39.3 percent) concurrent satisfaction across the business and family domains, once again a substantial proportion (37.3 percent) was deemed as having expressed full concurrent perceived satisfaction (in other words, scores of at least 80 out of 100 on each of the three constituent items).

WORK–FAMILY INTERFACE STRATEGIES AND EXPERIENCES

A growing body of entrepreneurship research has started to focus on entrepreneurs' experiences of the work–family interface (WFI), examining such considerations as a business owner's identification with the firm, dedication to business and household work, and factors consistent with two competing perspectives regarding individuals' WFI experiences; in other words, the work–family enrichment versus work–family conflict views (for example, Eddleston and Powell, 2012; Jennings et al., 2010; Jennings and McDougald, 2007; McGowan et al., 2012; Powell and Eddleston, 2013). Below, we use our survey findings to paint a picture of how entrepreneurs in China fare on these dimensions.

Identification

An 11-item Likert scale was used to measure an owner's identification with business, with each item measured from '1 = strongly disagree' to '5 = strongly agree.' Example items include, 'I am emotionally attached to the firm' and 'The firm reminds me who I am.' An initial Kaiser–Meyer–Olkin Measuring of Sampling Adequacy test (significance =.925) and Bartlett's

Test of Sphericity (significance = .001) both pointed to strong correlations among the 11 items, suggesting that factor analysis was appropriate for extracting common factors and thus reducing the number of variables included in model testing. Using the principal components method, one component was extracted based on the eigenvalues, which accounted for about 58.4 percent of the variance in the observed variables. The mean of the 11 items was 4.05, which indicates that the owner-managers in the China sample exhibited a very high degree of personal ownership and sense of belonging to their ventures.

Segmentation

In the WFI literature, researchers have also investigated the strategies that people use to cope with work and family role demands. The segmentation model hypothesizes that work and non-work are two distinct domains of life that are lived quite separately and have no influence on each other (for reviews see Edwards and Rothbard, 2000; Greenhaus and Parasuraman, 1999; Lambert, 1990). We asked the respondents not only about their ideal preference for work–family segmentation or integration but also about the extent to which they were able to separate the two domains in reality. We used three items to measure each scale, with each item measured on a 5-point scale from '1 = strongly disagree' to '5 = strongly agree.'

Our descriptive analysis revealed that the means for both scales were 3.41 and 3.31. These are higher than '3 = neutral,' which means that both ideally and in reality Chinese entrepreneurs prefer to segment work from family. Moreover, we found a 'good fit' between the actual and preferred levels of segmentation reported by our respondents, with approximately two-thirds reporting that they prefer to segment work and family and are able to do so in reality. We further observed that the maximum gap between ideality and reality (on either the positive or negative side) was very limited.

Hours and Household Help

In the WFI literature, the number of hours spent in the business and family domains is often considered as an antecedent of work–family conflict (Jennings and McDougald, 2007). As shown in the top of Table 10.2, the entrepreneurs in our China sample spent an average of 48.1 hours working in the business per week. Chinese labor law defines 44 working hours as an appropriate maximum; moreover, reviews of the literature on working hours and health provide some indication that when people work much beyond these hours, their health and performance can begin to deteriorate (for example, Guest, 2002). It thus appears that the Chinese entrepreneurs

Table 10.2   Work–family interface strategies and experiences (China sample)

	Mean	Std. deviation	Min	Max
Working hours per week	48.1	24.1	2.0	120
Hours spent on household tasks	11.4	10.7	0.0	72

	Shop for groceries	Cook dinner	Do the laundry	Take care of sick
Always or usually the woman	49.0%	42.7%	50.3%	28.3%
Equally	39.3%	36.0%	31.0%	50.3%
Always or usually the man	5.3%	8.3%	7.0%	6.7%
A third person (other family members)	3.3%	2.7%	3.0%	4.3%
A third person (hired help)	3.0%	10.3%	8.7%	10.3%

	Mean	Std. deviation	Min	Max
Work–family conflict	3.08	0.79	1	5
Work–family enrichment	3.78	0.64	1.67	5

in our sample have crossed that border and are burdened with an intense workload. Moreover, they reported spending an additional 11.4 hours on household tasks per week.

The findings reported in the middle of Table 10.2 shed even further insight into the households of owner-managers in China. As indicated, within almost half of such households, it is always or usually the female who shops for groceries (49.0 percent), decides what to have for dinner (42.7 percent) or does the laundry (50.3 percent). Within another third or so of such households, such tasks tend to be divided equally. In less than 1 in 10 households is it the man who always or usually takes responsibility for these household tasks. When it comes to caring for the sick, however, 50.3 percent of the respondents reported that the husband and wife shared this responsibility equally. Overall, then, these findings suggest that within enterprising households in China, women usually assume the lion's share of daily household tasks. Urgent events such as taking care of the sick, however, tend to be shared more equally between husbands and wives.

Egalitarianism and Fairness

After responding to the above-noted questions, the respondents were asked to comment upon the perceived fairness of their household division of labor. Only 4.0 percent felt that it was very unfair, whereas 30.3 percent felt that it was somewhat unfair, 37.7 percent felt that it was somewhat fair, and 28.0 percent felt that it was very fair. In general, then, approximately two-thirds of the business owners in the China sample perceived the division of domestic labor within their households to be at least somewhat fair.

Family Support Towards Business

Family support refers to instrumental support provided by family members for the respondent's role of business owner. It was measured by the factor loading of a 5-item Likert-type scale developed by Powell and Eddleston (2013). Illustrative items include: 'The members of my family who do not officially work in the business can be counted on to help out if something unexpected happens in this business' and 'The members of my family who do not officially work in the business often give me useful feedback and ideas concerning this business.'

Our survey findings show that owner-managers in China tend to receive considerable instrumental and emotional support from family members who do not officially work in the business. More specifically, 58.3 percent reported that such family members contributed to the business without expecting to be paid, 68.7 percent reported that these family members often offered useful feedback and ideas concerning the business, 64.7 percent reported that their family members could be counted on to help out if something unexpected happened in the business, and 54.7 percent reported their family members often went above and beyond what was normally expected in order to help the business succeed. Indeed, a high of 71.3 percent reported that their family members often tried to understand when they felt frustrated with their business.

Family-to-Business Conflict and Enrichment

The bottom row of Table 10.2 reports the items and findings for our measures of family-to-business conflict and enrichment. The mean and median for the degree of work–family conflict suffered by the Chinese entrepreneurs in our sample are in the middle of the 5-point Likert scale, which suggests that work–family conflict is controllable for owner-managers in this country. Notably, the observations were fairly evenly distributed across the three levels of 'very low to low level of conflict' (values of 1 or 2), 'medium level of conflict' (values of 3), and 'high to very high level of conflict' (values of 4 or 5), with approximately one third of the respondents falling into each of these categories.

In terms of family-to-business enrichment, the results reveal that Chinese entrepreneurs feel that their involvement in family life makes them a better businessperson. The means and medians of the six items, for instance, are all above neutral. Furthermore, the frequencies indicate that over 60 percent of the respondents agreed or strongly agreed that their involvement in the family domain enriches their business work.

FACTORS ASSOCIATED WITH PERCEIVED EFFECTIVENESS AND SATISFACTION

Table 10.3 and Table 10.4 contain the results of the regression analyses that we conducted to assess the effects of some of the above-noted family-to-business strategies and experiences on the Chinese entrepreneurs' perceived effectiveness and satisfaction as owner-managers, family members and in achieving work–life balance. We adopt an OLS regression to estimate the parameters because the outcome is a continuous variable ranging from 0 to 100. As indicated, we examined the effects of the family-to-business strategies and experiences net of several control variables. The effects of one demographic control variable, in particular, warrants mention. The female entrepreneurs in the China sample perceived a lower level of satisfaction as business owner-managers in comparison with their male counterparts ($\beta = -0.15, p < 0.01$).

The results for hours spent in the business domain indicate that this variable has a negative cross-domain effect on entrepreneurs' family lives. The more hours that they spend on the business, the less effective and satisfied they perceive themselves as a family member ($\beta = -0.27, p < 0.001$; $\beta = -0.33, p < 0.001$) and in balancing work and life ($\beta = -0.26, p < 0.001$; $\beta = -0.29, p < 0.001$). In contrast, greater time spent on household tasks helped to enhance the entrepreneurs' perception of being an effective family member ($\beta = 0.11, p < 0.001$), and of being effective and satisfied with their work–life balance ($\beta = 0.16, p < 0.05$; $\beta = 0.18, p < 0.01$). However, the time spent on household tasks did not show any significant impact on their perception of being satisfied as a family member.

With regards to the work–family interface (WFI) variables, we found that work–family conflict didn't have any effect on the Chinese entrepreneurs' perceptions of being effective or satisfied in the work and family domains. However, work–family enrichment showed significant and

Table 10.3 OLS regressions for perceived effectiveness with business, family and work–life balance (China sample)

	Effectiveness as a business person	Effectiveness as a family member	Effectiveness in balancing work and life
Controls			
Gender[a]	−0.09†	−0.00	−0.02
Education level	0.03	0.07	0.05
Married	−0.07	0.01	−0.02
Number of kids	0.02	−0.09	−0.04
Employee of another org	−0.07	0.03	0.02
Family support	0.12	0.01	0.06
Firm age	0.09	−0.03	−0.04
Working hours	−0.01	−0.27***	−0.26***
Household hours	−0.03	0.11***	0.16*
WFI variables			
Work–family conflict	0.01	0.08	0.01
Work–family enrichment	0.20**	0.15†	0.17*
Segmentation	0.01	0.04	0.10
Identification	0.20**	0.09	0.13†
Model *F*	8.03***	3.70***	5.04***
Adjusted *R* square	0.23	0.11	0.15

Notes:
a   coded 1 = male, 2 = female.
$\dagger$ $p \le .10$, * $p \le .05$, ** $p \le .01$, *** $p \le .001$.

positive effects on perceived effectiveness as a business person ($\beta = 0.20$, $p < 0.01$) and in balancing work and life ($\beta = 0.17$, $p < 0.05$), as well as a marginal significant and positive effects on perceived effectiveness as a family member ($\beta = 0.15$, $p < 0.1$). Moreover, work–family enrichment has a significant and positive effect on perceived satisfaction as a business person ($\beta = 0.33$, $p < 0.01$), a family member ($\beta = 0.20$, $p < 0.01$) and in balancing the work and life ($\beta = 0.23$, $p < 0.01$) (see Table 10.4). The findings imply that positive WFI experiences have beneficial across-domains spillover effects whereas negative WFI experiences, such as work–family conflict, don't seem to be influential.

As for the WFI strategies of segmentation and identification, segmentation strategy's effects were non-significant. Identification showed a positive and significant effect on perceived effectiveness ($\beta = 0.20$, $p < 0.05$) and satisfaction as a business person ($\beta = 0.17$, $p < 0.05$).

Table 10.4   OLS regressions for perceived satisfaction with business, family and work–life balance (China sample)

	Satisfaction as a business person	Satisfaction as a family member	Satisfaction in balancing work and life
Controls			
Gender[a]	−0.15**	−0.02	−0.03
Education level	−0.02	0.04	0.06
Married	−0.04	−0.01	−0.05
Number of kids	0.02	−0.06	0.03
Employee of another org	−0.08	−0.06	−0.07
Family support	0.02	0.05	0.07
Firm age	0.01	0.02	−0.02
Working hours	−0.05	−0.33***	−0.29***
Household hours	0.01	0.09	0.18**
WFI variables			
Work–family conflict	0.03	0.11[†]	0.16
Work–family enrichment	0.33***	0.20**	0.23**
Segmentation	0.06	0.10	0.07
Identification	0.17*	0.01	0.10
Model F	8.20***	6.24***	6.33***
Adjusted R square	0.24	0.19	0.19

Notes:
a   coded 1 = male, 2 = female.
† $p \leq .10$, * $p \leq .05$, ** $p \leq .01$, *** $p \leq .001$.

Table 10.5 contains the results of the multinomial logistic regression analyses that we conducted on the composite indicators of perceived effectiveness and satisfaction. Focusing on the findings for full concurrent effectiveness/satisfaction, two of the demographic control variables warrant mention. For one, the male entrepreneurs in the China sample were significantly more likely to report full concurrent satisfaction than the female entrepreneurs ($\beta = 0.90$, $p < 0.05$). This finding is consistent with that presented in the most recent GEM report, which indicated that females who are engaged in entrepreneurial activity in China tend to be less satisfied with their lives overall than their male counterparts (Amoró and Bosma, 2014: 66). Second, a consistent pattern was found between firm age and the entrepreneurs' perceived well-being, with those heading older firms significantly more likely to report full concurrent effectiveness and satisfaction across the business and family domains ($\beta = 0.09$, $p < 0.10$; $\beta = 0.07$, $p < 0.10$).

Table 10.5 *Multinomial logistic regressions on composite measures of perceived effectiveness and satisfaction (China sample)*

	Concurrent Perceived Effectiveness		Concurrent Perceived Satisfaction	
	Partial	Full	Partial	Full
Controls				
Gender = male	0.17	0.45	0.98**	0.90*
Education = high school	19.86***	0.85	1.29	1.44
Education = professional college	18.80***	−1.04	0.73	0.09
Education = 3 bachelor degree	19.11***	0.06	0.98	0.56
Education = 4 Master/MBA	19.35	0.50	0.70	0.82
Married = no	0.45	1.02†	−0.23	0.32
Employee of other org = no	0.25	0.55	−0.37	0.42
Number of kids	−0.33	−0.16	−0.21	−0.17
Family support	0.23	0.23	−0.09	0.27
Firm age	0.10**	0.09†	0.09*	0.07†
Working hours	−0.01	−0.03**	−0.01	−0.03***
Household hours	0.02	0.01	0.06**	0.04
WFI variables				
Work–family conflict	−0.29	−0.25	−0.07	0.09
Work–family enrichment	0.75**	0.91***	0.85***	1.01***
Segmentation	0.32	0.38†	0.17	0.17
Identification	0.11	0.23	0.28	0.15
Chi-square	104.93***		107.85***	
−2 Log Likelihood	633.37		644.66	
Cox and Snell R-sq	0.30		0.30	
Observations	300		300	

Note:
† $p \le .10$, * $p \le .05$, ** $p \le .01$, *** $p \le .001$.

Hours spent in the business and family spheres were also influential. Those who spent longer hours at work were significantly less likely to report full concurrent effectiveness and satisfaction ($\beta = -0.03$, $p < 0.01$; $\beta = -0.03$, $p < -0.01$). In contrast, those who spent more time on household tasks were more likely to report a partial degree of concurrent satisfaction ($\beta = 0.06$, $p < 0.01$).

With regards to the WFI variables, we found similar results to those reported above. That is, experienced conflict between the work and family domains didn't show any significant effects on the entrepreneurs' concurrent effectiveness and satisfaction. In contrast, experienced work–family enrichment contributed positively and significantly to these indicators of personal well-being. Entrepreneurs who pursued a segmentation strategy were more likely to report full concurrent effectiveness but, interestingly, not full concurrent satisfaction. Strong identification with the role of business owner was once again a non-significant determinant of these psychological outcomes.

DISCUSSION

Summary

How do SME owner-managers in transitional economies such as China perceive the balance in their work and family domains? In this chapter, we documented the characteristics of 300 Chinese owner-managers and how they perceived the interface between work and family. Our research extends prior studies on the inner working mechanisms of firms in emerging economies, specifically in a SME setting.

Our research shows that approximately 35 percent of business owner-managers in China consider themselves to be highly and concurrently effective and/or satisfied across the business and family domains. As for their strategies for managing the work–family interface and their experienced work–family conflict and enrichment, we found that time spent in the business domain has a negative cross-domain effect on entrepreneurs' family lives, while the time spent on household tasks generally helped to enhance entrepreneurs' perception of being effective family members and of being balanced with respect to work and life. Furthermore, positive WFI experiences like work–family enrichment have beneficial across-domains spillover effects whereas negative WFI experiences, such as work–family conflict, don't seem to be influential.

Limitations

It is important, however, to note the limitations of our study. For instance, the cross-sectional design may limit the inferences drawn from our analyses. We therefore encourage future research to collect longitudinal data and further examine the causal mechanisms. Additionally, we excluded public and large family companies from our sampling frame. As such, it is important to keep in mind that our findings pertain primarily to small and medium-sized enterprises in China. It would be interesting to examine the extent to which our findings hold within large, publicly traded firms as well.

Conclusion

Despite its limitations, our study contributes to research on the WFI experiences of entrepreneurs. Our survey first reveals that the majority of respondents perceived effectiveness in both work and family domains. More importantly, our analyses seem to support the work–family enhancement perspective (Greenhaus and Parasuraman, 1999), or the positive spillover model described within Guest's (2002) review of the five main models used to explain the relationship between work and life outside work. Derived from research on role accumulation, the essence of this view is that multiple roles can be beneficial, with the potential for positive spillover of emotions, attitudes, and behaviors. Our study reveals that, in China, work–family enrichment enhances entrepreneurs' perceived effectiveness and satisfaction within and between the work and family domains. In contrast, work–family conflict doesn't appear to detract from the perceived effectiveness and satisfaction of business owners in this country.

ACKNOWLEDGEMENTS

We acknowledge the financial support from the research center of entrepreneurial management of Nankai University and the National Natural Science Foundation Young Scholar Project (71102051).

REFERENCES

Amoró, J.E. and N. Bosma (2014), 'Global Entrepreneurship Monitor 2013 global report.'

Chinese Statistic Yearbook (2013), retrieved from http://www.stats.gov.cn/tjsj/ndsj/2013/indexce.htm (accessed February 6, 2015).

Eddleston, K.A. and G.N. Powell (2012), 'Nurturing entrepreneurs' work–family balance: A gendered perspective,' *Entrepreneurship Theory and Practice*, **26** (3), 513–541.

Edwards, J. and N. Rothbard (2000), 'Mechanisms linking work and family: Clarifying the relationship between work and family construct,' *Academy of Management Review*, **25** (1), 178–199.

Forbes China (2013), 'Chinese Family Business Survey 2013,' retrieved from http://www.forbeschina.com/review/201309/0028419.shtml (accessed September 8, 2013).

Greenhaus, J. and S. Parasuraman (1999), 'Research on work, family and gender: Current status and future directions.' In G.N. Powell (ed.), *Handbook of Gender and Work*: 391–412. Thousand Oaks, CA: Sage Publications.

Guest, D.E. (2002), 'Perspectives on the study of work–life balance,' *Social Science Information*, **41** (2), 255–279.

Jennings, J.E. and C.G. Brush (2013), 'Research on women entrepreneurs: Challenges to (and from) the broader entrepreneurship literature?,' *The Academy of Management Annals*, **7**, 661–713.

Jennings, J. and M. McDougald (2007), 'Work–family interface experiences and coping strategies: Implications for entrepreneurship research and practice,' *Academy of Management Review*, **32**, 747–760.

Jennings, J.E., R.S. Breitkreuz, and A.E. James (2013), 'When family members are also business owners: Is entrepreneurship good for families,' *Family Relations*, **62** (3), 472–489.

Jennings, J.E., K. Hughes, and P.D. Jennings (2010), 'The work–family interface strategies of male and female entrepreneurs: Are there any differences?' In C.G. Brush, E.J. Gatewood, A.M. de Bruin, and C. Henry (eds), *Women's Entrepreneurship and Growth Influences: An International Perspective*: 163–186. Cheltenham, UK and Northampton, MA, Edward Elgar Publishing.

Jennings, J.E., P.D. Jennings and M. Sharifian (forthcoming), 'Living the dream? Assessing the "entrepreneurship as emancipation" perspective in developed region,' *Entrepreneurship Theory and Practice*.

Lambert, S.J. (1990), 'Processes linking work and family: A critical review and research agenda,' *Human Relations*, **43**, 239–257.

McGowan, P., C.L. Redeker, S.Y. Cooper, and K. Greenan (2012), 'Female entrepreneurship and the management of business and domestic roles: Motivations, expectations and realities,' *Entrepreneurship and Regional Development*, **24** (1–2), 53–72.

Peng, M.W. (2004), 'Kinship networks and entrepreneurs in China's transitional economy,' *The American Journal of Sociology*, **109** (5), 1045–1074.

Powell, G.N. and K.A. Eddleston (2013), 'Linking family-to-business enrichment and support to entrepreneurial success: do female and male entrepreneurs experience different outcomes?,' *Journal of Business Venturing*, **28** (2), 261–280.

Puffer, S.M., D.J. McCarthy, and M. Boisot (2010), 'Entrepreneurship in Russia and China: The impact of formal institutional voids,' *Entrepreneurship Theory and Practice*, **May**, 441–467.

Rindova, V., D. Barry, and D. Ketchen (2009), 'Entrepreneuring as emancipation,' *Academy of Management Review*, **34** (3), 477–491.

Rothbard, N.P. (2001), 'Enriching or depleting? The dynamics of engagement in work and family roles,' *Administrative Science Quarterly*, **46**, 655–684.

Waismel-Manor, R., P. Moen, and S. Sweet (2002), 'Managing and thriving: What factors predict dual-earner middle-class couples feeling highly successful in their jobs, families and balancing both?' BLCC Working Paper #02-20.

Zhang Y.L., J. Yang, K. Au, and P. Reynolds (2011), 'Anatomy of business creation in China: Initial assessment on Chinese panel study of entrepreneurial dynamics.' In Paul Reynolds and Richard Curtin (eds), *New Business Creation: An International Overview*: 95–121. New York: Springer.

11. Entrepreneuring families in Brazil: the need for support at home and for the business

Ravi Sarathy, Tales Andreassi, Maria José Tonelli and Kimberly A. Eddleston

INTRODUCTION

Brazil is an interesting country in which to study the work–family interface of entrepreneurs because the family is the foundation of the Brazilian social structure (Watson, Barreira, and Watson, 2000) and the country has recently experienced a surge in entrepreneurial activity (Zacharakis, 2013; GEM, 2013), spurred by market reforms and the restoration of political and monetary stability (Fishlow, 2013). In addition, changes in the role of women in the workplace and family domain in Brazil have influenced how work and family demands are managed (Costa, Sorj, Bruschini, and Hirata, 2008). For example, 31 percent of Brazilian families are now headed by women (Costa et al., 2008). This chapter explores the family-to-business strategies, experiences and outcomes of enterprising families in Brazil, which are defined as households with at least one individual who is involved in owning and managing a business. The EY-G20 Entrepreneurship Barometer (2013), reports that Brazil has 27 million people involved in entrepreneurial activity, including 10.4 million women. The Global Entrepreneurship Monitor (GEM) suggests that Brazil is rated tenth out of 67 countries in entrepreneurship with 30 percent of its active workforce between the ages of 18 and 64 involved in entrepreneurial activities, helping to lower unemployment and to increase living standards (Zacharakis, 2013).

After several years of Brazilian currency stabilization, economic reforms, and advances in privatization and legal structures, the country has experienced a surge in entrepreneurship and business growth. For example, the PRIME program invests in startups that focus on innovation which has helped to generate new jobs. Small and medium-sized enterprises (SMEs) in Brazil are responsible for 96 percent of jobs and they comprise about

98 percent of all companies (Endeavor Brazil, 2011). However, Brazil's complex tax system and regulatory environment create obstacles to growth. The World Bank ranks Brazil 116 among 189 countries in terms of 'ease of doing business' in its 'Doing Business 2014' report, an improvement from its ranking of 129 in 2006. It takes the typical Brazilian entrepreneur 2600 hours per year to manage and pay taxes while those in the US spend 175 hours per year. This helps to explain the large informal sector in Brazil, which accounts for about 40 percent of its GNP, versus just 9 percent in the US (the world average is 33 percent) (Zacharakis, 2013).

Other issues which appear to stall entrepreneurial growth in Brazil are the lack of entrepreneurship education—less than 10 percent of Brazilians aged 18–64 receive any type of entrepreneurship training (Amoros et al., 2014)—and access to financing. The EY-G20 study revealed that 43 percent of entrepreneurs under age 40 report that access to funding in Brazil is 'very difficult' (EY-G20, 2013).

While Brazilian entrepreneurship is on the rise, we know little about how entrepreneurship affects the family domain. Brazil has one of the highest rates of entrepreneurship in the world, particularly female entrepreneurship—49.6 percent of all new businesses are led by women (GEM Brasil, 2012)—and yet we do not know how they are able to manage both their work and family domains. Further, data indicates that many individuals in Brazil may be drawn to entrepreneurship out of a necessity to support their families (GEM Brasil, 2012), and may need to rely on family assistance (Smith-Hunter and Leone, 2010). This is not surprising as Brazil's social structure is founded on the family and kinship plays a central role in business interactions (Watson et al., 2000). Given recent research showing that family support is vital to entrepreneurs' success and satisfaction (Powell and Eddleston, 2013) and that family members are expected to contribute to the family's welfare in Brazil (Watson et al., 2000), the work–family interface of entrepreneurs in Brazil is an important area for study.

This chapter investigates the characteristics of business-owning households within Brazil, and seeks to offer Brazil-specific insight to the question posed by Jennings, Breitkreuz, and James (2013): 'Is entrepreneurship "good" for families?' Additionally, as suggested by Powell and Eddleston (2013), we seek to understand: 'Are families "good" for entrepreneurship?' Beginning with demographic data on the participating business owners, we report information on their effectiveness in family and business aspects of their lives, followed by details on their work–family interface experiences and strategies. Multivariate analyses shed light on the factors associated with perceived effectiveness within and across the family and business domains.

METHODOLOGY

The data for this chapter was obtained from surveys, administered face-to-face, and completed by entrepreneurs participating in university entrepreneurship programs in Sao Paulo, Brazil, over the period September 2012 to September 2013. Surveys were administered in Portuguese, translated from the English version used in the US study. A prototype was tested and back-translated to check for accuracy before being used with respondents.

DEMOGRAPHIC CHARACTERISTICS OF BUSINESS OWNERS AND THEIR HOUSEHOLDS

Of the 219 survey respondents, 56 percent (118) identified themselves as 'family firms' and the remaining firms were deemed to be non-family firms (94), with a few firms unable to be characterized due to missing data. The vast majority of the family firms (73 percent) and non-family firms (80 percent) were very small; that is, they reported only 1 to 10 full-time employees. Only three family firms and one non-family firm reported having more than 251 full-time employees. The Brazilian firms that provided industry information were primarily in the service industry (71 percent of the sample).

Sixty-four (approximately 30 percent) of the respondents were male and 150 (approximately 70 percent) were female (5 values were missing). The high proportion of women in our sample may stem from the large number of workshops for women entrepreneurs conducted by the university. The family firms were approximately five times larger than the non-family firms, with an average of 56 versus 12 employees, respectively. The family firms were also significantly older than the non-family firms, with respective average ages of 11.08 versus 4.72 years. The family firm owner-managers were more likely to be married and less likely to be highly educated or the founder of their firm in comparison with the non-family firm owner-managers.

The majority of the business owners in the Brazil sample were reasonably educated with 83 percent of the respondents reporting that they had completed at least some university studies, and 28 percent reporting a master's or doctorate degree; only 17 percent had education less than or up to a high school degree. Viewed by gender, 88 percent of men and 81.5 percent of women had a university education. Therefore, our results are somewhat different from those of the EY-G20 study that found that only 18 percent of women and 11 percent of men have a university degree in Brazil. This difference is likely due to our research sample, which was drawn from university entrepreneurship programs.

Additionally, 61 percent of the participating owner-managers indicated that they have a spouse or marital-like partner and 49 percent reported having children under the age of 18 living in their household. The number of children ranged from 1 to 4, with the majority of respondents indicating that they have one or two children (44 and 41 respondents respectively). Single parent households constituted 8 percent of the sample.

KEY NON-ECONOMIC OUTCOMES: PERCEIVED EFFECTIVENESS AND SATISFACTION

As noted in the introduction to this chapter, necessity, or the lack of alternative sources of income, may motivate individuals in lower income countries to initiate entrepreneurial ventures. Yet, even in such economically constrained environments, entrepreneurship offers socio-emotional benefits beyond economic returns since entrepreneurs are able to create organizations that allow them to pursue personally defined goals (Eddleston and Powell, 2008; Powell and Eddleston, 2008). For example, researchers have long acknowledged that women often turn to entrepreneurship as a means to balance work and family (Brush, 1992; Eddleston and Powell, 2012; Kepler and Shane, 2007). Additionally, scholars have recognized how the 'family feeds the fire of entrepreneurship' (Rogoff and Heck, 2003: 559) by playing an important role in influencing an entrepreneur's satisfaction and the new venture's success (Powell and Eddleston, 2013; Cruz, Justo, and De Castro, 2012). However, while progress has been made in understanding how the family contributes to entrepreneurship, little is known about how entrepreneurship affects the family (Jennings et al., 2013). Hence, we consider the impact of entrepreneurial activity on families, and analyze key non-economic outcomes. We specifically discuss findings for perceived effectiveness within and across the domains of family and business.

To measure *perceived effectiveness*, we asked respondents to report how effective they considered themselves: (1) as a family member, (2) as a business owner-manager, and (3) in balancing the various aspects of their lives. Following Waismel-Manor, Moen, and Sweet (2003), each of the three items was rated on a scale ranging from 0 to 100. We then created a composite measure to assess *concurrent perceptions of effectiveness* within and across the family and business domains. Following Jennings, Jennings, and Sharifian (forthcoming), we first recoded each of the items dichotomously, assigning respondents a value of 1 if they reported a score of at least 80 out

Table 11.1   Perceived effectiveness within and across family and business domains (Brazil sample)

Indicators and Levels of Composite Measures	N	Mean/%	S.D.	Min	Max	% with score ≥ 80
Perceived Effectiveness						
Separate Constituent Indicators						
Perceived effectiveness as a family member	218	71.11	22.98	0	100	29.4%
Perceived effectiveness as a business owner	219	71.60	21.07	0	100	26.5%
Perceived effectiveness in balancing family and business	217	63.82	24.66	0	100	19.8%
Levels of Composite Measure						
Low concurrent perceived effectiveness	61	28.2%				
Moderate concurrent perceived effectiveness	106	49.1%				
High concurrent perceived effectiveness	49	22.7%				

of 100 on the item, and 0 if not. We then summed the three dichotomous measures and recoded the aggregate score such that a sum of 0 was deemed to reflect 'low concurrent perceived effectiveness,' sums of 1 or 2 were deemed to reflect 'moderate concurrent perceived effectiveness,' and a sum of 3 was deemed to reflect 'high concurrent perceived effectiveness.'

Table 11.1 shows that while 29.4 percent of the respondents feel that they have been highly effective as a family member, only about a quarter (26.5 percent) feel that they have been highly effective as a business owner (scores ≥ 80). These rates are very low compared with their US counterparts' perceived effectiveness as a business owner and family member, at 59.5 percent and 68.6 percent respectively.

In regards to their perceived effectiveness at balancing family and business, only 19.8 percent of respondents reported a high score (scores ≥ 80), whereas 52.4 percent of the US respondents reported feeling highly effective at balancing family and business. However, 39.6 percent of the Brazilian entrepreneurs reported feeling moderately effective (scores ≥ 70) at balancing work and family. The mean scores for each category of effectiveness are also lower in Brazil versus the US (effectiveness as a family member 71.1 percent in Brazil versus 80.2 percent in the US; effectiveness as business owner 71.6 percent in Brazil versus 77.1 percent in the US; effectiveness at balance 63.8 percent in Brazil versus 74.3 percent in the US). Further, three-quarters of the Brazilian sample reported either a low or moderate level of concurrent perceived effectiveness as a family member, business owner, and balancing family and business.

In sum, the Brazilian entrepreneurs perceive only moderate concurrent perceived effectiveness within and across the family and business domains. The lower scores in Brazil relative to the US may reflect the difficulties of doing business in an emerging market. These results are distressing since research has recently suggested that when entrepreneurs are successful at managing the business–family interface, they are more likely to experience positive business outcomes (Powell and Eddleston, 2013) and well-being (Eddleston and Powell, 2012). Work–family enrichment theory depicts work and family as 'allies' and explains how resources generated in one domain can be applied to the other (Greenhaus and Powell, 2006). This view of entrepreneurship is in line with the family embeddedness perspective of entrepreneurship (Aldrich and Cliff, 2003) which emphasizes the importance of the family to entrepreneurship and suggests that the family can enrich an entrepreneur's well-being. Conversely, work–family conflict theory depicts work and family as competing entities (Greenhaus and Beutell, 1985). This view of the work–family interface proposes that work–family conflict occurs because of competing time demands and behavioral expectations as well as spillover of stress from one role to the other (Greenhaus and Beutell, 1985). Next, we explore work–family conflict, enrichment and strategies of the entrepreneurs in our study.

WORK–FAMILY INTERFACE EXPERIENCES AND STRATEGIES

In this section, we present data on the degree of family-to-business conflict and enrichment experienced by business owners in Brazil, followed by descriptive information on a number of associated variables including: (1) time devoted to the family versus business spheres; (2) individual-level strategies of segmentation and identification; and (3) household-level considerations such as instrumental support provided by family members as well as traditionalism and fairness in the division of domestic labor. We use multivariate regression analysis to determine those factors that are most strongly related to family-to-business conflict and/or enrichment. Our descriptive findings and multivariate regression results are presented in Tables 11.2 and 11.3.

The various scales used, as listed in Table 11.2, appear valid in Brazil as the scale alphas are .80 or higher. The establishment of strong alpha scores is important given that the survey was translated to Brazilian Portuguese. Following standard practice, each item on the survey was translated by

Table 11.2 *Work–family interface experiences and strategies (Brazil sample)*

Variables	α	Mean	S.D.	Min	Max	% with Score
Family-to-business conflict	.83	3.69	1.52	1	7	≥ 5 (agree) = 20.4%
Family-to-business enrichment	.90	5.33	1.33	1	7	≥ 5 (agree) = 59.9%
Time devoted to the family sphere	n/a	11.23	10.05	0	60	≥ 20 hrs/wk = 11.9%
Time devoted to the business sphere	n/a	44.45	19.72	0	110	≥ 40 hrs/wk = 58.5%
Segmentation of family and business roles (actual)	.87	4.05	1.73	1	7	≥ 5 (agree) = 26.6%
Identification with the business	.83	5.88	.9	1	7	≥ 5 (agree) = 82.1%
Instrumental support from family members	.88	4.62	1.7	1	7	≥ 5 (agree) = 44.4%
Traditionalism in the division of household labor	.84	3.43	.87	1	5	≥ 4.5 (mainly fair) = 8.1%
Perceived fairness in the division of household labor	n/a	3.33	1.18	1	5	≥ 5 (very fair) = 25.5%

Table 11.3   *Determinants of family-to-business conflict and enrichment (Brazil sample)*

Variables	Family-to-Business Conflict		Family-to-Business Enrichment	
	Model 1	Model 2	Model 3	Model 4
Individual and household-level control variables				
Female	−0.038	−0.067	0.217**	0.149*
Education level	−0.049	−0.058	0.094	0.075
Married or marital-like relationship	−0.034	−0.202†	−0.065	−0.005
Number of children in household	0.126	0.173†	−0.02	−0.017
Firm-level control variables				
Founder-led firm	−0.065	−0.069	0.073	0.050
Family firm	0.052	0.062	0.126†	0.093
Firm age	−0.055	−0.084	0.043	0.026
Firm size	−0.136†	−0.194*	0.013	0.015
Firm performance	−0.055	−0.081	0.119†	0.103†
High-growth orientation	−0.153†	−0.121	0.051	0.022
Manufacturing firm	−0.001	0.004	0.097	0.099
General service firm	−0.008	0.067	−0.022	0.001
Work–family interface experiences and strategies				
Time devoted to the family sphere		−0.065		0.02
Time devoted to the business sphere		0.013		−0.077
Segmentation of family and business roles		−0.075		−0.08
Identification with the business		0.097		−0.01
Instrumental support from family members		−0.165†		0.396***
Traditional division of household labor		−0.168		0.073
Fairness in the division of household labor		−0.283**		0.168**
Overall model *F*	1.063	1.764*	1.891*	4.615***
R squared	.07	.25	.10	.31

Notes:
Values in the table are standardized OLS regression coefficients (beta values).
† $p \leq .10$, * $p \leq .05$, ** $p \leq .01$, *** $p \leq .001$ (two-tailed tests).

Brazilian native speakers and then translated back to English to verify that the translations captured the substance of the original English scale items. Additionally, some of the scales used, namely family-to-business conflict, enrichment, segmentation, identification and support, used 7-point

Likert-type scales in capturing responses. Therefore, the means are higher for these items relative to the 5-point item scales used in the US study. Hence, it is more useful to rely on the last column, indicating percentage of responses in the highest category, as a basis for assessing Brazilian responses, and comparing them to the US responses.

Family-to-Business Conflict and Enrichment

Family-to-business conflict was measured by the mean of a 6-item, Likert-type scale ($\alpha = .83$) with each item rated from '1 = strongly disagree' to '7 = strongly agree.' Three of the items tapped behavioral conflict. An example is: 'Household/family commitments interfere with my ability to perform business-related duties.' These were drawn from Netemeyer, Boles, and McMurrian (1996). The other three items tapped affective conflict, with an example being: 'I feel frustrated when my household/family responsibilities interfere with my work.' These were developed specifically for this study. The findings reported in Table 11.2 indicate that most of the business owners were experiencing an intermediate degree of family-to-business conflict. The sample mean of 3.69, for example, is just above the scale's midpoint of '3.5 = neither agree nor disagree.' Moreover, in only 20.4 percent of the cases was the respondent's score at or above '5 = agree.' However, a higher proportion of the Brazilian respondents are in the highest category of family-to-business conflict in comparison with those from the US (20.4 percent from Brazil versus 13.3 percent from the US).

Family-to-business enrichment was measured by the mean of a 6-item, Likert-type scale ($\alpha = .90$) with each item rated from '1 = strongly disagree' to '7 = strongly agree.' As in the above case, three of the items tapped perceived behavioral enrichment. An example is: 'My involvement in my family requires me to be as focused as possible at work, which helps make me a better businessperson.' Likewise, the other three items tapped perceived affective enrichment. An example here is: 'My involvement with my family makes me cheerful and this helps me be a better businessperson.' All six items were drawn from Carlson, Kacmar, Wayne, and Grzywacz (2006). The findings reported in Table 11.2 indicate that the majority of the business owners experienced a high degree of family-to-business enrichment. The sample mean of 5.33, for example, is above the scale value of '5 = agree'; moreover, 59.9 percent of the respondents scored at or above this value. Thus, nearly three-fifths of Brazilian respondents reported a high level of family-to-business enrichment. These results are comparable with the US sample, in which 55 percent reported a high level of family-to-business enrichment.

Time Devoted to the Family and Business Spheres

Time devoted to the family sphere was measured by a single item—the number of hours that the respondent estimated spending per week on household-related tasks. Although there are recognized weaknesses in this measure, such as susceptibility to over-estimation and discrepancy between marital partners it has nevertheless been used in previous studies of entrepreneurship and the work–family interface (for example, Cliff, 1998; Jennings et al., 2013).

Time devoted to the business sphere was measured by a parallel item— the number of hours that the respondent estimated spending per week on business-related tasks. This measure has been used in other studies of entrepreneurship and the work–family interface (for example, Jennings et al., 2013; Jennings et al., forthcoming; Powell and Eddleston, 2013). As indicated in Table 11.2, participants estimated spending 44.45 hours per week, on average, in the business sphere. Indeed, well over half the respondents (58.5 percent) were actively involved with their business on at least a full-time basis, putting in 40 hours or more during a typical week.

Considering the time devoted to the family and business spheres, the average number of hours devoted to the family is measurably lower for Brazil, at 11.23 hours per week versus 16.47 hours in the US. Further, only 11.9 percent reported devoting more than 20 hours a week to the family versus 38.5 percent in the US sample, suggesting that extended-family and third-party assistance may allow entrepreneurs in Brazil to focus more on their business. Indeed, the average time devoted to one's business per week was somewhat higher in Brazil, at 44.5 hours versus 43.1 hours in the US. However, when we consider entrepreneurs who devote at least 40 hours per week to their business, the results showed that while 58.5 percent of Brazilian entrepreneurs devote in excess of 40 hours to their business, 65.4 percent of American entrepreneurs do so too.

Individual-level Segmentation and Identification

The individual-level, work–family interface strategy of *segmentation* was measured by the mean of a 3-item, Likert-type scale ($\alpha = .87$) with each item rated from '1 = strongly disagree' to '7 = strongly agree.' The items were adapted from several studies (Carlson, Kacmar, and Williams, 2000; Kreiner, 2006; Powell and Greenhaus, 2010). An illustrative item is, 'In reality, I often leave household/family issues behind when I'm at work.' The phrase 'In reality' was inserted at the beginning of each item to help focus the respondent on their actual experiences rather than their preferred degree of segmentation between family and business roles. As indicated in Table 11.2, the sample mean, at 4.05, was above the scale's midpoint of '3.5 = neither agree nor disagree.' Approximately one-quarter of the participants (26.6 percent) could be deemed as enacting a segmentation strategy, with scores at or above the value of '5 = agree.' This is very similar to the US data, which revealed that 26.5 percent of the American respondents enact a segmentation strategy.

We measured the degree of an owner-manager's *identification* with his/her business by the mean of a 12-item, Likert-type scale (α = .83) with each item rated from '1 = strongly disagree' to '7 = strongly agree.' An example is: 'If I were describing myself, the firm would likely be something I would mention.' The items were adapted from O'Reilly and Chatman (1986), as suggested by Berrone, Cruz and Gómez-Mejía (2012). The findings reported in Table 11.2 indicate that the majority of the business owners identified very highly with their firms. Not only did the sample mean of 5.88 fall above the scale value of '5 = agree,' but a large percentage of the respondents (82.1 percent) scored at or above this value. In comparison, 70.2 percent of US respondents indicated a high degree of identification with their business.

Household-level Support, Traditionalism and Fairness

We measured the *instrumental support provided by family members* for the respondent's role of business owner by the mean of a 7-item, Likert-type scale (α = .88), developed by Powell and Eddleston (2013), with each item rated from '1 = strongly disagree' to '7 = strongly agree.' An illustrative item is: 'The members of my family who do not officially work in the business can be counted on to help out if something unexpected happens in this business.' The findings reported in Table 11.2 indicate that many of the business owners experience a reasonable level of instrumental support from the members of their families. Not only did the sample mean of 4.62 fall above the scale's midpoint, but 44.4 percent of the respondents had a score at or above the scale value of '5 = agree.' Thus, levels of support from family are roughly similar to that in the US, with 44.4 percent from Brazil and 40.5 percent from the US reporting a high degree of instrumental family support.

When perceived fairness of division of household tasks is considered, only 25.5 percent of Brazilian respondents consider the division of household labor as fair, compared with 50.5 percent in the US. Therefore, in Brazil, despite the prevalence of third-party contracted household help, other tasks which cannot be delegated to such household help or third-party family members may fall on one spouse, thus creating a perception of unfairness.

Determinants of Family-to-Business Conflict and Enrichment

We now investigate the associations between the work–family interface experiences and strategies and the extent of family-to-business conflict and enrichment reported by the business owners. The results of our multivariate ordinary least squares (OLS) analyses are presented in Table 11.3.

Table 11.3 considers factors affecting both family-to-business conflict and family-to-business enrichment. Models 1 and 3 focus solely on control variables, drawn from individual, household and firm domains. Models 2 and 4 add independent variables associated with the work–family interface and strategies, including hours per week devoted to family and business activities, segmentation of family and business roles, identification with the business, support from the family, division of labor in the household, and perceived fairness of the division of household labor.

Three of the four models are significant, with the R^2 for the models with the addition of independent variables being significant (family-to-business conflict $R^2 = .25$ and family-to-business enrichment $R^2 = .31$). The R^2 for the models increased significantly when moving from the controls-only model to those with the independent variables, for example, R^2 increasing from .07 to .25 for family-to-business conflict, and from .10 to .31 for family-to-business enrichment.

With regard to family-to-business conflict (Models 1 and 2), firm size is marginally significant as a control. Further, when the independent variables are introduced into the model (Model 2), marriage and number of children become marginally significant. In Model 2, firm size is shown to be significantly negatively related to family-to-business conflict. Regarding the independent variables, instrumental support from family members and fairness in the division of household labor were found to be negatively related to family-to-business conflict, although instrumental support from family members was only marginally significant. Therefore, those Brazilian entrepreneurs who received greater instrumental support from family members and perceived a fairer division of household labor reported the least amount of family-to-business conflict.

Turning to family-to-business enrichment, Model 3 indicates three significant or marginally significant control variables. Female entrepreneurs reported significantly more family-to-business enrichment than the male entrepreneurs. Additionally, family firm status and firm performance were marginally positively related to family-to-business enrichment. In regards to the independent variables, instrumental support from family members and perceived fairness in the division of household labor were shown to be positively related to family-to-business enrichment.

Taken together, our results demonstrate the importance of one's family in predicting a Brazilian entrepreneur's family-to-business conflict and enrichment. While instrumental support from family members and perceived fairness in the division of household labor were shown to lessen family-to-business conflict, these two variables were also shown to increase family-to-business enrichment. Thus, Brazilian entrepreneurs who are able to harness the support from family members, both at work and at home, appear best able to manage the family-to-business interface. These results are in line with research that emphasizes how social support can prevent stress and contribute to well-being (in other words, Cohen and Wills, 1985; Uchino, 2009). In particular, they demonstrate the important role that an entrepreneur's family plays, both at work and at home, in supporting an entrepreneur's ability to manage the work–family interface. Notably, however, the owner-managers who considered themselves to be heading family firms experienced neither higher nor lower family-to-business conflict nor enrichment than those heading non-family firms.

FACTORS ASSOCIATED WITH PERCEIVED EFFECTIVENESS

Having explored the factors associated with family-to-business conflict and enrichment, we turn now to investigate how they relate with perceived effectiveness, focusing on the composite measure; in other words, concurrent effectiveness within and across the family and business domains. Given that the composite measure consisted of three ordinal levels (low, moderate and high), the models were estimated by multinomial logistic regression. We ran three models for the outcome measure: (1) a baseline model of controls; (2) a model with the controls plus the work–family interface variables; and (3) a full model containing all of these variables plus family-to-business conflict and enrichment. Two columns of estimates corresponding to the moderate and high outcome levels are provided for the model (the low level was selected as the referent category). The complete set of models appears in Table 11.4.

Table 11.4 is concerned with factors that affect the perceived effectiveness of the entrepreneur in both the business and family spheres. In considering controls only (Model 1 in Table 11.4), the model is not significant. While no controls are significant for the moderate level of composite effectiveness, for the group reporting high levels of composite effectiveness, firm performance is *positively* significant.

In Model 2, where the independent variables involving the work–family interface and strategies are added, the Nagelkerke R^2 increases to .26 and is significant. At a moderate level of effectiveness, none of the controls are

Table 11.4 *Factors associated with perceived effectiveness (composite measure), Brazil sample*

Variables	Model 1		Model 2		Model 3	
	Moderate	High	Moderate	High	Moderate	High
Control variables						
Female	0.062	0.273	0.058	0.258	−0.217	−0.237
Education level	0.11	0.246	0.096	0.346	0.08	0.287
Married or marital-like relationship	0.2	0.4	0.354	0.294	0.388	0.314
Founder-led firm	0.152	−0.13	−0.131	−0.306	−0.174	−0.378
Firm size	−0.001	0.000	−0.001	0.000	−0.001	0.000
Firm performance	0.166	0.425*	0.178	0.372†	0.214	0.334
High-growth orientation	0.006	0.033	−0.016	−0.003	−0.014	0.000
Manufacturing firm	−0.959	1.894†	−1.12	1.958†	−1.007	2.023
Service firm	−0.001	−0.295	0.045	0.245	−0.058	0.181

Table 11.4 (continued)

Variables	Model 1		Model 2		Model 3	
	Moderate	High	Moderate	High	Moderate	High
Work–family interface experiences and strategies						
Time devoted to the family sphere			0.032	0.04	0.044†	0.053†
Time devoted to the business sphere			−0.005	−0.008	−0.011	−0.016
Segmentation of family and business roles			0.149	0.123	0.119	0.092
Identification with the business			0.173	0.281	0.206	0.391
Instrumental support from family members			0.123	0.460**	0.096	0.343†
Fairness in the division of household labor			0.477*	0.819**	0.415*	0.604*
Family-to-business conflict and enrichment						
Family-to-business conflict					−0.237†	−0.555**
Family-to-business enrichment					0.133	0.372
−2LL Chi-square	21.57		45.463*		58.048**	
Nagelkerke R-square	.12		.26		.32	

Notes:
Values in the table are unstandardized multinomial logistic regression coefficients.
† $p \leq .10$, * $p \leq .05$, ** $p \leq .01$, *** $p \leq .001$ (two-tailed tests).

significant, but, fairness in the division of household labor is significant and *positively* associated with a moderate level of concurrent effectiveness. In regards to a high level of concurrent effectiveness, the control variable firm performance is marginally significant. In addition, instrumental support from family members and fairness in the division of household labor are significant and positively contribute to a high level of concurrent effectiveness.

Finally, in Model 3 we added family-to-business conflict and enrichment. With the introduction of these variables, the overall model continues to be significant, and the R^2 increases to .32. For moderate concurrent effectiveness, family-to-business conflict is marginally negatively related to concurrent effectiveness. In addition, fairness in the division of household labor and time devoted to the family sphere are positively related to a moderate level of concurrent effectiveness, although time devoted to the family sphere is marginally significant. In regards to a high level of concurrent effectiveness a similar pattern of results is found, with a negative association for family-to-business conflict, and positive associations for time devoted to the family sphere, and fairness in the division of household labor, all being significant or marginally significant. Additionally, instrumental support from family members was shown to marginally contribute to a high level of concurrent effectiveness.

Taken together, the three models suggest that concurrent effectiveness in the family and business domains is positively influenced by fairness in the division of household labor and time devoted to the family sphere, and negatively associated with family-to-business conflict. Further, instrumental support from family members appears to distinguish those entrepreneurs with the highest level of concurrent effectiveness. Among controls, strong firm performance was shown to distinguish high concurrent effectiveness. Therefore, those Brazilian entrepreneurs who perceive a high level of concurrent effectiveness in the family and business domains are able to lead successfully performing firms while also devoting a significant amount of time to their families without instigating family-to-business conflict. Further, these entrepreneurs appear best able to harness the support of their families, both at work and at home, as demonstrated by the significant effects of instrumental support from family members for the business and fairness in the division of household labor.

DISCUSSION

Summary

While Brazil has seen a surge in entrepreneurship that has contributed to the country's economy (EY-G20, 2013; Zacharakis, 2013), we know little about how it has affected the entrepreneurs' well-being and family life. Our study sought to fill this gap by exploring the work–family interface of Brazilian entrepreneurs.

The results of our research revealed both good and bad news for the well-being and work–family balance of entrepreneurs in Brazil. While the entrepreneurs reported only a modest level of *concurrent* effectiveness in their business and family domains, they reported a high level of family-to-business enrichment, identification with the business, and support from family members for the business. Further, although half of the sample perceived a moderate level of perceived effectiveness as a family member or as a business owner, less than 40 percent felt moderately effective in balancing their family and business roles. Finally, while our study suggested that the vast majority of respondents did not have a traditional division of labor in the household, only one-quarter felt that the division of labor was very fair.

By comparing the Brazilian data with that from the US, our study revealed that Brazilian entrepreneurs report greater family-to-business conflict than US entrepreneurs. However, they also reported greater family-to-business enrichment and instrumental support from family members than their American counterparts. The Brazilian sample's relatively higher family-to-business conflict and lower perceived effectiveness in balancing their family and business roles required further investigation since they also reported significantly fewer hours devoted to the family domain than the US entrepreneurs (11.9 percent versus 38.5 percent). Additional analysis from our study revealed that greater instrumental support from family members and fairness in the division of household labor decreases the family-to-business conflict of Brazilian entrepreneurs. Regarding family-to-business enrichment, instrumental support from family members and fairness in the division of household labor significantly contributed to an entrepreneur's enrichment. Thus, for Brazilian entrepreneurs, family support at home and for the business is key to reducing family-to-business conflict and enhancing enrichment.

These two factors were also shown to distinguish the Brazilian entrepreneurs with the highest perceived concurrent effectiveness. Additionally, similar to the US study, family-to-business conflict was found to diminish perceived concurrent effectiveness. Our results show that the Brazilian entrepreneurs with the highest perceived concurrent effectiveness within and across the family and business domains reported fairness in the division of household labor, much instrumental support from family members, greater time to devote to the family sphere, and low family-to-business conflict.

These results suggest that Brazilian entrepreneurs, who are able to foster a symbiotic relationship between work and family, whereby the family supports the entrepreneur at work and at home, and the entrepreneur is able to spend more time with their family, feel that they are most effective in managing their work and family roles. However, unfortunately, less than a quarter of the Brazilian respondents were categorized as perceiving high concurrent effectiveness. The family appears to be a resource, both at home and at work, that can lessen entrepreneurs' family-to-business conflict and increase their family-to-business enrichment and perceived concurrent effectiveness. These results help validate the view of the family as 'the fire that feeds the oxygen of entrepreneurship' (Rogoff and Heck, 2003) and confirm that models of entrepreneurship are incomplete unless they include work–family considerations (Jennings and McDougald, 2007).

Implications

This study provides several implications for research and practice. Most fundamentally, it demonstrates how the family can be an important source of support, both at home and at work, that contributes to entrepreneurs' well-being and perceived effectiveness. Research that views work and family as opposing forces may not adequately capture the work–family interface of Brazilian entrepreneurs. An enrichment perspective that acknowledges the synergy and cooperation between the two domains should also be considered.

Given that our study took place in an emerging market with a high percentage of necessity entrepreneurs, the support of the family appears essential to an entrepreneur's work–family experience. However, our results also revealed that less than a quarter of the Brazilian entrepreneurs perceived high concurrent effectiveness in managing their family and business. Future research should explore specific ways in which family members can support an entrepreneur at work and at home, and ways to reduce conflict. By applying recent research on the work–family enrichment perspective of entrepreneurship (Powell and Eddleston, 2013) to emerging markets we may gain a better understanding of the unique challenges and needs of necessity entrepreneurs. Such understanding is important because losing struggles to achieve work–family balance or a sense of well-being may ultimately hurt an entrepreneur's business and willingness to remain a business owner. The low perceived effectiveness that we discovered among our respondents may help explain why so many entrepreneurs in Brazil close the doors to their business within two years of operation (EY-G20, 2013).

Limitations

As with most studies, our research has limitations that should be acknowledged. First, because we used a university to assist with the data collection, our sample is not necessarily representative of all business owners in Brazil. Second, our reliance on self-report data is a limitation. It would have been beneficial if we had been able to corroborate certain variables, such as performance, with independent sources. Additional data on firm performance and family-related factors such as the time devoted to household responsibilities would have been useful. It would also have been useful if we had data on the earnings of other individuals in the entrepreneur's household and how the family functions within the household.

Conclusion

Brazil has been referred to as a country of contradictions (EY-G20, 2013). Our study on the work–family interface of Brazilian entrepreneurs supports this depiction. While our respondents reported high family-to-business enrichment, identification with their business, and instrumental support from family members, very few perceived high concurrent effectiveness in managing the work and family domains. When considering which factors contributed to Brazilian entrepreneurs' family-to-business conflict, enrichment, and perceive effectiveness, a consistent pattern emerged: instrumental support from family members and fairness in the division of household labor are fundamental resources that contribute to their work–family interface. Thus, those Brazilian entrepreneurs' who receive support from their families at work and at home may be most inclined to feel that entrepreneurship is 'good' for their family and that their family is 'good' for entrepreneurship.

REFERENCES

Aldrich, H.E. and J.E. Cliff (2003), 'The pervasive effects of family on entrepreneurship: Toward a family embeddedness perspective,' *Journal of Business Venturing*, **18** (5), 573–596.
Amoros, J.E., N. Bosma and Global Entrepreneurship Research Association

(2014), 'Global Entrepreneurship Monitor 2013 Global Report,' Wellesley, MA: Babson College.

Berrone, P., C. Cruz, and L.R. Gómez-Mejía (2012). 'Socioemotional wealth in family firms theoretical dimensions, assessment approaches, and agenda for future research,' *Family Business Review*, **25** (3), 258–279.

Brush, C.G. (1992), 'Research on women business owners: Past trends, a new perspective and future directions,' *Entrepreneurship Theory and Practice*, **16** (4), 5–30.

Carlson, D.S., K.M. Kacmar, and L.J. Williams (2000), 'Construction and initial validation of a multidimensional measure of work–family conflict,' *Journal of Vocational Behavior*, **56**, 249–276.

Carlson, D.S., K.M. Kacmar, J.H. Wayne, and J.G. Grzywacz (2006), 'Measuring the positive side of the work–family interface: Development and validation of a work–family enrichment scale,' *Journal of Vocational Behaviour*, **68**, 131–164.

Cliff, J. E. (1998), 'Does one size fit all? Exploring the relationship between attitudes towards growth, gender and business size,' *Journal of Business Venturing*, **13** (6), 523–543.

Cohen, S. and T.A. Wills (1985), 'Stress, social support, and the buffering hypothesis,' *Psychological Bulletin*, **98**, 310–357.

Costa, A.O., B. Sorj, C. Bruschini, and H. Hirata (2008), *Mercado de Trabalho e Gênero: comparações internacionais*. Rio de Janeiro, Brazil: Editora FGV.

Cruz, C., R. Justo, and J.O. De Castro (2012), 'Does family employment enhance MSEs performance?: Integrating socio-emotional wealth and family embeddedness perspectives,' *Journal of Business Venturing*, **27** (1), 62–76.

Eddleston, K.A. and G.N. Powell (2008), 'The role of gender identity in explaining sex differences in business owners' career satisfier preferences,' *Journal of Business Venturing*, **23** (2), 244–256.

Eddleston, K.A. and G.N. Powell (2012), 'Nurturing entrepreneurs' work–family balance: A gendered perspective,' *Entrepreneurship Theory and Practice*, **36** (3), 513–541.

Endeavor Brazil (2011), 'Brazil,' retrieved from http://www.endeavor.org/network/affiliates/brazil/1(accessed August 1, 2014).

EY-G20 (2013), 'Entrepreneurship Barometer Brazil,' retrieved from http://www.ey.com/Publication/vwLUAssets/EY-G20-country-report-2013-Brazil/$FILE/EY-G20-country-report-2013-Brazil.pdf (accessed August 1, 2014).

Fishlow, A. (2013), *Starting Over: Brazil since 1985*. Washington, DC: Brookings Institution Press.

GEM (2013), 'Global Entrepreneurship Monitor Report,' retrieved from http://www.gemconsortium.org/docs/3106/gem-2013-global-report (accessed July 15, 2014).

GEM Brasil (2012), 'Global Entrepreneurship Monitor. Empreendedorismo no Brasil,' IBQP, Instituto Brasileiro de Qualidade e Produtividade, Curitiba, retrieved from http://www.gemconsortium.org/docs/download/2806 (accessed January 1, 2014).

Greenhaus, J.H. and N.J. Beutell (1985), 'Sources of conflict between work and family roles,' *Academy of Management Review*, **10** (1), 76–88.

Greenhaus, J.H. and G.N. Powell (2006), 'When work and family are allies: A theory of work–family enrichment,' *Academy of Management Review*, **31** (1), 72–92.

Jennings, J.E. and M.S. McDougald (2007), 'Work–family interface experiences and coping strategies: Implications for entrepreneurship research and practice,' *Academy of Management Review*, **32** (3), 747–760.

Jennings, J.E., R.S. Breitkreuz, and A.E. James (2013), 'When family members are also business owners: Is entrepreneurship good for families?,' *Family Relations*, **62**, 472–489.

Jennings, J.E., P.D. Jennings, and M. Sharifian (forthcoming), 'Living the dream? Assessing the "entrepreneurship as emancipation" perspective in a developed region,' *Entrepreneurship Theory and Practice*.

Kepler, E. and S. Shane (2007), 'Are male and female entrepreneurs really that different?,' Office of Advocacy, US Small Business Administration, retrieved from http://archive.sba.gov/advo/research/rs309tot.pdf (accessed August 1, 2014).

Kreiner, Glen E. (2006), 'Consequences of work–home segmentation or integration: A person–environment fit perspective,' *Journal Of Organizational Behavior*, **27** (4), 485–507.

Netemeyer, R.G., J.S. Boles, and R. McMurrian (1996), 'Development and validation of work–family conflict and family–work conflict scales,' *Journal of Applied Psychology*, **81** (4), 400–410.

O'Reilly, C. and J. Chatman (1986), 'Organizational commitment and psychological attachment: The effects of compliance, identification, and internalization on prosocial behavior,' *Journal Of Applied Psychology*, **71** (3), 492–499.

Powell, G.N. and K.A. Eddleston (2008), 'The paradox of the contented female business owner,' *Journal of Vocational Behavior*, **73** (1), 24–36.

Powell, G.N. and K.A. Eddleston (2013), 'Linking family-to-business enrichment and support to entrepreneurial success: Do female and male entrepreneurs experience different outcomes?,' *Journal of Business Venturing*, **28** (2), 261–280.

Powell, Gary N., and J.H. Greenhaus (2010), 'Sex, gender, and the work-to-family interface: Exploring negative and positive interdependencies,' *Academy of Management Journal*, **53** (3), 513–534.

Rogoff, E.G. and R.K.Z. Heck (2003), 'Evolving research in entrepreneurship and family business: Recognizing family as the oxygen that feeds the fire of entrepreneurship,' *Journal of Business Venturing*, **18** (5), 559–566.

Smith-Hunter, A. and J. Leone (2010), 'Evidence on the characteristics of women entrepreneurs in Brazil: An empirical analysis,' *International Journal of Management and Marketing Research*, **3** (1), 85–102.

Uchino, B.N. (2009), 'Understanding the links between social support and physical health: A life-span perspective with emphasis on the separability of perceived and received support,' *Perspectives on Psychological Science*, **4**, 236–255.

Waismel-Manor, R., P. Moen, and S. Sweet (2003), 'Winning couples: Predicting conjoint perceptions of work, family and balancing success,' *Academy of Management Proceedings*, F1 F6.

Watson, S.R., A.M. Barreira, and T.C. Watson (2000), 'Perspectives on quality of life: The Brazilian experience,' in K.D. Keith and R.L. Schalock (eds), *Cross-cultural Perspectives on Quality of Life*. Washington, DC: AAMR, pp. 112–139.

World Bank (2012), 'Doing business 2012: Doing business in a more transparent world,' retrieved from http://www.doingbusiness.org/reports/global-reports/doing-business-2012 (accessed June 20, 2014).

Zacharakis, A. (2013), 'Entrepreneurship in Brazil: Unlimited potential,' *Forbes Online*, April 10, retrieved from http://www.forbes.com/sites/babson/2013/04/10/entrepreneurship-in-brazil-unlimited-potential/ (accessed August 1, 2014).

12. Enterprising families in India: are their businesses and families enemies?

Ravi Sarathy, K. Kumar and Kimberly A. Eddleston

INTRODUCTION

This chapter focuses on the family-to-business strategies, experiences, and outcomes of enterprising families in India. Enterprising families refer to those households comprised of at least one individual who is involved in owning and managing a business. There are multiple sources of statistical data on the demographic and livelihood patterns in India, such as the national population census, the economic census, annual survey of industries, as well as sponsored reports on entrepreneurial activity. However, the various sources provide incomplete and different perspectives on the involvement of households operating a business. While the specific rate of entrepreneurship within India tends to vary depending on the source of data, most sources report that the rate of entrepreneurship is persistently growing.

The latest Global Entrepreneurship Monitor (GEM) report indicates that, in 2013, 10.0 percent of the adult population in India is involved in launching a nascent or new business and that 20.6 percent operate a young or established firm. Accordingly, 30.6 percent of the Indian population surveyed reported that they were involved in entrepreneurship. In comparison, earlier GEM reports indicated that 19.3 percent and 27.9 percent of the Indian population were involved in entrepreneurship in 2001 and 2008, respectively. Research indicates that the number of small firms is growing by about 5 percent to 8 percent per year (Koster and Rai, 2008; Yu and Tandon, 2012). Some of this growth is likely due to India's large and growing consumer market and the country's active efforts to promote the image of entrepreneurs (Ernst & Young, 2013). For example, in the Ernst & Young G20 Entrepreneurship Barometer study, 69 percent of entrepreneurs in India reported that their country encourages entrepreneurship compared with about 57 percent across the other G20 countries.

According to the latest NSS report from 2005, 21.8 million households in India operate 'own account enterprises.' That is, they operate a business that does not employ outside labor. If these 'own account enterprises' are treated as enterprising families, then in 2005 it can be inferred that approximately 10.5 percent of households in India included a self-employed individual. In contrast, Gallup research from 2012 indicated that 16 percent of adults in India owned a business (Yu and Tandon, 2012). This research also uncovered that only 22 percent of the entrepreneurs surveyed reported that they formally registered their business. Unregistered businesses may be common in India given that 46 percent of entrepreneurs surveyed by Gallup feel that their government's bureaucracy makes it difficult to start a business. Indeed, the World Bank ranks India 166 among 183 countries in terms of ease of doing business in its 'Doing Business 2012' report (World Bank, 2012).

Despite the difficulties in operating a business, a survey by the National Knowledge Commission (NKC) indicated that 99.4 percent of entrepreneurs in India do not want to change vocations to secure a routine job (NKC, 2008). Further, almost 75 percent of the entrepreneurs surveyed felt that their family supported their entrepreneurial endeavors. Indeed, in India 61.4 percent of the population aged 18–64 view entrepreneurship as a good career choice (GEM, 2013). Additionally, 55.7 percent of this population feel that they have the capabilities to operate a business and 22.7 percent have intentions to start a business. In comparison, the GEM study showed that while 55.7 percent of the American population aged 18–64 feel that they have the capabilities to operate a business, only 12.2 percent of that population have intentions to start a business. Therefore, although business obstacles that hamper the 'ease of doing business' are prevalent, the Indian population still views entrepreneurship positively and the rate of business ownership continues to grow. However, while multiple reports reveal that more and more households in India can be described as 'enterprising families,' little is known about how business ownership affects the family domain and the owner-manager's ability to balance work and family.

This chapter seeks to fill these gaps by exploring the work–family interface and personal well-being of business owners in India. The results reported in this chapter are based on a survey of 245 owner-managers primarily located in and around Bangalore. After presenting basic demographic data on the participating business owners, we present descriptive information on the extent to which they consider themselves to be effective and satisfied in their family and business domains. We then present details on their family-to-business strategies and experiences.

METHODOLOGY AND SAMPLE

The data for this chapter were obtained from an online survey completed in 2012–2013 by a sample of 245 owner-managers heading firms that were primarily located in Bangalore, India. Approximately one-third (34.0 percent) were primarily manufacturing firms while 47 percent were primarily in the service industry (other firms reported being involved in both manufacturing and service). The average firm size was 148 employees and firm age was 14.15 years. When asked whether they considered their firm to be a family firm, 44 percent of the respondents indicated their firm to be a family firm. Furthermore, 87 percent of the non-family firms were led by their founders, suggesting the possibility that these latter firms might well become family firms in the future. If we add founder-led non-family firms to the family firm group, fully 93 percent of the sample can be seen as family firms. Regarding family ownership, 44 percent of the businesses had family shareholders while 56 percent did not. Of those businesses with family shareholders, the average percentage of family equity was 74.5 percent.

DEMOGRAPHIC CHARACTERISTICS OF THE BUSINESS OWNERS AND THEIR HOUSEHOLDS

Of the 245 participating owner-managers, 172 (73.5 percent) indicated that they were male and 62 (26.5 percent) indicated that they were female. It is not surprising that the proportion of women entrepreneurs in the sample is low, given the prevalent male-dominated cultural norms in this country and the cultural expectation of traditional female roles within the home. For example, census data from 2001 shows that while 68.4 percent of the workforce is male, 31.6 percent is female. However, the rate of women entrepreneurs has been growing: in 1994 only 9 percent of manufacturing businesses were led by women, but by 2005 that figure increased to 19 percent (Ghani, Kerr, and O'Connell, 2013). Further, the 2013 GEM report revealed that 13 percent of men and 6 percent of women in India were involved in starting a new business or running a business less than 3.5 years old. In the US, those figures were 15 percent and 10 percent for men and women, respectively.

Regarding education, 97 percent of respondents indicated that they had completed a bachelor's degree or higher at a college or university. Only one respondent reported having earned a high school diploma. Further, 52.1 percent reported that they obtained a master's or doctorate degree. On balance, then, the majority of the business owners in the Indian sample were highly educated.

The vast majority of the participating owner-managers (81.1 percent) indicated that they had a spouse or marital-like partner. Most (70.3 percent) had at least one child under the age of 18 living in their household. The number of children ranged from zero to three, with most respondents reporting two children. With regard to income, respondents reported an average personal income of $39,900, and an average household income of $47,600 (amounts converted to US dollars from Indian rupees).

KEY INDICATORS OF PERSONAL WELL-BEING: PERCEIVED EFFECTIVENESS AND SATISFACTION

Even though income derived from entrepreneurial activity is an important economic consideration in developing countries, particularly given the high percentage of 'necessity' entrepreneurs in India (38.8 percent) who are pushed to start a business because they lack options for work (GEM, 2013), entrepreneurship also affords business owners other benefits beyond a paycheck. Thus, following calls for a more holistic approach to the conceptualization of outcomes associated with business ownership (Davidsson, 2004; Shane, 2012) and the need to consider how entrepreneurship impacts one's family life (Jennings, Breitkreuz, and James, 2013; Eddleston and Powell, 2012; Powell and Eddleston, 2013), in this section we focus upon important non-economic outcomes that are believed to contribute to an entrepreneur's psychological well-being. More specifically, we concentrate on perceived effectiveness and satisfaction within and across the domains of family and business.

For the separate indicators of *perceived effectiveness*, we asked the respondents to report how effective they considered themselves to date: (1) as a family member, (2) as a business owner-manager, and (3) balancing the business and family aspects of their lives. Following Waismel-Manor, Moen, and Sweet (2002), each of the three items was rated on a scale ranging from 0 to 100. To assess the extent to which the respondents possessed *concurrent perceptions of effectiveness* within and across the family and business domains, we created a composite measure as follows. Following Jennings, Jennings and Sharifian (forthcoming), we first recoded each of the three constituent items dichotomously, assigning respondents a value of 1 if they reported a score of at least 80 out of 100 on the item, 0 if not. We then summed the three dichotomous measures and recoded the aggregate score such that a sum of 0 was deemed to reflect 'low concurrent perceived effectiveness,' sums of 1 or 2 were deemed to reflect 'moderate concurrent perceived effectiveness,' and a sum of 3 was deemed to reflect 'high concurrent perceived effectiveness.' A parallel procedure was adopted

Table 12.1   Perceived effectiveness and satisfaction within and across family and business domains (India sample)

Indicators and Levels of Composite Measures	N	Mean/%	S.D.	Min	Max	% with Score ≥ 80
Perceived Effectiveness						
Separate Constituent Indicators						
Perceived effectiveness as a family member	170	71.77	18.5	10	100	50.6%
Perceived effectiveness as a business owner	171	73.86	16.57	30	100	50.0%
Perceived effectiveness in balancing family and business	170	69.06	20.27	10	100	49.7%
Levels of Composite Measure[a]						
Low concurrent perceived effectiveness	98	58.3%				
Moderate concurrent perceived effectiveness	53	31.5%				
High concurrent perceived effectiveness	17	10.1%				
Perceived Satisfaction						
Separate Constituent Indicators						
Perceived satisfaction as a family member	168	75.42	19.39	20	100	60.7%
Perceived satisfaction as a business owner	168	70.83	19.40	20	100	66.8%
Perceived satisfaction in balancing family and business	168	70.83	21.82	10	100	52.1%
Levels of Composite Measure[a]						
Low concurrent perceived satisfaction	86	51.2%				
Moderate concurrent perceived satisfaction	49	29.2%				
High concurrent perceived satisfaction	33	19.6%				

Note:
a   Composite measures were created by recoding each constituent item dichotomously, assigning respondents a value of 1 if they reported a score of at least 80 out of 100 on the item, 0 if not. The three dichotomous measures were then summed so that 0 was deemed to reflect 'low,' sums of 1 or 2 were deemed to reflect 'moderate', and a sum of 3 was deemed to reflect 'high'.

to create the *separate indicators of perceived satisfaction* as well as the *concurrent satisfaction measure*.

The findings reported in the top half of Table 12.1 provide insight into the question: 'To what degree do owner-managers in India consider themselves *effective* within and across the domains of family and business?' The results presented in the first three rows suggest that the answer to this question is: 'To some degree.' As indicated, about half of the respondents

(50.6 percent, 50.0 percent, and 49.7 percent respectively) reported a score of at least 80 out of 100 on the separate indicators of perceived effectiveness as a family member, business owner and in balancing the two roles. The findings for the composite measure, however, are quite revealing. Notably, only about one-tenth (10.1 percent) were coded as expressing a high level of concurrent perceived effectiveness (in other words, scores of at least 80 out of 100 on each of the three constituent items). The majority of respondents (58.3 percent) reported low concurrent perceived effectiveness.

The findings reported in the bottom half of Table 12.1 offer insight into the question: 'To what extent are owner-managers in India *satisfied* within and across the domains of family and business?' As in the above case, on first blush the results suggest that the answer is: 'More satisfied than not.' As indicated, on each of the *separate* indicators of perceived satisfaction, the majority of the respondents reported a score at or above 80 out of 100. Notably, however, only about one-fifth (19.6 percent) were deemed to exhibit a high level of concurrent perceived satisfaction (in other words, scores of at least 80 out of 100 on each of the three constituent items). Further, 51.2 percent were coded as possessing low concurrent perceived satisfaction.

In sum, approximately 10 percent of the business owners who participated in the Indian study considered themselves to be highly and concurrently *effective* within and across the family and business domains. However, almost twice as many respondents considered themselves to be highly and contemporaneously *satisfied* within and across the two domains. The implication is that approximately 8 in 10 did not perceive themselves to be highly and simultaneously effective or satisfied as family members, business owners and in balancing the two roles. The remainder of this chapter is dedicated to exploring the factors associated with perceived effectiveness and satisfaction in the family and business domains amongst business owners in India.

FAMILY-TO-BUSINESS EXPERIENCES AND STRATEGIES

Considerations of how business owners experience and manage the overlapping spheres of family and business are central to several prominent models of family enterprise (for example, Gersick, Davis, McCollom Hampton, and Lansberg, 1997; Lansberg, 1983; Stafford, Duncan, Danes, and Winter, 1999). Attention to work–family interface considerations is also evident in conceptual frameworks depicting relationships between family factors and entrepreneurial processes and outcomes (for example,

Jennings and McDougald, 2007). Additionally, recent research reveals that the work–family interface significantly affects business owners' satisfaction with their business as well as economic indicators of success (Powell and Eddleston, 2013).

Cognizant of the debate about whether work and family are 'allies' or 'enemies' (Greenhaus and Powell, 2006), we adopt an agnostic stance in this chapter. We start by presenting data on the degree of family-to-business conflict *and* enrichment experienced by Indian business owners in our study. We then provide descriptive information on a number of theoretically associated variables. Guided primarily by Jennings and McDougald's (2007) framework these include: (1) time devoted to the family versus business spheres; (2) individual-level strategies of segmentation and identification; and (3) household-level factors such as the instrumental support provided by family members and the traditionalism and fairness in the division of domestic labor. We conclude this section with a multivariate regression analysis to assess which factors are most strongly related to family-to-business conflict and/or enrichment. Our results are presented in Tables 12.2 and 12.3.

Family-to-Business Conflict and Enrichment

Family-to-business conflict was measured by the mean of a 6-item, Likert-type scale ($\alpha = .81$) with each item rated from '1 = strongly disagree' to '5 = strongly agree.' Three of the items were drawn from Netemeyer, Boles, and McMurrian's (1996) measure that assessed behavioral conflict. An example is: 'Household/family commitments interfere with my ability to perform business-related duties.' The other three items assessed affective conflict, with an example being: 'I feel frustrated when my household/family responsibilities interfere with my work.' These were developed specifically for this study. The findings reported in Table 12.2 indicate that most of the business owners were not experiencing a high degree of family-to-business conflict. The sample mean of 2.70 is below the scale's midpoint of '3 = neither agree nor disagree.' Moreover, in only 3.6 percent of the cases was the respondent's score at or above '4 = agree.'

Family-to-business enrichment was similarly measured by the mean of a 6-item, Likert-type scale ($\alpha = .87$) with each item rated from '1 = strongly disagree' to '5 = strongly agree.' As in the above case, three of the items tapped perceived behavioral enrichment. An example is: 'My involvement in my family requires me to be as focused as possible at work, which helps make me a better businessperson.' Likewise, the other three items assessed perceived affective enrichment. An example is: 'My involvement with my family makes me cheerful and this helps me be a better businessperson.'

Table 12.2 Work–family interface experiences and strategies (India sample)

Variables	α	Mean	S.D.	Min	Max	% with Score
Family-to-business conflict	.81	2.70	0.71	1	5	≥ 4 (agree) = 3.6%
Family-to-business enrichment	.87	3.81	0.67	2	5	≥ 4 (agree) = 51.2%
Time devoted to the family sphere	n/a	17.28	14.02	0	90	≥ 20 hrs/wk = 35.8%
Time devoted to the business sphere	n/a	54.66	17.73	7	100	≥ 40 hrs/wk = 80.7%
Segmentation of family and business roles (actual)	.83	3.48	0.82	2	5	≥ 4 (agree) = 43.5%
Identification with the business	.90	4.03	0.64	1	5	≥ 4 (agree) = 52.8%
Instrumental support from family members	.85	3.53	0.85	1	5	≥ 4 (agree) = 39.4%
Traditionalism in the division of household labor	.63	3.22	0.65	1	4	≥ 3.5 (mainly F) = 48.8%
Perceived fairness in the division of household labor	n/a	2.94	0.78	1	4	≥ 4 (very fair) = 25.1%

Table 12.3 Determinants of family-to-business conflict and enrichment (India sample)

Variables	Family-to-Business Conflict		Family-to-Business Enrichment	
	Model 1	Model 2	Model 3	Model 4
Individual and household-level control variables				
Female	0.02	0.08	0.05	0.07
Married or marital-like relationship	−0.04	0.01	−0.08	0.04
Number of children in household	−0.06	−0.10	0.12	0.20†
Firm-level control variables				
Founder-led firm	0.16	0.08	0.14	0.08
Family firm	0.02	0.00	0.07	−0.09
Firm age	0.08	0.19	−0.04	−0.01
Firm size	−0.20	−0.23†	0.08	0.10
Firm performance	0.01	−0.04	0.06	0.10
High-growth orientation	0.03	0.09	−0.03	−0.17
Work–family interface experiences and strategies				
Time devoted to the family sphere		0.06		0.10
Time devoted to the business sphere		0.07		0.12
Segmentation of family and business roles		−0.00		−0.08
Identification with the business		−0.03		0.20*
Instrumental support from family members		0.07		0.44***
Traditional division of household labor		0.03		−0.04
Fairness in the division of household labor		−0.20†		0.02
Overall model *F*	0.83	0.80	0.62	3.37***
R squared	.06	.13	.05	.39

Notes:
Values in the table are standardized OLS regression coefficients (beta values).
† $p \le .10$, * $p \le .05$, ** $p \le .01$, *** $p \le .001$ (two-tailed tests).

All six items were adapted from Carlson, Kacmar, Wayne, and Grzywacz (2006). The findings reported in Table 12.2 indicate that the majority of the business owners experience a high degree of family-to-business enrichment. The sample mean of 3.81 is very close to the scale value of '4 = agree'; moreover, 51.2 percent of the respondents scored at or above this value.

Individual-level Strategies

Time devoted to the family sphere was measured by a single item—the number of hours that the respondent estimated spending per week on household-related tasks. Although there are recognized weaknesses in this measure, such as susceptibility to over-estimation and discrepancy between marital partners (Yodanis, 2005), it has nevertheless been used in previous studies of entrepreneurship and the work–family interface (for example, Cliff, 1998; Jennings, Hughes, and Jennings, 2010). As indicated in Table 12.2, participants estimated spending 17.3 hours per week, on average, on household-related tasks. Over one-third (35.8 percent) reported that they dedicated at least 20 hours per week to household-related tasks.

Time devoted to the business sphere was measured by a parallel item—the number of hours that the respondent estimated spending per week on business-related tasks. This measure has been used in other studies of entrepreneurship and the work–family interface (for example, Jennings et al., 2010; Jennings et al., forthcoming; Powell and Eddleston, 2013). As indicated in Table 12.2, participants estimated spending 54.7 hours per week, on average, in the business sphere. Further, almost four-fifths (80.7 percent) were actively involved with their business on at least a full-time basis, putting in 40 hours or more during a typical week.

Segmentation was measured by the mean of a 3-item, Likert-type scale (α = .83) with each item rated from '1 = strongly disagree' to '5 = strongly agree.' The items were adapted from several studies on work–family segmentation (Carlson, Kacmar, and Williams, 2000; Kreiner, 2006; Powell and Greenhaus, 2010). An illustrative item is, 'In reality, I often leave household/family issues behind when I'm at work.' The phrase 'In reality' was inserted at the beginning of each item to focus the respondent on their experienced rather than preferred degree of segmentation between family and business roles. As indicated in Table 12.2, the sample mean of 3.48 was just above the scale's midpoint of '3 = neither agree nor disagree.' Approximately four-tenths of the participants (43.5 percent) could be deemed as enacting a segmentation strategy, with scores at or above the value of '4 = agree.'

We measured the degree of an owner-manager's *identification* with his/her business by the mean of a 12-item, Likert-type scale (α = .90) with each item rated from '1 = strongly disagree' to '5 = strongly agree.' The items were adapted from O'Reilly and Chatman (1986), as suggested by Berrone, Cruz, and Gómez-Mejía (2012). An example is: 'If I were describing myself, the firm would likely be something I would mention.' The findings reported in Table 12.2 indicate that the majority of the business owners identified highly with their firms. Not only did the sample mean of

4.03 fall above the scale value of '4 = agree,' but over half of the respondents (52.8 percent) scored at or above this value.

Household-level Considerations

We measured the *instrumental support provided by family members* for the respondent's business by the mean of a 5-item, Likert-type scale ($\alpha = .85$), developed by Powell and Eddleston (2013), with each item rated from '1 = strongly disagree' to '5 = strongly agree.' An illustrative item is: 'The members of my family who do not officially work in the business can be counted on to help out if something unexpected happens in this business.' The findings reported in Table 12.2 indicate that many of the business owners experienced a high level of instrumental support from the members of their families. Not only did the sample mean of 3.53 fall above the scale's midpoint, but 39.4 percent of the respondents had a score at or above the scale value of '4 = agree.'

We measured *traditionalism in the division of household labor* by the mean of a 6-item scale ($\alpha = .63$), based on Yodanis (2005), which was developed for capturing the distribution of housework. The respondent indicated who was responsible for six tasks (for example, shopping for groceries, deciding what to have for dinner, doing the laundry and caring for the sick) by checking one of the following responses: '4 = always or usually the woman,' '3 = equally,' '2 = always or usually the man,' or '1 = a third person (hired help).' As indicated in Table 12.2, the sample mean of 3.22 ended up being very close to the value of '3 = equally.' A sizeable proportion of the respondents (48.8 percent), however, could be deemed as living in a traditional household, given that their scores fell at or above 3.5.

Perceived fairness in the division of household labor was measured by the respondent's response to the follow-up question, 'How fair do you feel that this division of household labor is for yourself?' The response categories ranged from '1 = very unfair' to '4 = very fair.' This question was adapted from Milkie and Peltola (1999). The findings reported in Table 12.2 reveal that many of the business owners considered the division of labor in their households to be somewhat *unfair*. Not only did the sample mean of 2.94 fall below the value of '3 = somewhat fair,' but only a quarter of the participants (25.1 percent) perceived the division of labor in their households to be very fair.

Determinants of Family-to-Business Conflict and Enrichment

In this subsection we investigate the associations between the above-noted set of work–family interface experiences and strategies and the extent of family-to-business conflict and enrichment reported by the business owners. More specifically, we are interested in determining which factors are most influential above and beyond standard demographic characteristics of the owner-managers and their households as well as key characteristics of their firms. The results of our multivariate ordinary least squares (OLS) analysis are presented in Table 12.3.

The findings summarized within Models 1 and 2 of Table 12.3 reveal surprisingly few statistically significant relationships for family-to-business *conflict*. Only the division of household labor emerged as a marginally significant covariate. As indicated by its negative coefficient, business owners who perceived greater fairness in the way that tasks were divided within their households tended to report lower levels of family-to-business conflict. Notably, those who considered themselves to be heading family firms did not report significantly higher (or lower) family-to-business conflict.

In contrast, the findings reported in Models 3 and 4 of Table 12.3 reveal more statistically significant associations for family-to-business *enrichment*. While number of children is the only (marginally) significant control variable in the full model, among the work–family interface variables, both identification with the business and instrumental family support are statistically significant. More specifically, business owners who reported a higher level of family-to-business enrichment tended to identify more with their business and to receive more instrumental support from family for the business. As indicated by the beta coefficients, the most influential of these was the instrumental support from family variable. As above, those heading family firms did not report a significantly higher or lower degree of family-to-business enrichment.

FACTORS ASSOCIATED WITH PERCEIVED EFFECTIVENESS AND SATISFACTION

Having explored the factors associated with family-to-business conflict and enrichment, we now turn to investigate their relationships with perceived effectiveness and satisfaction. In each case we focus upon the composite measure of the outcome variable; in other words, the degree to which a business owner considers him/herself to be concurrently effective or concurrently satisfied within and across the family and business domains. Given that these composite measures consisted of three ordinal levels (low, moderate and high), the models were estimated by multinomial logistic regression. We ran three models for each outcome measure: (1) a baseline model of controls; (2) a model with the controls plus the addition of work–family interface experience and strategy variables; and (3) a full model containing all of these variables plus family-to-business conflict and enrichment. Two columns of estimates corresponding to the moderate and high outcome levels are provided for each model (the low level was selected as the referent category). The complete set of models appears in Tables 12.4 and 12.5.

As indicated in Table 12.4, among the control variables, gender, educational level, firm age, and whether the business was a family firm were significantly associated with a high level of *concurrent effectiveness*. Among the work–family interface experience and strategy variables, segmentation of family and business roles, identification with the business, and the fair division of household labor were shown to be positively (marginally) related to high levels of concurrent effectiveness. Time devoted to the business was negatively related to high levels of concurrent effectiveness. However, once family-to-business conflict and enrichment were added to the model, only segmentation of family and business roles remained significant. Family-to-business conflict was shown to be negatively related while family-to-business enrichment was positively, although marginally, related to high levels of concurrent effectiveness. Notably, the family firm indicator remained a significant of perceived effectiveness, with owner-managers heading businesses of this type perceiving themselves to be less effective than owner-managers of non-family firms.

As indicated in Table 12.5, one of the controls in the business domain, firm age, and one of the controls in the family domain, marital status, was associated with a moderate level of *concurrent satisfaction*. None of the controls was significantly related to a high level of concurrent satisfaction. Of the work–family interface experience and strategy variables, only segmentation of the family and business was positively associated with high concurrent satisfaction. Both family-to-business conflict and enrichment emerged as significant. Family-to-business enrichment exhibited a positive, but marginal, association with concurrent satisfaction. Family-to-business conflict was negatively associated with a high degree of concurrent satisfaction. In other words, business owners in India who reported a high level of concurrent satisfaction within and across the family and business domains tended to report lower levels of family-to-business conflict and higher levels of family-to-business enrichment, and, segmentation of the family and business.

DISCUSSION

Summary

The results of our study paint a somewhat bleak picture of the personal well-being of owner-managers in India. Specifically, only 10 percent

Table 12.4 Factors associated with composite measure of perceived effectiveness (India sample)

Variables	Model 1		Model 2		Model 3	
	Moderate	High	Moderate	High	Moderate	High
Control variables						
Female	0.85	1.56†	0.54	1.27	0.87	6.96†
Education level	−0.19	0.77	−0.07	0.94	−0.12	5.50*
Married or marital-like relationship	0.87	17.12	0.40	1.43	1.21	10.55
Number of children in household	−0.30	0.09	0.00	0.00	−0.31	3.47
Founder-led firm	0.00	0.00	–	–	–	–
Family firm	−0.82	−1.50	−0.72	−2.34*	−1.40*	−7.27†
Firm age	−0.02	0.02	0.00	0.03	0.02	0.41†
Firm size	0.00†	0.00†	0.00	0.00	0.00	0.00
Firm performance	0.22	−0.06	−0.00	−0.34	0.06	−3.13
High-growth orientation	−0.03	0.01	−0.01	0.00	−0.05	−0.34

Work–family interface experiences and strategies				
Time devoted to family sphere	0.01	0.02	0.00	0.06
Time devoted to business sphere	-0.02	-0.07*	-0.02	-0.07
Segmentation of family and business	0.59†	1.06†	0.76*	9.03*
Identification with the business	0.23	1.53†	0.19	1.31
Instrumental support from family	0.25	-0.28	0.23	1.77
Traditional division of household labor	-0.19	-0.65	-0.20	0.51
Fair division of household labor	0.17	1.30†	-0.01	-0.03
Family-to-business conflict and enrichment				
Family-to-business conflict			-0.07	-13.63*
Family-to-business enrichment			0.30	6.39†
-2LL Chi-square	24.39	37.69		65.19***
Nagelkerke R-square	.22	.34		.57

Notes:
Values in the table are unstandardized multinomial logistic regression coefficients.
† $p \leq .10$, * $p \leq .05$, ** $p \leq .01$, *** $p \leq .001$ (two-tailed tests).

Table 12.5 *Factors associated with composite measure of perceived satisfaction (India sample)*

Variables	Model 1		Model 2		Model 3	
	Mod	High	Mod	High	Mod	High
Control variables						
Female	0.17	0.76	0.05	0.30	-0.08	0.47
Education level	-0.35	0.34	-0.33	0.52	-0.40	0.45
Married or marital-like relationship	2.38*	0.96	1.87	1.47	2.09	1.03
Number of children in household	-0.22	-0.02	-0.19	0.09	-0.38	-0.08
Household income	0.00	0.00	0.00	0.00	0.00	0.00
Founder-led firm	0.00	0.00	0.00	0.00	0.00	0.00
Family firm	0.09	-0.89	-0.19	-0.77	-0.14	-1.06
Firm age	-0.06*	-0.01	-0.06†	0.00	-0.06†	0.02
Firm size	0.00	0.00	0.00	0.00	0.00	0.00
Firm performance	0.22	0.31	0.16	0.10	0.20	-0.02
High-growth orientation	-0.06	-0.07	-0.10	-0.10	-0.07	-0.06

Work–family interface experiences and strategies			
Time devoted to the family sphere	0.02	0.02	0.02
Time devoted to the business sphere	0.15	0.00	-0.01
Segmentation of family and business	0.43	0.59	0.99*
Identification with the business	0.36	0.90	0.85
Instrumental support from family	-0.05	-0.50	-0.63
Traditional division of household labor	0.19	-0.12	-0.12
Fairness division of household labor	0.25	0.48	0.02
Family-to-business conflict and enrichment			
Family-to-business conflict		-0.22	-1.10*
Family-to-business enrichment		1.18*	1.25†
-2LL Chi-square	23.95	35.46	48.19†
Nagelkerke R-square	.22	.34	.44

Notes:
Values in the table are unstandardized multinomial logistic regression coefficients.
† $p \le .10$, * $p \le .05$, ** $p \le .01$, *** $p \le .001$ (two-tailed tests).

229

reported a high level of concurrent effectiveness and less than 20 percent reported a high level of concurrent satisfaction within and across the family and business domains. For both concurrent effectiveness and satisfaction, more than half of the sample reported low levels (58.3 percent and 51.2 percent, respectively). In examining the individual indicators of effectiveness and satisfaction, it appears that the majority of Indian owner-managers only feel effective or satisfied in one facet. Since being able to effectively and satisfactorily balance work and family enhances individuals' psychological well-being (Greenhaus and Allen, 2011) and represents some of the potential benefits of entrepreneurship (Eddleston and Powell, 2012; Jennings and McDougald, 2007), our results suggest that entrepreneurship may not be 'good' for the personal experiences of owner-managers in India.

By further exploring the work–family experiences and strategies of our respondents, we see that while their reported family-to-business conflict is low (2.70), the average time they devote to their business is quite high (54.66 hours per week). In fact, more than 80 percent of our sample reported that they worked more than forty hours per week. In comparison, the US sample reported an average work week of 43.1 hours and 65.4 percent revealed that they worked more than forty hours per week.

Although it could be expected that such long work-hours exacerbated Indian owner-managers' family-to-business conflict, and reduced concurrent effectiveness and satisfaction, this was not the case. The only significant variable found to be marginally associated with family-to-business conflict was the perceived fairness in the division of household labor. In our sample, only 25 percent felt that their household's division of labor was very fair. In turn, it was those owner-managers who had a fair division of labor that reported the least family-to-business conflict. Interestingly, hours devoted to the family or business sphere was not related to family-to-business conflict. Therefore, taken together, this suggests that how owner-managers in India negotiate the division of household responsibilities with their spouse/partner is a key indicator of their degree of family-to-business conflict.

Regarding family-to-business enrichment, factors distinct from those associated with family-to-business conflict were revealed to be most important. In line with recent research, this supports the argument that conflict and enrichment are not opposite ends of a continuum and that both should be considered when studying the work–family interface (Chen, Powell, and Cui, 2014; Powell, 2011). Our results showed that owner-managers' identification with the business and instrumental support from family for the business were significantly related to family-to-business enrichment.

Finally, when we look at those Indian owner-managers who reported the highest levels of concurrent effectiveness and satisfaction, we see a distinct pattern of work–family relationships. Specifically, segmentation of the family and business, family-to-business enrichment, and family-to-business conflict were all significantly related to concurrent effectiveness and satisfaction. Therefore, it appears that the intersection of work and family best explains Indian owner-managers' sense of effectiveness and satisfaction within and across the family and business domains.

Implications

These findings have several important implications for research on entrepreneurs and the work–family interface, particularly as they relate to an emerging market context. Entrepreneurship research, which has predominantly focused on developed economies (Felzensztein, Gimmon, and Aqueveque, 2013; Steier, 2009) often portrays the ability to balance work and family as a potential benefit and source of satisfaction from business ownership (Buttner and Moore, 1997; Eddleston and Powell, 2012; Heilman and Chen, 2003). Yet, when almost 40 percent of the entrepreneurship population is motivated by necessity as opposed to opportunity, as seen in India (GEM, 2013), it may be more difficult to achieve a sense of effectiveness and satisfaction within and across both work and family domains. Further, because India is experiencing a growing consumer market and increasing middle class (Ernst & Young, 2013), Indian owner-managers may be experiencing new pressures to be both strong income providers *and* active family members. Therefore, as the quality of life in India improves, entrepreneurs may feel greater pressure to be effective family members as well as family breadwinners.

Our results indicate that those owner-managers who are best able to manage the intersection of work and family report the greatest concurrent effectiveness and satisfaction. In other words, we did not find that factors exclusively linked to one domain or the other contributed to concurrent effectiveness or satisfaction, but rather, it was those factors that jointly took into account *both* domains that best characterized high concurrent effectiveness and satisfaction (segmentation of the family and business, family-to-business enrichment, and family-to-business conflict). As such, it appears that Indian owner-managers are quite cognizant of the relationship between the two domains and when assessing their concurrent effectiveness and satisfaction, they consider how the two domains synchronize and complement each other.

Our findings also contribute to the debate on whether work and family are best portrayed as 'allies' or 'enemies' (Greenhaus and Powell, 2006). Those owner-managers who reported low family-to-business conflict and high family-to-business enrichment expressed the greatest concurrent effectiveness and satisfaction within and across the two domains. However, we also found that a greater segmentation strategy is associated with the highest levels of concurrent effectiveness and satisfaction. Thus, the linkages between work and family can be complex for Indian owner-managers. While it seems important to foster positive and beneficial relationships between the two domains, it is also necessary to ensure that the two domains are kept distinct and do not become highly integrated.

Limitations

It is important to consider the preceding summary and implications in light of the study's limitations. One pertains to the fact that the sample is not necessarily representative of all business owners in India. This is attributable to two factors. The first was our reliance upon a sample drawn principally from Bangalore, a large, fast-growing southern Indian city marked by the presence of several quality institutes of higher education in science, engineering, software and business, and with a reputation for rapid economic growth rooted in both knowledge-based and traditional industries, a context which may not be representative of the universe of Indian entrepreneurs. The second was the deliberate attempt to over-sample female-led firms so as to yield a reasonable representation of such businesses in the overall sample.

Another limitation is our reliance upon self-report data from the business owners. Although such individuals are clearly well-qualified to provide information on their firms and households, it would have been ideal if we had been able to corroborate certain variables through different sources. This is especially so for the allocation of time to the business and family spheres, division of household tasks and firm performance data. Related to the preceding point, the ideal design for shedding insight into the overarching question of whether entrepreneurship is 'good' for families would have involved collecting data from other household members in addition to the business owner.

Conclusion

Our study gives a rare glimpse into the work–family experiences, strategies and outcomes of business owners in India. While India's strong growth in GDP and size of its consumer market have helped to spur the rate of entrepreneurship, the country is still dominated by 'necessity' entrepreneurs who turn to business ownership to earn an income rather than to pursue an opportunity (GEM, 2013). We suspect that this emerging market context plays a role in the Indian owner-manager's sense of concurrent effectiveness and satisfaction within and across the family and business domains.

In comparison with the US sample, the Indian owner-managers devoted a much greater number of hours per week to their business (43.1 versus 54.7 hours, respectively). Additionally, while half of the US sample felt that their household's division of labor was very fair, in India only a quarter of the respondents felt this way. In turn, in both samples fairness in the division of household labor was significantly related to family-to-business conflict. However, the greatest difference between the two samples appears to lie at the proportion of owner-managers who felt high concurrent effectiveness and satisfaction. In the US, approximately 40 percent of the sample reported high concurrent effectiveness and satisfaction. However, in India, only 10.1 percent reported high concurrent effectiveness and 19.6 percent reported concurrent satisfaction. More than half of the Indian sample scored *low* on concurrent effectiveness and satisfaction. As such, there appears to be important differences between the work–family experiences of Indian and US owner-managers.

For Indian owner-managers, factors at the intersection of work and family were most associated with concurrent effectiveness and satisfaction; specifically, segmentation of the family and business, family-to-business enrichment, and family-to-business conflict. As such, for Indian owner-managers to achieve a sense of concurrent effectiveness and satisfaction, they needed to create synergy and cooperation between the two domains while also keeping them distinct. This contrasts with the US study, which did not find segmentation to be related to concurrent effectiveness or satisfaction. Additionally, family-to-business enrichment did not contribute to the concurrent effectiveness of American owner-managers. Therefore, how Indian owner-managers approach the work–family interface appears to be unique. Further, given the results of our study, which are embedded in the emerging market context that Indian owner-managers face, it appears that these entrepreneurs need to make much more progress in learning how to balance work and family, before it can be said that entrepreneurship is 'good' for their families.

REFERENCES

Berrone, P., C. Cruz, and L.R. Gómez-Mejía (2012), 'Socioemotional wealth in family firms: Theoretical dimensions, assessment approaches, and agenda for future research,' *Family Business Review*, **25**, 258–279.
Buttner, E.H. and D.P. Moore (1997), 'Women's organizational exodus to

entrepreneurship: Self-supported motivations and correlations with success,' *Journal of Small Business Management*, **35**, 34–46.

Carlson, D.S., K.M. Kacmar, and L.J. Williams (2000), 'Construction and initial validation of a multidimensional measure of work–family conflict,' *Journal of Vocational Behavior*, **56**, 249–276.

Carlson, D.S., K.M. Kacmar, J.H. Wayne, and J.G. Grzywacz (2006), 'Measuring the positive side of the work–family interface: Development and validation of a work–family enrichment scale,' *Journal of Vocational Behavior*, **68**, 131–164.

Chen, Z., G.N. Powell, and W. Cui (2014), 'Dynamics of the relationships among work and family resource gain and loss, enrichment, and conflict over time,' *Journal of Vocational Behavior*, **84**, 293–302.

Cliff, J.E. (1998), 'Does one size fit all? Exploring the relationship between attitudes between growth, gender and business size,' *Journal of Business Venturing*, **13**, 523–542.

Davidsson, P. (2004), *Researching Entrepreneurship*. Boston, MA, USA: Springer.

Eddleston, K.A. and G.N. Powell (2012), 'Nurturing entrepreneurs' work–family balance: A gendered perspective,' *Entrepreneurship Theory and Practice*, **36**, 513–541.

Ernst & Young (2013), 'EY G20 Entrepreneurship Barometer,' retrieved from http://www.ey.com/GL/en/Services/Strategic-Growth-Markets/The-EY-G20-Entrepreneurship-Barometer-2013 (accessed June 20, 2014).

Felzensztein, C., E. Gimmon, and C. Aqueveque (2013), 'Entrepreneurship at the periphery: Exploring framework conditions in core and peripheral locations,' *Entrepreneurship Theory and Practice*, **37**, 815–835.

GEM (2013), 'Global Entrepreneurship Monitor Report,' retrieved from http://www.gemconsortium.org/docs/3106/gem-2013-global-report (accessed July 15, 2014).

Gersick, K., J. Davis, M. McCollom Hampton, and I. Lansberg (1997), *Generation to Generation: Life Cycles in Family Business*. Boston, MA, USA: Harvard University Press.

Ghani, E., W.R. Kerr, and S.D. O'Connell (2013), 'Local industrial structures and female entrepreneurship in India,' *Journal of Economic Geography*, **13**, 929–964.

Greenhaus, G.H. and T.D. Allen (2011), 'Work–family balance: A review and extension of the literature,' in L. Tetrick and J.C. Quick (eds), *Handbook of Occupational Health Psychology*. Washington, DC: American Psychological Association, pp. 165–183.

Greenhaus, J.H. and G.N. Powell (2006), 'When work and family are allies: A theory of work–family enrichment,' *Academy of Management Review*, **31**, 72–92.

Heilman, M.E. and J.J. Chen (2003), 'Entrepreneurship as a solution: The allure of self-employment for women and minorities,' *Human Resource Management Review*, **13**, 347–364.

Jennings, J.E. and M.S. McDougald (2007), 'Work–family interface experiences and coping strategies: Implications for entrepreneurship research and practice,' *Academy of Management Review*, **32**, 747–750.

Jennings, J.E., R.S. Breitkreuz, and A.E. James (2013), 'When family members are also business owners: Is entrepreneurship good for families?,' *Family Relations*, **62**, 472–489.

Jennings, J.E., K.D. Hughes, and P.D. Jennings (2010), 'The work–family inter-face strategies of male and female entrepreneurs: Are there any differences?,' in C.G. Brush, A. de Bruin, E.J. Gatewood, and C. Henry (eds), *Women Entrepreneurs and the Global Environment for Growth*. Cheltenham, UK and Northampton, MA, USA: Edward Elgar Publishing, pp. 163–186.

Jennings, J.E., P.D. Jennings, and M. Sharifian (forthcoming), 'Living the dream? Assessing the "entrepreneurship as emancipation" perspective in a developed region,' *Entrepreneurship Theory and Practice*.

Koster, S. and S.K. Rai (2008), 'Entrepreneurship and economic development in a developing country: a case study of India,' *Journal of Entrepreneurship*, **17**, 117–137.

Kreiner, G.E. (2006), 'Consequences of work–home segmentation or integration: A person-environment fit perspective,' *Journal of Organizational Behavior*, **27**, 485–507.

Lansberg, I. (1983), 'Managing human resources in family firms: The problem of institutional overlap,' *Organizational Dynamics*, Summer, 29–38.

Milkie, M.A. and P. Peltola (1999), 'Playing all the roles: Gender and the work–family balancing act,' *Journal of Marriage and the Family*, **61**, 476–490.

National Knowledge Commission (NKC) (2008), 'Entrepreneurship in India,' retrieved from http://knowledgecommission.gov.in/downloads/documents/NKC_Entrepreneurship.pdf (accessed June 20, 2014).

Netemeyer, R.G., J.S. Boles, and R. McMurrian (1996), 'Development and valida-tion of work–family conflict and family–work conflict scales,' *Journal of Applied Psychology*, **81**, 400–410.

O'Reilly, C. and J. Chatman (1986), 'Organizational commitment and psychologi-cal attachment: The effects of compliance, identification, and internalization on prosocial behavior,' *Journal of Applied Psychology*, **71**, 492–499.

Powell, G.N. (2011), *Women and Men in Management*. Los Angeles, CA, USA: Sage Publications.

Powell, G.N. and K.A. Eddleston (2013), 'Linking family-to-business enrich-ment and support to entrepreneurial success: Do female and male entre-preneurs experience different outcomes?,' *Journal of Business Venturing*, **28**, 261–280.

Powell, G.N. and J.H. Greenhaus (2010), 'Sex, gender, and the work-to-family interface: Exploring negative and positive interdependencies,' *Academy of Management Journal*, **53**, 513–534.

Shane, S. (2012), 'Reflections on the 2010 AMR decade award: Delivering on the promise of entrepreneurship as a field of research,' *Academy of Management Review*, **37** (1), 10–20.

Stafford, K., K. Duncan, S. Danes, and M. Winter (1999), 'A research model of sustainable family businesses,' *Family Business Review*, **12**, 197–208.

Steier, L.P. (2009), 'Familial capitalism in global institutional contexts: Implications for corporate governance and entrepreneurship in East Asia,' *Asia Pacific Journal of Management*, **26**, 513–535.

Waismel-Manor, R., P. Moen, and S. Sweet (2002), 'Managing and thriving: What factors predict dual-earner middle-class couples feeling highly successful in their jobs, families and balancing both?' BLCC Working Paper 02-20.

World Bank (2012), 'Doing business 2012: Doing business in a more transpar-ent world,' retrieved from http://www.doingbusiness.org/reports/global-reports/doing-business-2012 (accessed June 20, 2014).

Yodanis, C. (2005), 'Divorce culture and marital gender equality: A cross-national study,' *Gender and Society*, **19**, 644–659.

Yu, D. and Y. Tandon (2012), 'India's big problem: Nurturing entrepreneurs,' *Gallup Business Journal*, August, retrieved from http://www.gallup.com/business-journal/156143/india-big-problem-nurturing-entrepreneurs.aspx (accessed June 20, 2014).

13. Part II summary: is entrepreneurship 'good' for families? It depends on the country

Kimberly A. Eddleston, Jennifer E. Jennings, P. Devereaux Jennings and Ravi Sarathy

Around the globe, entrepreneurship is an important driver of economic growth. While the vast majority of entrepreneurship research has been performed in developed countries (Bruton, Ahlstrom, and Obloj, 2008; Felzensztein, Gimmon, and Aqueveque, 2013), studies on emerging markets highlight how pro-market reforms have recently spurred entrepreneurship and, in turn, how entrepreneurship has contributed to the growth of the middle class (Bruton et al., 2008; Manolova, Eunni, and Gyoshev, 2008; Peng, 2001). Although research has examined the economic benefits of entrepreneurship to developed and emerging markets, few studies have taken a cross-cultural approach to understand how entrepreneurship affects the *entrepreneur*. Yet, as a career, entrepreneurship is quite unique because it allows individuals to create businesses that reflect their personal preferences, interests and needs (Carter, Gartner, Shaver, and Gatewood, 2003; Eddleston and Powell, 2008). For example, researchers studying developed markets have acknowledged how many individuals turn to entrepreneurship in search of achieving greater work–family balance (Caputo and Dolinsky, 1998; De Martino and Barbato, 2003; Eddleston and Powell, 2012). They also recognize that managing the work–family interface is important to entrepreneurs' career satisfaction and personal well-being (Jennings and McDougald, 2007; Powell and Eddleston, 2013).

However, in an emerging market context with a high proportion of 'necessity' entrepreneurs who turn to entrepreneurship because of a need to financially provide for themselves and their families (GEM, 2013), is work–family balance important or an elusive luxury? Further, do entrepreneurs in emerging markets gain a sense of work–family effectiveness and satisfaction in the same way as their counterparts in developed markets? Accordingly, the Part II chapters sought to explore if entrepreneurship is 'good' for families in developing and emerging market contexts. We now look to identify similarities and differences among the entrepreneurs from our previous five chapters to determine if there are any 'universal' factors that encourage positive linkages between work and family and to explore the unique cultural elements that reflect the double embeddedness of a business being embedded within a family that is embedded within a country.

The family embeddedness perspective (Aldrich and Cliff, 2003) recognizes how an entrepreneur's business and family are often inextricably intertwined. Research applying this perspective often focuses on how the family is a resource for the entrepreneur's business (Powell and Eddleston, 2013) and serves as the 'oxygen that feeds the fire of entrepreneurship' (Rogoff and Heck, 2003: 559). Research in this vein argues that family characteristics influence new business creation and processes, and as a result, the business' performance and survival (Powell and Eddleston, 2013; Rogoff and Heck, 2003). While progress in applying the family embeddedness perspective to entrepreneurship has been made, almost no research has considered how entrepreneurship affects the family domain (as noted in the review by Jennings, Breitkreuz, and James, 2013). This is particularly so in a cross-country context.

Besides exploring entrepreneurs' concurrent effectiveness and satisfaction in their business and family domains, the studies in Part II of this book also considered both positive and negative linkages between the business and family. While most research on the work–family interface has employed a conflict perspective that depicts work and family as 'enemies' (Jennings and McDougald, 2007), recently a positive view has been offered that views work and family as 'allies' (Greenhaus and Powell, 2006; Powell and Eddleston, 2013). The enrichment perspective proposes that beneficial linkages can exist between work and family that enhance an individual's effectiveness and well-being. Therefore, in comparing the Part II chapters, we look to explore if work and family can be better described as 'enemies' or 'allies' in each country.

PERCEIVED CONCURRENT EFFECTIVENESS WITH BUSINESS AND FAMILY

Perceived concurrent effectiveness assesses the extent to which owner-managers feel that they are highly effective in both their business and family domains as well as in balancing the two spheres. Our results, which are displayed in Figure 13.1, reveal that the US had the greatest proportion of owner-managers (38.2 percent) who perceived themselves as possessing a high level of concurrent effectiveness (in other words, scores of at least 80 out of 100 on perceived effectiveness in the business domain,

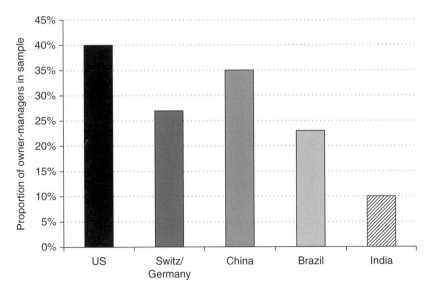

*Figure 13.1   Incidence of high concurrent effectiveness within and across
business and family domains by country*

in the family domain and in balancing the two). China closely followed
with 34.7 percent of owner-managers feeling highly concurrently effective.
In sharp contrast, only 10.1 percent of Indian owner-managers reported
that they felt highly effective within and across both their business and
family domains. And only about one-quarter of the owner-managers in
Switzerland/Germany (27.3 percent) and Brazil (22.7 percent) reported a
high degree of concurrent effectiveness. Moreover, across the five studies,
the results showed that most owner-managers felt more effective in one
domain than the other. It is also important to note that in no country did
more than half of the respondents report high concurrent effectiveness
within and across the business and family domains.

When examining the predictors of high concurrent effectiveness across
the countries a few patterns emerged. Family-to-business conflict and/or
family-to-business enrichment proved to be significantly associated with
high concurrent effectiveness for all countries except Switzerland/Germany.
While family-to-business conflict detracted from the concurrent effectiveness of owner-managers in the US, Brazil and India, family-to-business
enrichment increased it in China and India. As such, negative spillover
from family-to-business hurt the concurrent effectiveness of American,
Brazilian and Indian owner-managers, while positive spillover benefitted
the concurrent effectiveness of Chinese and Indian owner-managers.

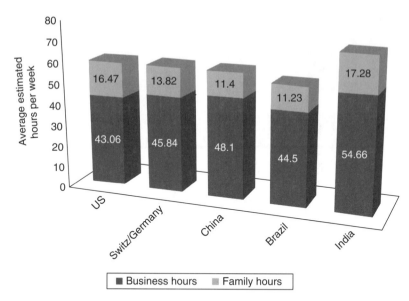

*Figure 13.2   Estimated time devoted to tasks in business and family
          domains by country*

Time devoted to one's business and/or family was also important within
all countries except Switzerland/Germany. Information on the average
time devoted to the business and family for each country are displayed in
Figure 13.2. Interestingly, while time devoted to one's business damaged
the concurrent effectiveness of owner-managers in China and India, time
devoted to one's family hurt the concurrent effectiveness of Americans
but benefitted the concurrent effectiveness of Brazilian owner-managers.
Thus, we see that for Americans to feel highly concurrently effective, their
business must not infringe on their family life and they must limit time in
their family domain. This is a very different picture from that in China, the
country with the second highest concurrent effectiveness. For the Chinese,
it appears a greater sense of family-to-business enrichment and less time
devoted to work promotes concurrent effectiveness. In comparison, India,
with the lowest rate of high concurrent effectiveness, was most affected by
both family-to-business conflict and enrichment. Thus, for Indian owner-
managers there appears to be much value on creating synergy between
work and family, and in particular, in strengthening the positive linkages
between the two domains while minimizing negative spillover.

While all of the countries except Switzerland/Germany were influenced
by work–family spillover (positive and/or negative) and devotion of time

to work or family, owner-managers in Switzerland/Germany were only affected by their identification with the business. That is, in order for Swiss/German owner-managers to perceive high concurrent effectiveness in their business and family roles, they needed to strongly identify with their business. Another distinct finding is in regards to firm performance. Firm performance was consistently, significantly related to US owner-managers' concurrent effectiveness as well as their satisfaction. The only other country in which firm performance was somewhat related to owner-managers' concurrent effectiveness was Brazil. Therefore, while our results across the five countries identified some similarities in factors that contribute to owner-managers' perceived concurrent effectiveness, we also found patterns that were unique and did not translate to owner-managers in other countries.

HIGH CONCURRENT SATISFACTION WITH BUSINESS AND FAMILY

Besides considering owner-managers' perceived effectiveness at managing their business and family it was also important to examine the degree to which they felt satisfied with both domains. Similar to the results on concurrent effectiveness, across the five countries most owner-managers felt more satisfied in one domain than the other. When considering those who were highly concurrently satisfied with both their business and family as well as with the balance between the two domains, Switzerland/Germany and the US were essentially tied for the highest score, with proportions of 40.3 percent and 40.1 percent, respectively. China closely followed with 37.3 percent, and then India with 19.6 percent (see Figure 13.3). Unfortunately, not enough data from Brazil was collected on these items to include them in this comparison. As such, considering the countries we studied, India has the lowest concurrent effectiveness and satisfaction with their business and family. These results suggest that entrepreneurship is not necessarily 'good' for the personal well-being and family role of Indian owner-managers.

When looking at predictors of all countries with data, results showed that family-to-business conflict and/or family-to-business enrichment discerned those owner-managers with the highest level of concurrent satisfaction. Similar to concurrent effectiveness, family-to-business conflict *and* enrichment affected Indian owner-managers' concurrent satisfaction. Additionally, hours devoted to the business lessened the concurrent satisfaction of Swiss/German and Chinese owner-managers.

While the majority of owner-managers in each of the countries were not

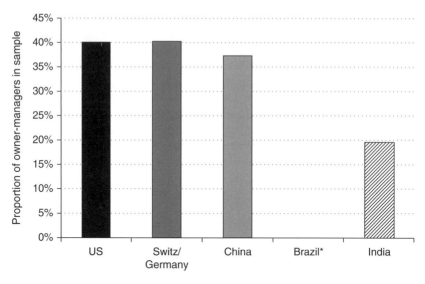

Note: * Sufficient data was not available from the Brazil study to report findings.

*Figure 13.3   Incidence of high concurrent satisfaction within and across
business and family domains by country*

concurrently satisfied with their businesses and families, once again, those
in India were the least likely to report concurrent satisfaction. Further,
it is interesting to note that although family-to-business conflict *and*
enrichment significantly contributed to their level of concurrent satisfaction, both of these factors also predicted high concurrent satisfaction for
American owner-managers, who in contrast, were the most likely to report
high concurrent satisfaction. This suggests that concurrent satisfaction is
similarly defined by American and Indian owner-managers. Given these
findings, we looked to see if the family-to-business conflict or enrichment
levels were strikingly different for the American and Indian respondents. Surprisingly, they were not. As such, it appears that Indian owner-
managers are more sensitive to the effects of family-to-business conflict
and enrichment than their American counterparts.

Additionally, we considered predictors of family-to-business conflict
and enrichment. While this information was not available from China,
a 'universally relevant' factor for each type of spillover was identified.
Specifically, fairness in the division of household labor significantly
predicted the family-to-business conflict of owner-managers in the US,
Switzerland/Germany, India and Brazil, and instrumental support from

the family for the business significantly predicted the family-to-business enrichment for each of these countries. When we looked at differences in the means of these variables across countries, we found that while India reported the highest mean for instrumental support from the family for the business, the US reported the highest mean for fairness in the division of household labor. Thus, it seems that while family-to-business conflict and family-to-business enrichment have a similar source for owner-managers in the US, Switzerland/Germany, China and India, the owner-managers' ability to obtain enough of these factors to lessen their work–family conflict or foster work–family enrichment, is not.

DISCUSSION

Our cross-country research suggests that many entrepreneurs across the globe struggle to achieve concurrent effectiveness and satisfaction in both their work and family lives (and in balancing the two). In no country did we find even *half* of the study respondents report high concurrent effectiveness or satisfaction with their business and family. These results highlight the need for further cross-country research on the work–family interface of entrepreneurs, and particularly, how their businesses impact their family lives and personal well-being. If entrepreneurs are unable to achieve a sense of effectiveness and satisfaction in managing their business and family roles, they may choose to turn away from entrepreneurship and pursue a different career, or limit the size and growth of their businesses (Eddleston and Powell, 2012; Jennings and McDougald, 2007). There are also likely to be negative effects on their families such as stress, depression, and even divorce (Clark, 2000; Frone, Russell, and Cooper, 1992).

While the quest for work–family balance is a common issue recognized by researchers studying individuals in developed countries, our findings show that entrepreneurs in emerging markets also struggle to achieve concurrent effectiveness and satisfaction in their business and family roles, and it appears that their struggles tend to be more intense. Further, a comparison of our chapters reveals that the country in which an owner-manager is embedded determines how linkages between work and family are viewed. While greater personal well-being (in other words, concurrent effectiveness and satisfaction) was enhanced for owner-managers from some countries when family-to-business conflict was minimized, for others work–family enrichment mattered more. Additionally, while owner-managers from some countries seemed to want to lessen their hours devoted to the business, for those from other countries it was time spent with family that most strongly influenced their well-being. Similarly, for owner-managers from some countries emphasis on the business role tended to be key to well-being, but for others it was emphasis on the family role that mattered most.

It is important to consider these findings and inferences, however, in light of the study's limitations. While the final chapter of this book outlines several limitations regarding the overall research design, including its limited sample of countries, cross-sectional nature and self-reported data (see Jennings, Eddleston, Jennings, and Sarathy, Chapter 14), there are also limitations that are specific to the Part II chapters and thus our efforts to compare each country's findings about the work–family interface of business owner-managers. First, due to missing data from some countries, we were not able to include all countries in our comparisons. For example, some data were missing from China and Brazil which limited our analyses. Second, given that owner-managers may have personal definitions of what it means to achieve work–family balance (Eddleston and Powell, 2012), qualitative data should have been gathered so that a clearer understanding of the work–family interface of entrepreneurs from diverse countries could be achieved. More specifically, what it means to be concurrently effective or satisfied within and across business and family domains may vary by country. Finally, we only have information from the owner-managers and not members of their family. To capture a more complete picture of how owner-managers manage work and family demands, future research should aim to also gather data from additional household members.

Despite these limitations, our results suggest that while the work–family interface for owner-managers from all of the countries we studied could be significantly improved, the steps to be taken for addressing this issue are likely to vary. Some countries appear to approach work and family more like 'enemies,' and thus should look to minimize negative spillover, whereas others approach work and family more like 'allies,' and thus should look to maximize positive spillover. Therefore, while the difficulties associated with managing the work–family interface appear to be a 'universal' issue for entrepreneurs, whether work and family can be described more as enemies or allies is not. In sum, the findings from the Part II chapters suggest that the answer to the question 'Is entrepreneurship "good" for families?' posed by Jennings et al. (2013) is: 'It depends on the country.'

REFERENCES

Aldrich, H.E. and J.E. Cliff (2003), 'The pervasive effects of family on entrepreneurship: Toward a family embeddedness perspective,' *Journal of Business Venturing*, **18** (5), 573–596.
Bruton, G.D., D. Ahlstrom, and K. Obloj (2008), 'Entrepreneurship in emerging

economies: Where are we today and where should the research go in the future,' *Entrepreneurship Theory and Practice*, **32**, 1–14.

Caputo, R.K. and A. Dolinsky (1998), 'Women's choice to pursue self-employment: The role of financial and human capital of household members,' *Journal of Small Business Management*, **36** (3), 8–17.

Carter, N.M., W.B. Gartner, K.G. Shaver, and E.J. Gatewood (2003), 'The career reasons of nascent entrepreneurs,' *Journal of Business Venturing*, **18** (1), 13–39.

Clark, S.C. (2000), 'Work/family border theory: A new theory of work/family balance,' *Human Relations*, **53** (6), 747–770.

De Martino, R. and R. Barbato (2003), 'Differences between women and men MBA entrepreneurs: Exploring family flexibility and wealth creation as career motivators,' *Journal of Business Venturing*, **18** (6), 815–832.

Eddleston, K.A. and G.N. Powell (2008), 'The role of gender identity in explaining sex differences in business owners' career satisfier preferences,' *Journal of Business Venturing*, **23** (2), 244–256.

Eddleston, K.A. and G.N. Powell (2012), 'Nurturing entrepreneurs' work–family balance: A gendered perspective,' *Entrepreneurship Theory and Practice*, **36** (3), 513–541.

Felzensztein, C., E. Gimmon, and C. Aqueveque (2013), 'Entrepreneurship at the periphery: Exploring framework conditions in core and peripheral locations,' *Entrepreneurship Theory and Practice*, **37**, 815–835.

Frone, M.R., M. Russell, and M.L. Cooper (1992), 'Antecedents and outcomes of work–family conflict: Testing a model of the work–family interface,' *Journal of Applied Psychology*, **77** (1), 65–78.

GEM (2013), 'Global Entrepreneurship Monitor Report,' retrieved from http://www.gemconsortium.org/docs/3106/gem-2013-global-report (accessed July 15, 2014).

Greenhaus, J.H. and G.N. Powell (2006), 'When work and family are allies: A theory of work–family enrichment,' *Academy of Management Review*, **31** (1), 72–92.

Jennings, J.E. and M.S. McDougald (2007), 'Work–family interface experiences and coping strategies: Implications for entrepreneurship research and practice,' *Academy of Management Review*, **32** (3), 747–760.

Jennings, J.E., R.S. Breitkreuz, and A.E. James (2013), 'When family members are also business owners: Is entrepreneurship good for families?,' *Family Relations*, **62**, 472–489.

Manolova, T.S., R.V. Eunni, and B.S. Gyoshev (2008), 'Institutional environments for entrepreneurship: Evidence from emerging economies in Eastern Europe,' *Entrepreneurship Theory and Practice*, **32** (1), 203–218.

Peng, M.W. (2001), 'How entrepreneurs create wealth in transition economies,' *Academy of Management Executive*, **15** (1), 95–108.

Powell, G.N. and K.A. Eddleston (2013), 'Linking family-to-business enrichment and support to entrepreneurial success: Do female and male entrepreneurs experience different outcomes?,' *Journal of Business Venturing*, **28**, 261–280.

Rogoff, E.G. and R.K.Z. Heck (2003), 'Evolving research in entrepreneurship and family business: Recognizing family as the oxygen that feeds the fire of entrepreneurship,' *Journal of Business Venturing*, **18** (5), 559–566.

14. Conclusion: reflections upon the double embeddedness of business enterprising

Jennifer E. Jennings, Kimberly A. Eddleston, P. Devereaux Jennings and Ravi Sarathy

The multi-country study featured in this book originated from our desire to respond to two increasingly voiced calls within both the entrepreneurship and family business literatures. One is the request for greater understanding of how the meso-level institution of family influences, and is influenced by, the operation and performance of owner-managed firms. The second is the call for enhanced appreciation of the macro-level environments in which such firms (as well as their owner-managers and families) are embedded.

In conjunction with our collaborators, we investigated this 'double embeddedness' of business enterprising by collecting difficult-to-obtain primary survey data on the firms and families of almost 1400 owner-managers. The participants were selected from five countries characterized by diverse economic, institutional, and cultural contexts: the United States, Switzerland/ Germany, China, Brazil and India. This concluding chapter summarizes our overarching findings regarding the double embeddedness notion, the caveats stemming from limitations inherent in the overall study design, and the contributions to and implications for existing and future work.

FINDINGS REGARDING THE DOUBLE EMBEDDEDNESS NOTION

To summarize the emergent pattern of cross-country findings, we recreated the conceptual frameworks that guided the analyses for Parts I and II of this book. In each augmented figure, we used arrows of varying types to signify the strength of evidence that was found for a particular focal relationship across the five country studies. These revised diagrams appear as Figures 14.1 and 14.2 respectively.

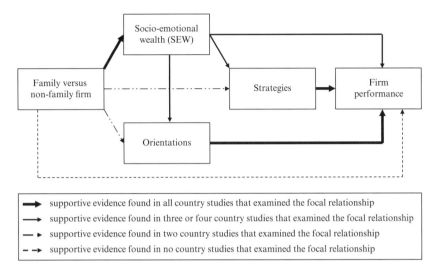

Figure 14.1   Summary of findings regarding family influences upon owner-managed businesses across focal countries

Family Influences upon Owner-managed Businesses Across Countries

The findings summarized in Figure 14.1 provide clear support for the influence of family-related factors upon owner-managed business operations and outcomes. Although none of the country studies revealed that the owner-manager's self-reported classification of the business as either a 'family firm' or 'non-family firm' was directly associated with perceived firm performance, supportive evidence was found for most of the indirect paths. Of especial interest are those pertaining to the family-related dimensions of socio-emotional wealth (SEW). Within every country study that distinguished between family and non-family firms, owner-managers of family firms reported a marginally higher emphasis upon SEW motivations than owner-managers of non-family firms. Moreover, SEW was found to be significantly associated with certain strategic orientations and business strategies—as well as with perceived firm performance—within at least three of the country studies in which such linkages were explicitly examined.

The findings summarized in Figure 14.1 also provide clear support for the impact of broader macro-level environments upon the operation of owner-managed businesses. More specifically, the different types of arrows featured in this figure signify that the influence of the focal family-related factors (and others) was not invariant across the five country contexts.

Indeed, we found it particularly interesting that SEW was most strongly associated with business orientations, strategies and performance in the US sample—yet rarely associated with these organizational processes and outcomes within the Brazil and India samples. This finding ran counter to our overarching expectation that family-related considerations such as the emphasis placed upon SEW motivations would be more influential within developing rather than developed economic regions. We were also surprised to find that the samples exhibited very little cross-country variation in the emphasis placed upon SEW, which tended to be rated highly, on average, by the owner-managers across the different countries in our study.

Family Influences upon Business Owner-Managers Across Countries

As illustrated by Figure 14.2, empirical support for the double embeddedness notion was also found when we turned our analytic lens to psychological indicators of well-being at the owner-manager level of analysis. Notably, as evidenced by the heavy arrows in this figure, in every study that examined the concurrent effectiveness and/or satisfaction reported by business owner-managers within and across the domains of work and family, at least one strategy for managing the work–family interface (WFI) emerged as a significant predictor. Moreover, the WFI experiences of family-to-business conflict and family-to-business enrichment were each found to be significant predictors of the psychological well-being measures within at least three of the country studies.

Besides demonstrating how the well-being of business owner-managers

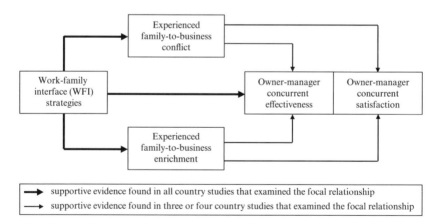

Figure 14.2   Summary of findings regarding family influences upon business owner-managers across focal countries

is impacted by the family systems in which they are embedded, the findings from the Part II analyses also reveal how these impacts vary by country context. Indeed, we found it especially interesting how each of the focal settings seems to possess a distinct profile in this regard. In the United States, the 'enemies' metaphor seems most apt, with the psychological well-being of business owner-managers being primarily (and negatively) influenced by family-to-business conflict than enrichment. In sharp contrast, the 'allies' metaphor applies most to the China sample, with the well-being of business owner-managers in this country benefiting from family-to-business enrichment and being unaffected by family-to-business conflict. The situation induced from the Switzerland/Germany findings is different yet again, with neither type of family-to-business experience making much of a difference to the perceived effectiveness and satisfaction of business owners in these countries. Yet this is far from the case in Brazil and India, countries in which our results suggest that the business and family spheres are highly enmeshed, with the well-being of owner-managers simultaneously benefitting and suffering from experienced family-to-business enrichment and conflict, respectively.

Although the above-noted pattern of results from the Part II analyses are intriguing, perhaps the most striking finding is that which emerged from the basic descriptive statistics. Notably, and rather alarmingly, in not a single sample did the majority of business owner-managers perceive themselves to be concurrently effective and/or satisfied within and across the work and family domains.

LIMITATIONS OF THE OVERALL STUDY DESIGN

In order to contextualize our study's contributions and implications, we think it is important to first discuss its limitations. The four raised here are largely around design choices. In a world where large-scale, publicly accessible databases containing information on numerous countries are appearing with increasing frequency, our five-country design is likely to come across as lacking in breadth. While we acknowledge that this is a weakness to a certain extent, the depth of data that was able to be collected through the custom-designed surveys administered by our collaborators is arguably a countervailing strength. Comparable, fine-grained data of the type featured herein is rarely available for privately-owned firms across multiple countries—let alone for the owner-managers of such businesses as well as their family structures. We were also careful to obtain samples from some of the most prominent examples of developed versus developing markets in the world. That being said, we definitely encourage replications of our study beyond the countries examined here. To facilitate such endeavors, Appendix A of this book contains English-language scale items for the focal constructs.

Although a highly standardized version of the survey instrument was utilized within each of the focal contexts (albeit in different languages), the disparate sampling frames and data collection approaches implemented by the study teams represents a second potential limitation. As noted in the country-specific chapters, and summarized in Appendix B, the resultant samples differed with respect to their geographic scope of country coverage, their focus upon family firms versus small and medium-sized enterprises (SMEs), and their proportional representation of businesses headed by women. Although this non-standardization complicates the comparability of the samples, it has resulted in variation that could be fruitfully exploited within subsequent pooled analyses. That being said, it is important to acknowledge that none of our samples can be considered fully representative of all privately-held firms in the focal country.

Some scholars might also critique our reliance upon single-source, self-reported data. The study informants, however, were owner-managers who arguably constitute the ideal source of information about the strategic orientations, business strategies and comparative performance of their privately-held enterprises. Moreover, each country team took care to assess and report the internal reliability (Cronbach alphas) of the measurement scales for the focal constructs. We recognize, however, that data from additional sources would have been ideal in some instances; specifically, for the emphasis upon family-related SEW motivations within the firm as well as for the work-family interface strategies implemented within the owner-manager's household. Future researchers interested in pursuing the 'Is entrepreneurship "good" for families?' theme evident within many of the Part II chapters are especially encouraged to collect data from family members beyond the owner-manager.

Finally, we were only able to obtain cross-sectional data for this study. Such a design is nevertheless useful for investigating associations between core constructs, which was our goal. Also, it is important to note that our data contains many cumulative measures; for example, firm size, firm age, 12-month performance and five (or three)-year performance in the business sphere, and (arguably) household size and income level in the family sphere. That being said, we encourage future researchers to consider longitudinal investigations of the 'firms within families within countries' notion.

CONTRIBUTIONS AND IMPLICATIONS

With the above limitations in mind, we conclude by raising some of the most noteworthy contributions and implications derived from our collaborative, multi-country study of the premise that firms are 'doubly embedded' within the meso and macro contexts, respectively, of business-owning families and broader economic, institutional and sociocultural environments. One set of contributions stems from our attention to a variety of family considerations, as called for by entrepreneurship and family business scholars alike. For the family business literature, in particular, we offer one of the first operationalizations of the multi-dimensional SEW construct as proposed by Berrone, Cruz and Gómez-Mejía (2012), demonstrating the reliability and validity of several constituent dimensions as well as of the aggregate measure. Substantively, the results of our study suggest that SEW motivations are more influential for the strategic orientations, business strategies and perceived performance of owner-managed enterprises than the simple categorical distinction between family and non-family firms utilized within most comparative studies to-date. That being said, our findings also offer at least some fodder for questioning whether SEW motivations are unique to—or even strikingly higher within—family than non-family firms. Our country-specific findings further reveal that a stronger concern for SEW is not always associated with strategic orientations and business strategies that are most easily inferred from this theoretical perspective. The key implication, then, is that while SEW motivations help address calls for greater attention to the heterogeneity amongst family firms (Sharma, Melin, and Nordqvist, 2014), there is room for considerably more conceptual refinement of this construct—potentially including, as a starting point, the distinction between the preservation versus enhancement of this family-centered, non-economic outcome.

For the entrepreneurship literature, our study is in step with the growing interest in non-economic outcomes such as the personal well-being of those who engage in business enterprising; see, for example, the special section within the most recent Global Entrepreneurship Monitor (GEM) report (Amoró and Bosma, 2014). Although not as extensive in country coverage as the GEM study, our investigation nevertheless offers contributions for furthering work on this societally important topic. Methodologically, for instance, we provide more holistic measures of well-being capturing the extent to which owner-managers consider themselves to be simultaneously effective and/or satisfied within and across the domains of work and family (see Appendix A of this book). Empirically, however, our overall findings demonstrate quite strikingly that only a minority of business owner-managers within developed and developing regions alike rate themselves highly on these psychological indicators—a result that sheds preliminary light on the provocative question posed by Jennings, Breitkreuz, and James (2013) of whether entrepreneurship is necessarily 'good' for family members. Our country-specific findings further suggest that the effects of certain family structures and processes on an owner-manager's well-being differ quite profoundly according to the broader context in which the business families are themselves embedded, not only acting as 'allies' in some situations yet 'enemies' in others (cf., Eddleston and Powell, 2012; Powell and Eddleston, 2013) but also, in some cases, as either 'double agents' or 'neutral parties.' Combined, these observations support the value of additional research consistent with the family embeddedness perspective (Aldrich and Cliff, 2003; Rogoff and Heck, 2003), and imply that such endeavors should be as attuned as possible to macro-level encircling influences.

Having returned to the book's overarching 'double embeddedness' theme, the following reflections seem an appropriate note on which to end. If interpreted strictly, the notion of double embeddedness implies doubly constrained behavior. Interestingly, however, not only did sufficient variation exist within each country sample to observe significant associations but the heterogeneous effects of the family-related factors, in particular, acted as means of breaking from broader macro-level constraints. Viewed in this manner, the families of entrepreneurs warrant a closer look specifically in future studies of the provocative 'entrepreneurship as emancipation' perspective recently formulated by Rindova, Barry, and Ketchen (2009). Another emergent perspective for which our study possesses implications is the call for greater attention to the role of community in entrepreneurial endeavors (Jennings, Greenwood, Lounsbury, and Suddaby, 2013). Our results suggest that this leap to the community level skips a key meso-level institution that should not be ignored in such quests; that is, families not only reflect communities but also constitute them. Finally, as scholars based in North America, we couldn't help but notice how the findings for the US sample were quite distinctive from those for the other featured countries within both sets of analyses (which raises concerns about the generalizability of much extant research within the entrepreneurship and family business literatures). Indeed, managing this collaboration convincingly demonstrated to us the importance of continuing to implement multi-country designs in order to generate insights that are more globally relevant. If our experience is any indication, such efforts are likely to prove challenging yet enlightening.

REFERENCES

Aldrich, H.E. and J.E. Cliff (2003), 'The pervasive effects of family on entrepreneurship: Toward a family embeddedness perspective,' *Journal of Business Venturing*, **18** (5), 573–596.

Amoró, J.E. and N. Bosma (2014), 'Global Entrepreneurship Monitor 2013 global report,' retrieved from http://www.gemconsortium.org/docs/download/3106 (accessed February 23, 2015).

Berrone, P., C. Cruz, and L.R. Gómez-Mejía (2012), 'Socioemotional wealth in family firms: Theoretical dimensions, assessment approaches, and agenda for future research,' *Family Business Review*, **25**, 258–279.

Eddleston, K.A. and G.N. Powell (2012), 'Nurturing entrepreneurs' work–family balance: A gendered perspective,' *Entrepreneurship Theory and Practice*, **36** (3), 513–541.

Jennings, J.E., R.S. Breitkreuz, and A.E. James (2013), 'When family members are also business owners: Is entrepreneurship good for families?,' *Family Relations*, **62**, 472–489.

Jennings, P.D., R. Greenwood, M.D. Lounsbury, and R. Suddaby (2013), 'Institutions, entrepreneurs, and communities: A special issue on entrepreneurship,' *Journal of Business Venturing*, **28** (1), 1–9.

Powell, G.N. and K.A. Eddleston (2013), 'Linking family-to-business enrichment and support to entrepreneurial success: Do female and male entrepreneurs experience different outcomes?,' *Journal of Business Venturing*, **28**, 261–280.

Rindova, V., D. Barry, and D.J. Ketchen (2009), 'Entrepreneuring as emancipation,' *Academy of Management Review*, **34** (3), 477–491.

Rogoff, E.G. and R.K.Z. Heck (2003), 'Evolving research in entrepreneurship and family business: Recognizing family as the oxygen that feeds the fire of entrepreneurship,' *Journal of Business Venturing*, **18** (5), 559–566.

Sharma, P., L. Melin, and M. Nordqvist (2014), 'Introduction: Scope, evolution and future of family business studies' in L. Melin, M. Nordqvist and P. Sharma (eds), *The Sage Handbook of Family Business*, 1–22. London: Sage Publications.

Appendix A: measurement scales for focal constructs (US version)

Table A.1   Scales for key variables in Part I

Family firm self-classification

Family firm   1. Do you consider this to be a family firm? Yes / No

Socio-emotional wealth dimensions

Family control (all items rated from 1 = strongly disagree to 5 = strongly agree)	1. I will never consider selling shares of the business outside my family.
	2. I will not engage in strategic actions that diminish my control over firm strategic decisions.
	3. I am reluctant to incorporate outsiders to the board of directors.
	4. In the business, most executive positions are occupied by family members.
	5. In the business, continuing the traditions of the current owner(s) is important.
	6. I wish that the future president of the business will be a family member.
	7. I see the business as a legacy to be transferred to the next generation.
Identification (all items rated from 1 = strongly disagree to 5 = strongly agree)	1. I am highly concerned about how the firm is viewed in the public.
	2. I will not engage in strategic actions that may damage the image of the business.
	3. I am committed to perpetuating a positive firm image.
	4. Customers often associate my name with products and/or services of this firm.
Bonds (all items rated from 1 = strongly disagree to 5 = strongly agree)	1. In the business, recruitment is often made through informal social networks.
	2. In the business, promotions are mainly based on seniority.
	3. In the business, employees are treated as if they are part of one family.
	4. In the business, we emphasize trust in relationships.
	5. In the business, relationships are based on reciprocal behavior (in other words, you scratch my back, I'll scratch yours).
	6. In the business, we prefer dealing with people we know.
	7. In the business, our networks provide us with many useful referrals.
	8. In the business, we often experience generous actions of network partners.
	9. In the business, our network allows us to pool resources.

Table A.1   (continued)

Socio-emotional wealth dimensions

| | 10. | In the business, thanks to our network, we receive reliable and useful information that helps our business. |

Emotion
(all items rated
from 1 = strongly
disagree to 5 =
strongly agree)

1. I am emotionally attached to the firm.
2. The firm reminds me of who I am.
3. If I were describing myself, the firm would likely be something I would mention.
4. If I lost the firm, I would feel like I had lost a little bit of myself.
5. People who know me might sometimes think of the firm when they think of me.

Renewal
(all items rated
from 1 = strongly
disagree to 5 =
strongly agree)

1. The firm is in the business for the long run.
2. I do not evaluate my firm's investments on a short-term basis.
3. The firm has the possibility to seize investment projects that take a longer time until payback.
4. The firm is able to wait and see how investments evolve over time.

Strategic orientations

Growth
orientation
(all items rated
from 1 = strongly
disagree to 5 =
strongly agree;
items 2, 4, 6 and
8 reverse-coded)

1. I have a strong desire to expand my business.
2. For me, the hassles of leading a large business would outweigh the benefits.
3. I aim to significantly grow the business in the next five years.
4. I have a maximum size in mind for my business that I would prefer not to exceed.
5. I have made significant investments to grow my business.
6. I do not want this firm to grow beyond a manageable size.
7. I am always searching for new ways to grow my business.
8. I see good reason for limiting the growth of the firm.

Entrepreneurial
orientation
(all items rated
from 1 = strongly
disagree to 5 =
strongly agree)

1. We were careful not to risk so much money that the company would be in real trouble financially if things did not work out.
2. We allowed the business to evolve as opportunities emerged.
3. We adapted what we were doing to the resources we had.
4. We were flexible and took advantage of opportunities as they arose.
5. We avoided courses of action that restricted our flexibility and adaptability.
6. We used a substantial number of agreements with customers, suppliers and other organizations and people to reduce the amount of uncertainty.
7. We used pre-commitments from customers and suppliers as often as possible.
8. The product/service that we now provide is substantially different than we first imagined.

Long-term
orientation
(all items rated
from 1 = strongly
disagree to 5 =
strongly agree)

1. The firm is in the business for the long run.
2. I do not evaluate my firm's investments on a short-term basis.
3. The firm has the possibility to seize investment projects that take a longer time until payback.
4. The firm is able to wait and see how investments evolve over time.
5. The incentive for our (middle) management is tied to the long-run performance of the firm.

Table A.1 (continued)

Business strategies

Exploration (all items rated from 1 = very unimportant to 5 = very important)	1. Introduce new generation of products. 2. Extend product range. 3. Open up new markets. 4. Enter new technology fields.
Exploitation (all items rated from 1 = very unimportant to 5 = very important)	1. Improve existing product quality. 2. Improve production flexibility. 3. Reduce production costs. 4. Improve yield or reduce material consumption.
Causation (all items rated from 1 = strongly disagree to 5 = strongly agree)	1. We selected long-run opportunities that we thought would provide the best returns. 2. We designed and planned business strategies. 3. We implemented control processes to make sure we met objectives. 4. We did meaningful competitive analysis to select target markets. 5. We planned production and marketing efforts.
Effectuation (all items rated from 1 = strongly disagree to 5 = strongly agree; item 2 reverse-coded)	1. We experimented with different products and/or business models. 2. The product/service that we now provide is essentially the same as originally conceptualized. 3. We tried a number of different approaches until we found a business model that worked. 4. We were careful not to commit more resources than we could afford to lose.

Firm performance

12-month performance (all items rated from 1 = worse to 7 = better with 4 = the same)	How would you rate your firm's performance relative to your competitors over the last twelve months (that is, your current performance)? 1. Growth in sales. 2. Growth in market share. 3. Growth in profitability. 4. Return on equity. 5. Return on total assets. 6. Profit margin on sales. 7. Ability to fund growth from profits.
3–5 year performance	Same as above with 'three to five years ago (if applicable)' instead of 'over the last twelve months (that is, your current performance)'

Table A.2   Scales for key variables in Part II

Work–family interface strategies

Segmentation of family and business roles (all items rated from 1 = strongly disagree to 5 = strongly agree)	1. In REALITY, I often leave household/family issues behind when I'm at work. 2. In REALITY, I often avoid thinking about family while I'm at work. 3. In REALITY, I often limit household/family issues from creeping into my work life.
Identification with business (all items rated from 1 = strongly disagree to 5 = strongly agree)	1. I am emotionally attached to the firm. 2. The firm reminds me of who I am. 3. If I were describing myself, the firm would likely be something I would mention. 4. If I lost the firm, I would feel like I had lost a little bit of myself. 5. People who know me might sometimes think of the firm when they think of me. 6. I sense that this is MY company. 7. This firm feels like an important possession to me. 8. I feel a very high degree of personal ownership for this organization. 9. Customers often associate my name with products and/or services of this firm. 10. I am highly concerned about how the firm is viewed in the public. 11. I am committed about perpetuating a positive firm image. 12. I will not engage in strategic actions that may damage the image of the business.
Instrumental support from family members (all items rated from 1 = strongly disagree to 5 = strongly agree)	The members of my family who do not officially work in the business. . . 1. Often contribute to this business without expecting to be paid. 2. Often give me useful feedback and ideas concerning this business. 3. Can be counted on to help out if something unexpected happens in this business. 4. Often go above and beyond what is normally expected in order to help this business succeed. 5. Often try to understand when I'm frustrated with this business.
Traditionalism in the division of household labor (responses for each item consisted of: 'always or usually the woman,' 'equally,' 'always or usually the man' and 'a third person (hired help)'	Who does the following household tasks in your family? 1. Shopping for groceries? 2. Deciding what to have for dinner? 3. Doing the laundry? 4. Caring for the sick?

Table A.2   (continued)

Work–family interface experiences

Family-to-business conflict (all items rated from 1 = strongly disagree to 5 = strongly agree)	1. I feel frustrated when my household/family responsibilities interfere with my work. 2. Things I want to do for my business don't get done because of the demands of my household/family. 3. I resent having to handle household/family issues while I am at work. 4. My home life interferes with my business responsibilities such as getting to work on time and accomplishing daily tasks. 5. I feel annoyed about having to deal with household/family matters when I'm at work. 6. Household/family commitments interfere with my ability to perform business-related duties.
Family-to-business enrichment (all items rated from 1 = strongly disagree to 5 = strongly agree)	My involvement in my family. . . 1. Helps me gain knowledge that makes me a better businessperson. 2. Puts me in a good mood and this mood helps make me a better businessperson. 3. Requires me to be as focused as possible at work, which helps make me a better businessperson. 4. Helps me acquire skills that make me a better businessperson. 5. Helps me gain perspective that makes me a better businessperson. 6. Makes me cheerful and this helps me be a better businessperson.

Psychological well-being

Perceived effectiveness (all items scored from 0 = poor to 100 = excellent)	Overall, how effective would you say you have been: 1. As a business owner-manager? 2. As a family member? 3. In balancing the various aspects of your life?
Perceived satisfaction (all items scored from 0 = completely dissatisfied to 100 = completely satisfied)	Overall, how satisfied would you say you are: 1. As a business owner-manager? 2. As a family member? 3. In balancing the various aspects of your life?

Appendix B: cross-country research design and sampling differences

As discussed in the introductory and concluding chapters of this book, each country-focused research team relied on the same basic survey instrument in order to obtain comparable data on business owner-managers and their firms and families (see Appendix A for the key scales appearing within the US version). Here we compare the sampling frames, data collection methods and nature of the samples across the five country-level studies.

The strata in the random samples were for size and type of firm, with size ranging from small (fewer than 10 employees), medium (between 10 and 250), large (250 to 500) to very large (500+), and type referring to family and non-family firms. In general, except in the case of the Switzerland/Germany study, it was easier to secure data from the small firms given their large representation in most countries as well as the interest of SME owner-managers in our study. In some cases, such as the US, additional large firms had to be contacted in order to round out the top two size strata in the sample. Where the type of firm was concerned, the willingness to respond varied considerably more by country. While both family and non-family owner-managers in the US and China were quite interested in completing the questionnaires, only the former type of firm was focused upon in the first wave of data collection within the Switzerland/Germany study. In India and Brazil, personal contacts with local academic institutions and businesses made entry into both family and non-family firms easier, if more time-consuming. Data was collected via an online survey in the US, Switzerland/Germany and India studies, via a mix of online and hardcopy surveys in China and via face-to-face interviews in Brazil.

Table B.1 reports the results of the data collection effort. The number of respondents varied between 212 and 319 respondents per country. Small firms were prevalent in the US and Brazil samples and constituted at least 30 percent of the China and India samples. In contrast, because of the focus upon long-lived family firms by the Switzerland/Germany study team, only 1.2 percent of this country's sample comprised of small firms, with 70 percent of the businesses having more than 250 employees.

Table B.1   A comparison of sample attributes for firms and families across the five countries

| | More Developed Economies | | | Emerging Economies | | | | | |
| | US | | Switz/Germany | China | | Brazil | | India | |
	Family	Non-family	Family	Family	Non-family	Family	Non-family	Family	Non-family
Number of respondents	213	93	319	107	186	118	94	81	102
Small firms	59.6%	46.2%	1.2%	33.6%	43.9%	72.9%	79.8%	18.5%	35.7%
Firm age	16.1	13.4	86.9	7.6	7.4	11.08	4.72	22.5	10.0
Male	52.7%	47.3	85.4%	62.6%	69.8%	34%	30%	75.3%	81.7%
Some university education	53.0%	68.5%	68.0%	58.9%	51.2%	93%	84%	97.5%	98.0%
Married	70.0%	57.0%	70.0%	86.0%	78.8%	83%	51%	74.0%	80.8%
Children in household	44%		51.9%	69.3%		49%		70.3%	

Family firms (as self-defined by the survey respondents) constituted approximately two-thirds of the US and China samples, essentially all of the Switzerland/Germany sample, and about half of the Brazil and India samples.

Turning to the firm and family demographics, the businesses in the Switzerland/Germany sample were much older than their counterparts from other countries because of the selected sampling frame, with an average age of nearly 87 years. The average firm age elsewhere ranged from 5 to 23 years. As the Part I chapters showed, service firms were dominant in the US, China and Brazil samples and in India's non-family subsample. Manufacturing firms were more dominant in the Switzerland/German sample and within India's family firm subsample. Also, as discussed in the Part I summary chapter (Jennings, Sarathy, Eddleston, and Jennings, Chapter 7), the perceptions of business performance were positive, with most managers rating it near 4.0 or above average.'

In the case of the family characteristics, approximately half of the owner-managers in the US and China samples were female. In contrast, in Germany and India, they were mostly male. Brazil was an anomaly due to the sampling procedures discussed in this country's chapters, with more than 70 percent female. Across the countries, education levels were generally high: over 50 percent of the owner-managers across all countries reported having at least some university training. The very high proportion within the India sample is attributable to the focused approach of targeting participants in university-based entrepreneurship and incubator programs. The majority of respondents in the countries were also married, though the proportion ranged from 53 percent to 86 percent, and with more family firm owner-managers being married than non-family firm owner-managers. Nearly half of all households in the sampled firms by country had children. Finally, although the owner-managers perceived their businesses to be performing well (as noted above), the proportion who considered themselves to be concurrently effective within and across the family and business domains ranged from a low of 10 percent in India to a high of only 40 percent in the US (as noted in the Part II summary chapter by Eddleston, Jennings, Jennings, and Sarathy, Chapter 13).

In sum, the stratified random sampling frame appeared to succeed in the sense of generating variation by firm size and type by country and also in terms of other key firm and family attributes. Variation is essential for testing and comparing the multivariate model across venues. Nevertheless, given some of the departures of our sample's demographics from their population means (for example, the sampled percentage of female-headed businesses in Brazil relative to the national average, the proportion of university-educated business owner-managers in India) as well as the geographically constrained nature of the Brazil and India samples, we acknowledge that the collected data cannot be considered representative in each country context (a point discussed in the limitations section of the book's concluding chapter).

Index

ambidexterity *see* business strategies

Brazil 3, 5, 7, 9, 73–94, 192–212, 239–43, 246, 248–9, 259–62
business strategies
  ambidexterity 19–23, 61–2, 64, 41, 43, 50, 105
  causation 7, 19–23, 27, 38, 40–41, 43, 47–8, 53, 61–2, 66, 77–80, 100–102, 109, 256
  effectuation 7, 19–23, 27, 38, 40–41, 43, 47–9, 53, 61–2, 66, 78, 83–4, 88, 100–102, 109, 256
  exploitation 7, 19–23, 27, 38, 40–41, 43, 47–50, 52–4, 61–2, 64–6, 256
  exploration 7, 19–23, 27, 38, 40–41, 43, 47–50, 52–4, 61–2, 64–6, 256

causation *see* business strategies
children 178, 137–9, 155, 163–4, 166, 168
China 3–4, 7, 9, 57–72, 176–91, 239–43, 246, 249, 259–62
conceptual framework 3, 6–8
concurrent effectiveness 132–5, 156–8, 179–80, 189, 238–41, 248–9, 258
concurrent satisfaction 146, 156–7, 172, 180, 189, 238–41, 248–9, 258
country contexts 2, 4–5, 75–7, 117–26, 259–62
cross-country comparisons 10, 117–24, 233, 238–44, 246–52, 259–62

division of household labor *see* household labor
double embeddedness 2, 123, 238, 246, 248, 252

education 59, 178
effectuation *see* business strategies

egalitarianism in division of household labor *see* household labor
emerging economies 3, 117–24, 237
enrichment perspective *see* work–family enhancement perspective
entrepreneurial context 96, 192–3, 213–14
entrepreneurial orientation *see* strategic orientations
exploitation *see* business strategies
exploration *see* business strategies

fairness in division of household labor 140, 159–60, 163–70, 184, 202, 223
family-to-business conflict 8, 135–7, 154, 159–60, 163–5, 167, 169–72, 184–5, 189–90, 199–200, 203–4, 219–21, 223–4, 231–2, 239, 241, 248–9, 258
family-to-business enrichment 135–7, 154, 159–61, 163–5, 167, 169–73, 184–6, 189–90, 199–200, 203–4, 239, 241, 248–9, 258
family embeddedness perspective 1, 147, 171, 238, 252
family firms
  comparison with non-family firms 64, 66–71, 76, 99–102, 106–7, 112, 247, 251
  demographics 17–18, 37, 59, 74, 96–9, 155, 194–5, 215–16
  proportion 37, 59, 178
family support 137, 159–60, 162–4, 167, 169–72, 184, 202, 223, 257
female entrepreneurs *see* gender
FIBER 42–5, 47–50, 53, 63, 66, 70
firm demographics
  age 39, 59, 155, 177

performance 7, 23–5, 28–9, 39, 59,
76, 82–9, 98, 104–7, 241, 246–8,
250, 256
size 39, 59, 64, 155
founder 17–18, 59,

gender 17–18, 24, 131, 165, 178, 187,
193, 215
Germany 3–4, 7, 9, 37–56, 153–75,
239–43, 246, 249
Global Entrepreneurship Monitor
(GEM) 1, 176, 251
growth orientation *see* strategic
orientations

hours spent on business/family *see* time
devoted to business/family
household help *see* household labor
household income *see* income
household labor/tasks 136–7, 140,
159–65, 167, 169–70, 182–3,
257

identification with business 38, 42–4,
46–8, 52, 136–9, 181–2, 186,
201–2, 222–3, 241, 254, 257
income
household 131, 152, 155, 178,
250
personal 155, 178,
India 3, 5, 7, 9, 95–113, 213–36,
239–43, 246, 248–9, 259–62
industry 17–18, 24, 59, 64, 178
institutional voids 73
instrumental support *see* family
support
integration *see* segmentation
international dispersion 59

limitations 32, 54, 70–71, 90–91, 148,
172, 189, 210, 232, 249–50
long-term orientation *see* strategic
orientations

macro context/environment 2, 4–5,
246, 251–2
marital status *see* married
married 17–18, 24, 59, 155, 178
meso context/environment 2, 246,
251–2

necessity entrepreneurs/
entrepreneurship 85, 96, 209,
237
non-family firm
demographics 17–19, 59
proportion 59

owner-manager well-being *see*
psychological well-being

perceived effectiveness 31, 60, 109–11,
133, 142, 179–80, 185–90, 195–7,
204–7, 216–18, 224–31, 249
perceived satisfaction 61, 109–11,
180–81, 185–90, 195–7, 216–18,
224–31, 249
personal income *see* income
personal well-being *see* psychological
well-being
positive spillover model 190
privately-owned enterprises/firms
17–18, 29, 57, 68, 177
psychological well-being 9, 156, 159,
171, 177, 237, 248

segmentation 139, 159–62, 164, 167,
169, 182, 186, 201–2, 222, 257
small- and medium-sized enterprises
(SMEs) 15–18, 57–9, 68–71, 176,
189, 250
socio-emotional wealth (SEW)
and firm performance 27–30, 44–8,
53–4, 66–8, 82–8, 103–9,
247–8
comparison between family and
non-family firms 28–9, 64,
66–71, 247
components 22–3, 32–4, 38, 43, 63,
81–2, 254
composite measure 32–4, 64, 66,
254
cross-country comparison 118–25,
247–8
definition 7, 42, 58
spouse *see* marital status
strategic orientations
entrepreneurial orientation 7, 21–2,
63, 66, 80, 86, 102, 247, 255
growth orientation 7, 21–2, 27, 80,
86, 102, 247, 255